SECTOR

AV7 **7** TRS

TRANSFORMERS

Sector 7: a shadowy agency
within the United States
government dedicated to
protecting the world from
threats too strange and
dangerous for the public to
ever learn of. Their existence
is known only by a few.

This is their story.

Written by
John Barber

Artwork by
Joe Suito & Lou Kang

Colors by
Andrew Crossley

Letters by
Chris Mowry

Original Series Edits by
Carlos Guzman and Andy Schmidt

Collection Edits by
Justin Eisinger

Collection Design & Production by
Shawn Lee & Chris Mowry

Special thanks to Hasbro's Aaron Archer, Michael Kelly, Amie Lozanski, Val Roca, Ed Lane, Michael Provost, Erin Hillman, Samantha Lomow, and Michael Verrecchia for their invaluable assistance.

 Licensed By:

ISBN: 978-1-60010-913-3
14 13 12 11   1 2 3 4
www.IDWPUBLISHING.com

Ted Adams, CEO & Publisher
Greg Goldstein, Chief Operating Officer
Robbie Robbins, EVP/Sr. Graphic Artist
Chris Ryall, Chief Creative Officer
Matthew Ruzicka, CPA, Chief Financial Officer

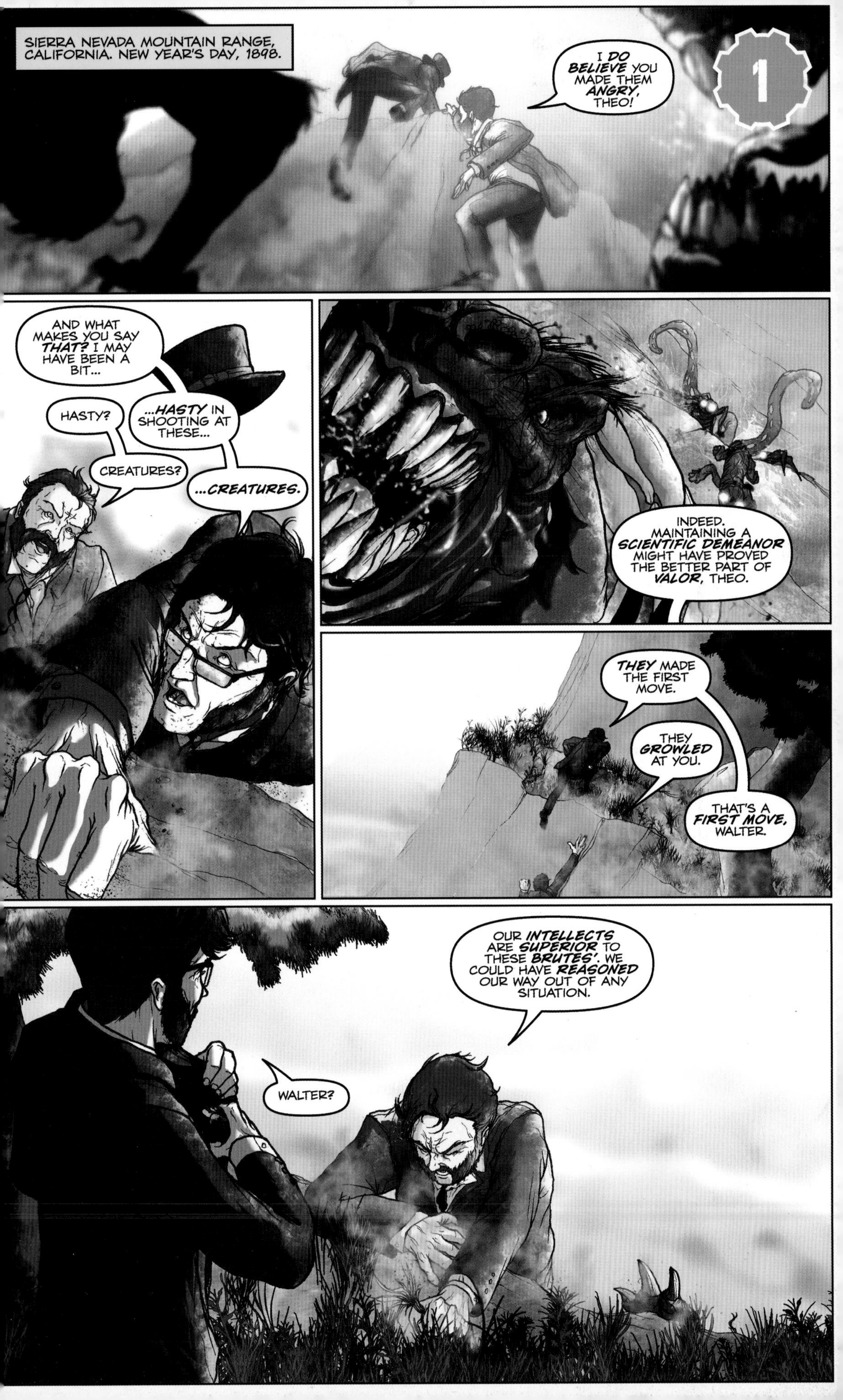
SIERRA NEVADA MOUNTAIN RANGE, CALIFORNIA. NEW YEAR'S DAY, 1898.
I DO BELIEVE YOU MADE THEM ANGRY, THEO!
1
AND WHAT MAKES YOU SAY THAT? I MAY HAVE BEEN A BIT...
HASTY?
...HASTY IN SHOOTING AT THESE...
CREATURES?
...CREATURES.
INDEED. MAINTAINING A SCIENTIFIC DEMEANOR MIGHT HAVE PROVED THE BETTER PART OF VALOR, THEO.
THEY MADE THE FIRST MOVE.
THEY GROWLED AT YOU.
THAT'S A FIRST MOVE, WALTER.
OUR INTELLECTS ARE SUPERIOR TO THESE BRUTES'. WE COULD HAVE REASONED OUR WAY OUT OF ANY SITUATION.
WALTER?

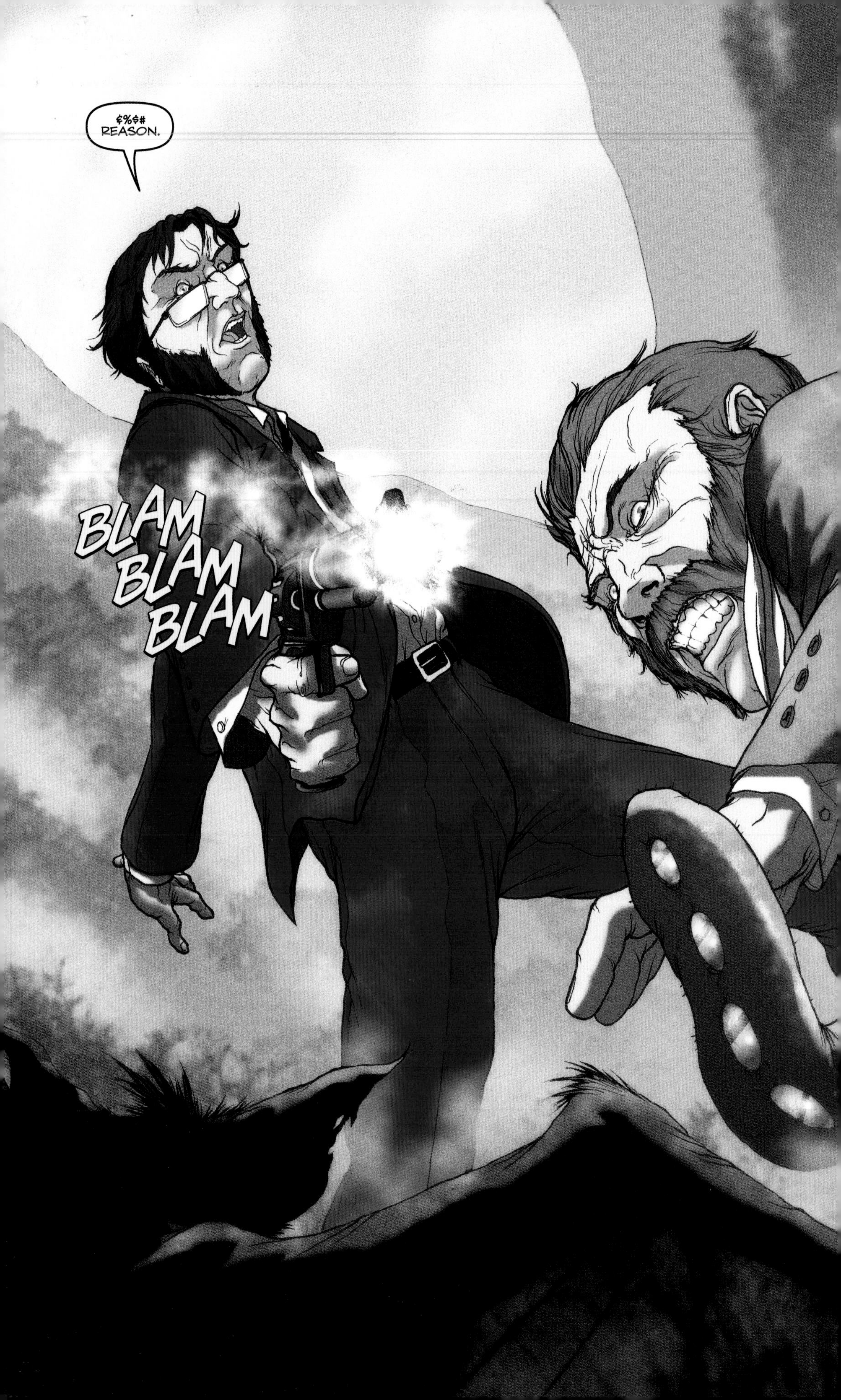
¢%$#
REASON.
BLAM
BLAM
BLAM

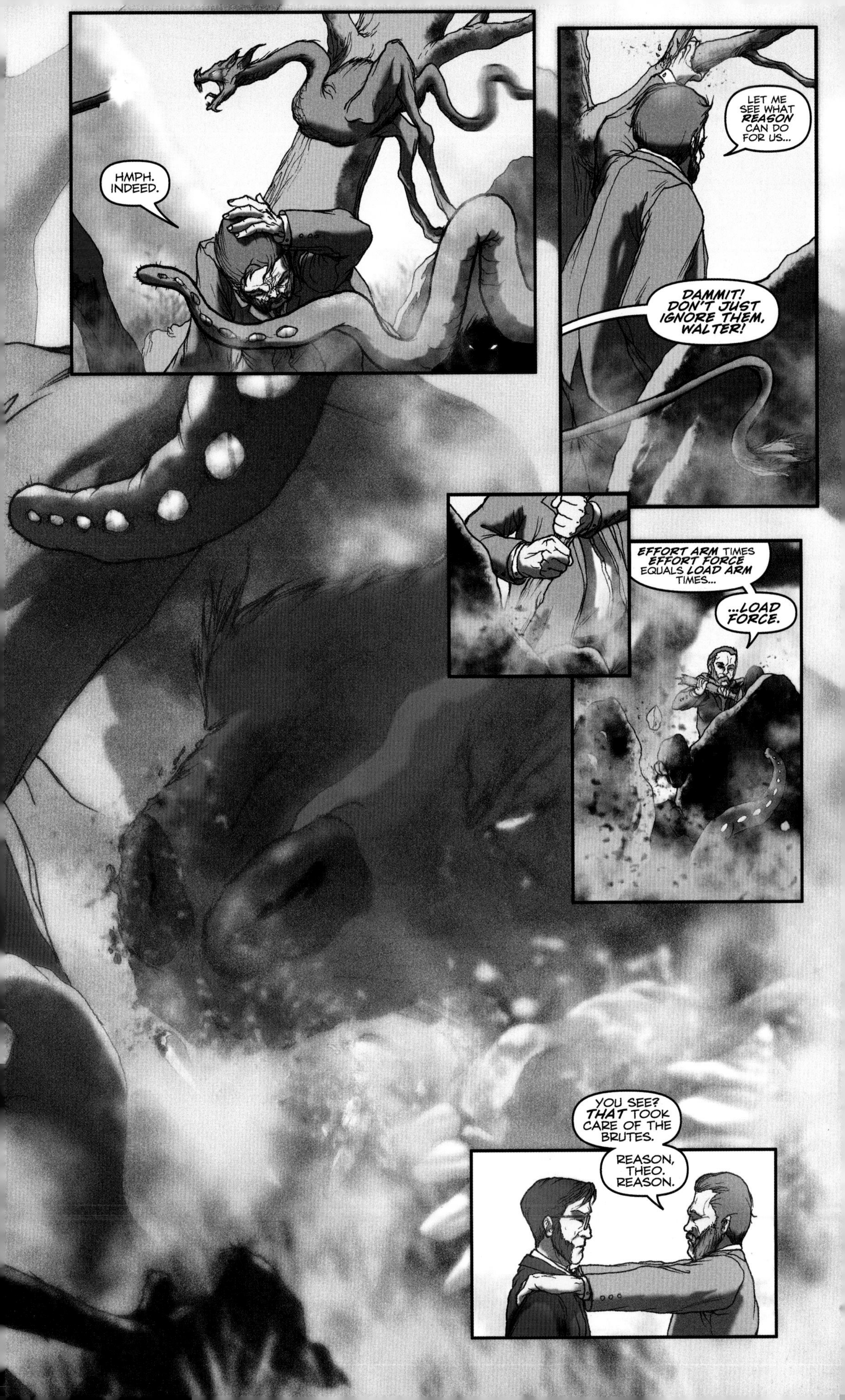
HMPH. INDEED.
LET ME SEE WHAT REASON CAN DO FOR US...
DAMMIT! DON'T JUST IGNORE THEM, WALTER!
EFFORT ARM TIMES EFFORT FORCE EQUALS LOAD ARM TIMES...
...LOAD FORCE.
YOU SEE? THAT TOOK CARE OF THE BRUTES.
REASON, THEO. REASON.

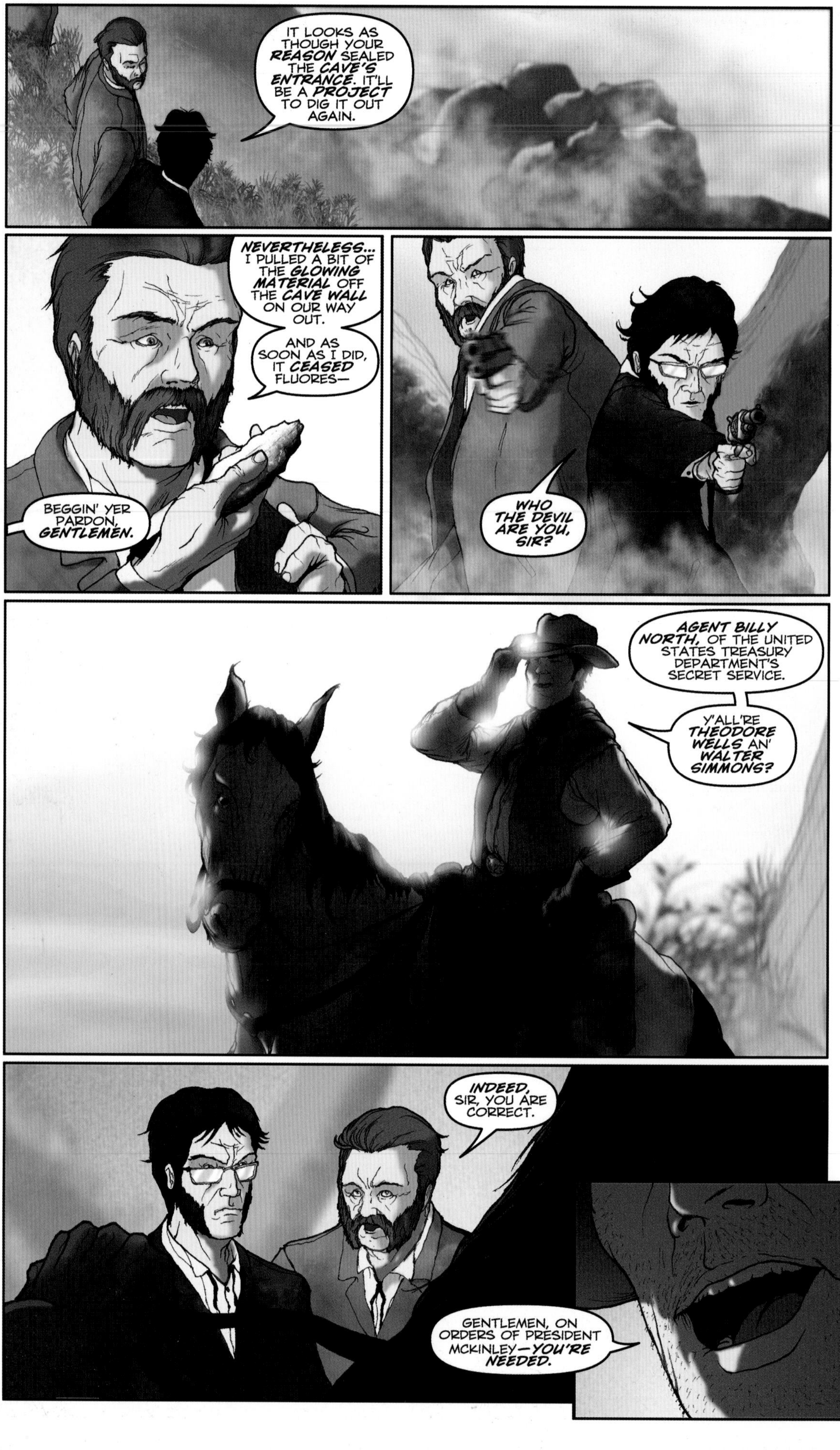
IT LOOKS AS THOUGH YOUR REASON SEALED THE CAVE'S ENTRANCE. IT'LL BE A PROJECT TO DIG IT OUT AGAIN.
NEVERTHELESS... I PULLED A BIT OF THE GLOWING MATERIAL OFF THE CAVE WALL ON OUR WAY OUT.
AND AS SOON AS I DID, IT CEASED FLUORES—
BEGGIN' YER PARDON, GENTLEMEN.
WHO THE DEVIL ARE YOU, SIR?
AGENT BILLY NORTH, OF THE UNITED STATES TREASURY DEPARTMENT'S SECRET SERVICE.
Y'ALL'RE THEODORE WELLS AN' WALTER SIMMONS?
INDEED, SIR, YOU ARE CORRECT.
GENTLEMEN, ON ORDERS OF PRESIDENT MCKINLEY—YOU'RE NEEDED.

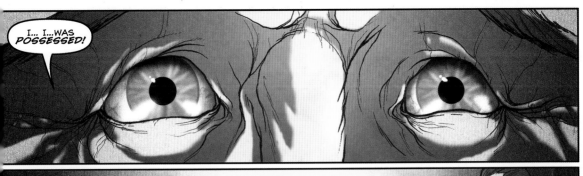

I... I...WAS *POSSESSED!*

BOSTON SECURE HOSPITAL, FIVE DAYS LATER.

THAT *THING...* LOOKED INTO MY *SOUL!* IT TURNED ME INSIDE OUT! MY MIND, MY BODY...

...WERE NO *LONGER* MY *OWN!* I—

YES, WELL...

WE'LL GET *BACK* TO YOU!

—I TELL YOU, I'VE *SEEN* IT! IT'S *REAL! MINE EYES!*

MINE EYES HAVE SEEN THE GLORY!

SO? WHAT'S THE *VERDICT,* PARDNERS?

UNFORTUNATELY, AGENT NORTH, ANOTHER *WOULD-BE ADVENTURE* HAS BEEN *STYMIED* BY *MADNESS.*

I'M NOT SO *SURE,* THEO.

OH, WALTER, PLEASE DON'T TELL ME YOU'RE *CONSIDERING...*

...A THIRTY-FOOT-TALL *STEEL MAN,* WHOSE VERY GAZE TURNED BLIND OUR UNFORTUNATE *CAPTAIN ARCHIBALD WIKETY?*

HEY! IT'S CAPTAIN *WITWICKY,* AND—

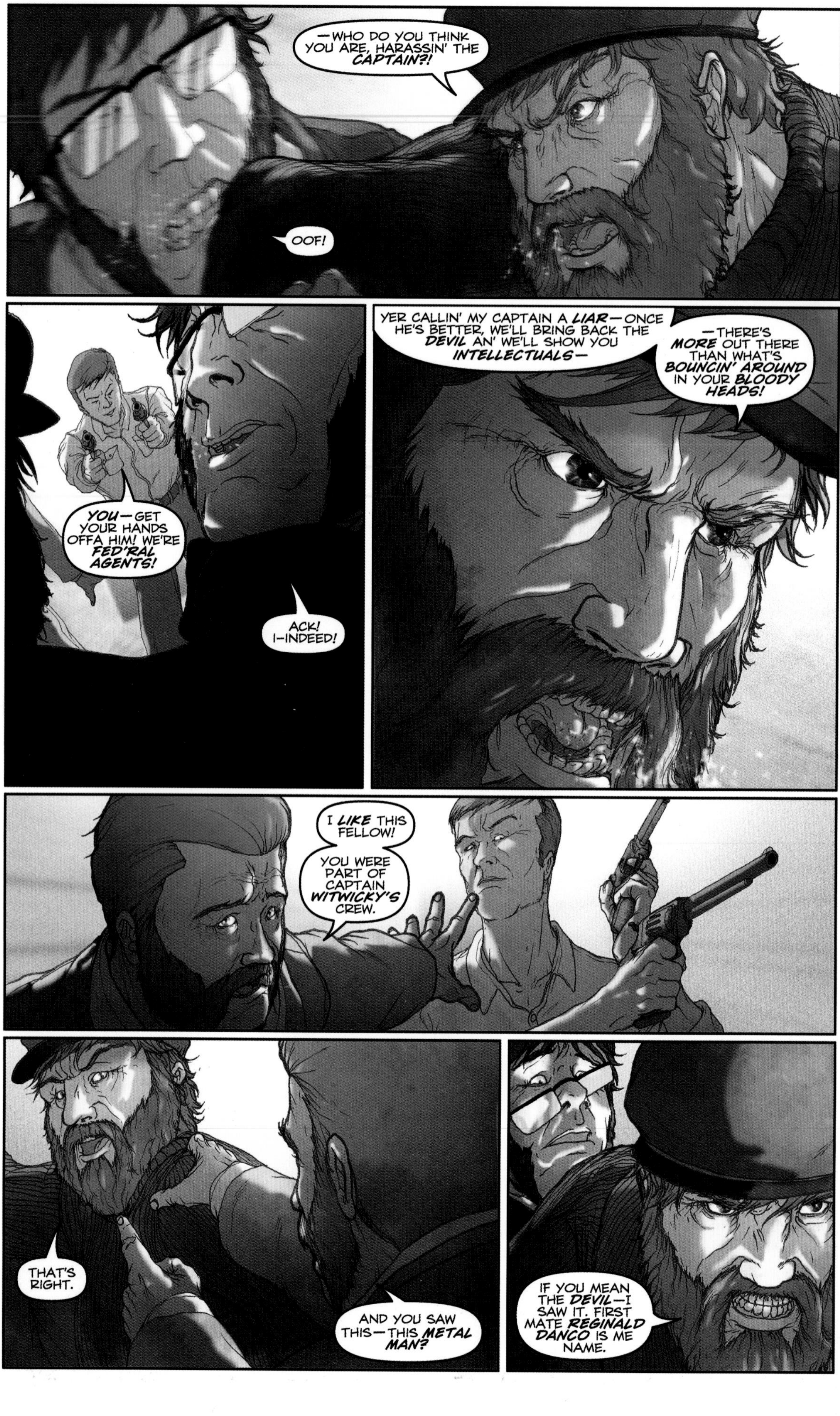
—WHO DO YOU THINK YOU ARE, HARASSIN' THE CAPTAIN?!
OOF!
YOU—GET YOUR HANDS OFFA HIM! WE'RE FED'RAL AGENTS!
ACK! I-INDEED!
YER CALLIN' MY CAPTAIN A LIAR—ONCE HE'S BETTER, WE'LL BRING BACK THE DEVIL AN' WE'LL SHOW YOU INTELLECTUALS—
—THERE'S MORE OUT THERE THAN WHAT'S BOUNCIN' AROUND IN YOUR BLOODY HEADS!
I LIKE THIS FELLOW!
YOU WERE PART OF CAPTAIN WITWICKY'S CREW.
THAT'S RIGHT.
AND YOU SAW THIS—THIS METAL MAN?
IF YOU MEAN THE DEVIL—I SAW IT. FIRST MATE REGINALD DANCO IS ME NAME.

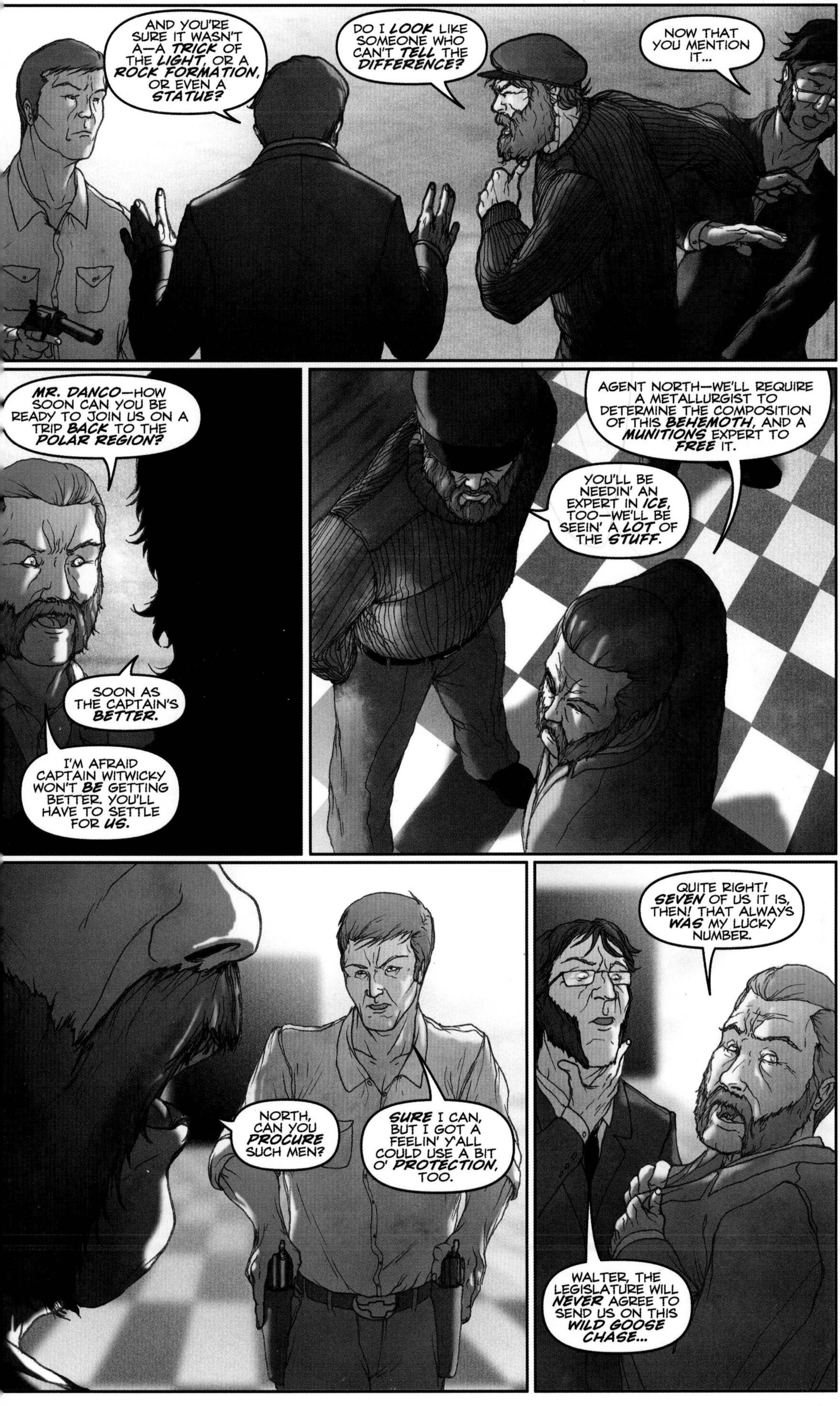
AND YOU'RE SURE IT WASN'T A—A TRICK OF THE LIGHT, OR A ROCK FORMATION, OR EVEN A STATUE?
DO I LOOK LIKE SOMEONE WHO CAN'T TELL THE DIFFERENCE?
NOW THAT YOU MENTION IT...
MR. DANCO—HOW SOON CAN YOU BE READY TO JOIN US ON A TRIP BACK TO THE POLAR REGION?
SOON AS THE CAPTAIN'S BETTER.
I'M AFRAID CAPTAIN WITWICKY WON'T BE GETTING BETTER. YOU'LL HAVE TO SETTLE FOR US.
AGENT NORTH—WE'LL REQUIRE A METALLURGIST TO DETERMINE THE COMPOSITION OF THIS BEHEMOTH, AND A MUNITIONS EXPERT TO FREE IT.
YOU'LL BE NEEDIN' AN EXPERT IN ICE, TOO—WE'LL BE SEEIN' A LOT OF THE STUFF.
NORTH, CAN YOU PROCURE SUCH MEN?
SURE I CAN, BUT I GOT A FEELIN' Y'ALL COULD USE A BIT O' PROTECTION, TOO.
QUITE RIGHT! SEVEN OF US IT IS, THEN! THAT ALWAYS WAS MY LUCKY NUMBER.
WALTER, THE LEGISLATURE WILL NEVER AGREE TO SEND US ON THIS WILD GOOSE CHASE...

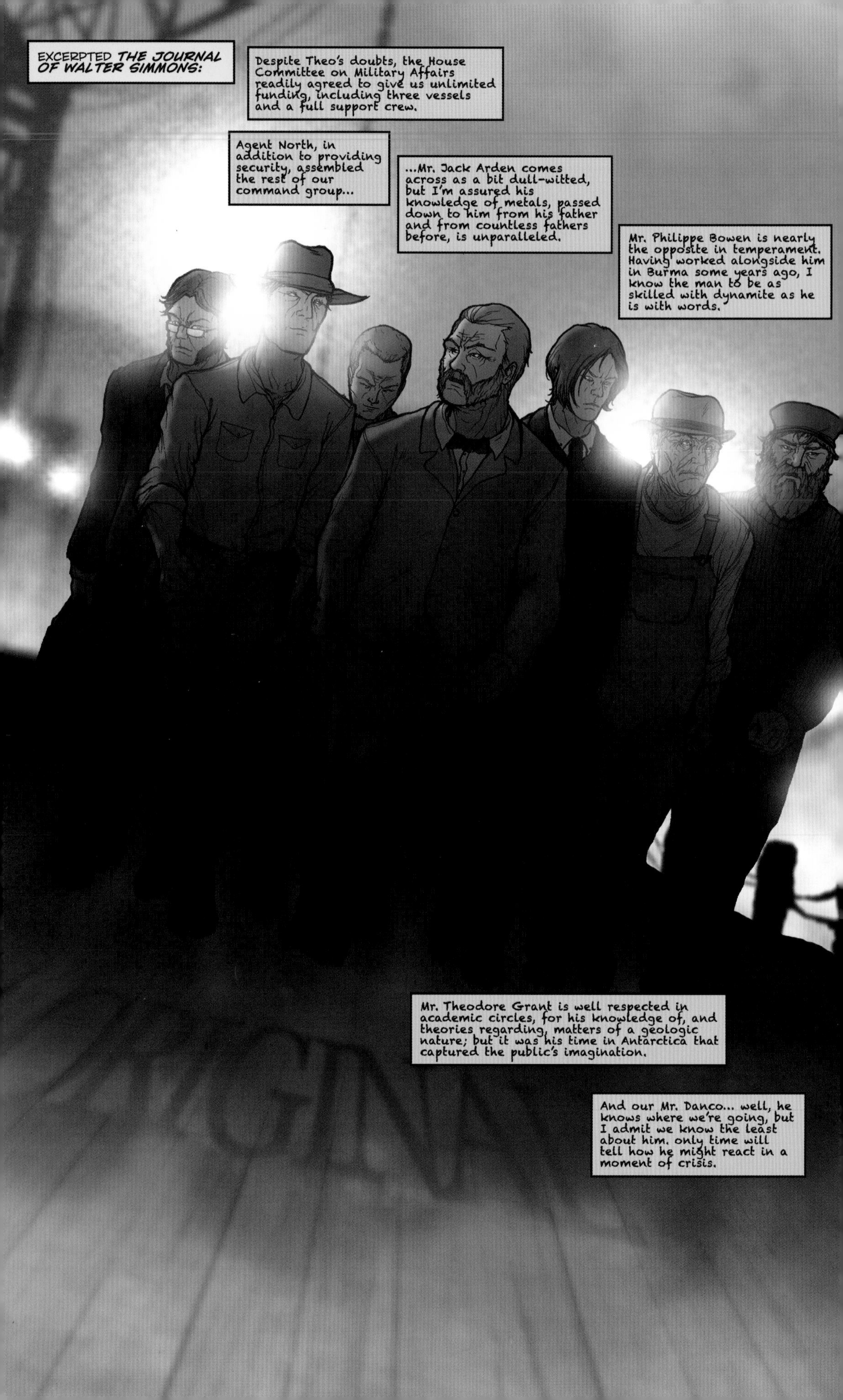
EXCERPTED THE JOURNAL OF WALTER SIMMONS:
Despite Theo's doubts, the House Committee on Military Affairs readily agreed to give us unlimited funding, including three vessels and a full support crew.
Agent North, in addition to providing security, assembled the rest of our command group...
...Mr. Jack Arden comes across as a bit dull-witted, but I'm assured his knowledge of metals, passed down to him from his father and from countless fathers before, is unparalleled.
Mr. Philippe Bowen is nearly the opposite in temperament. Having worked alongside him in Burma some years ago, I know the man to be as skilled with dynamite as he is with words.
Mr. Theodore Grant is well respected in academic circles, for his knowledge of, and theories regarding, matters of a geologic nature; but it was his time in Antarctica that captured the public's imagination.
And our Mr. Danco... well, he knows where we're going, but I admit we know the least about him. only time will tell how he might react in a moment of crisis.

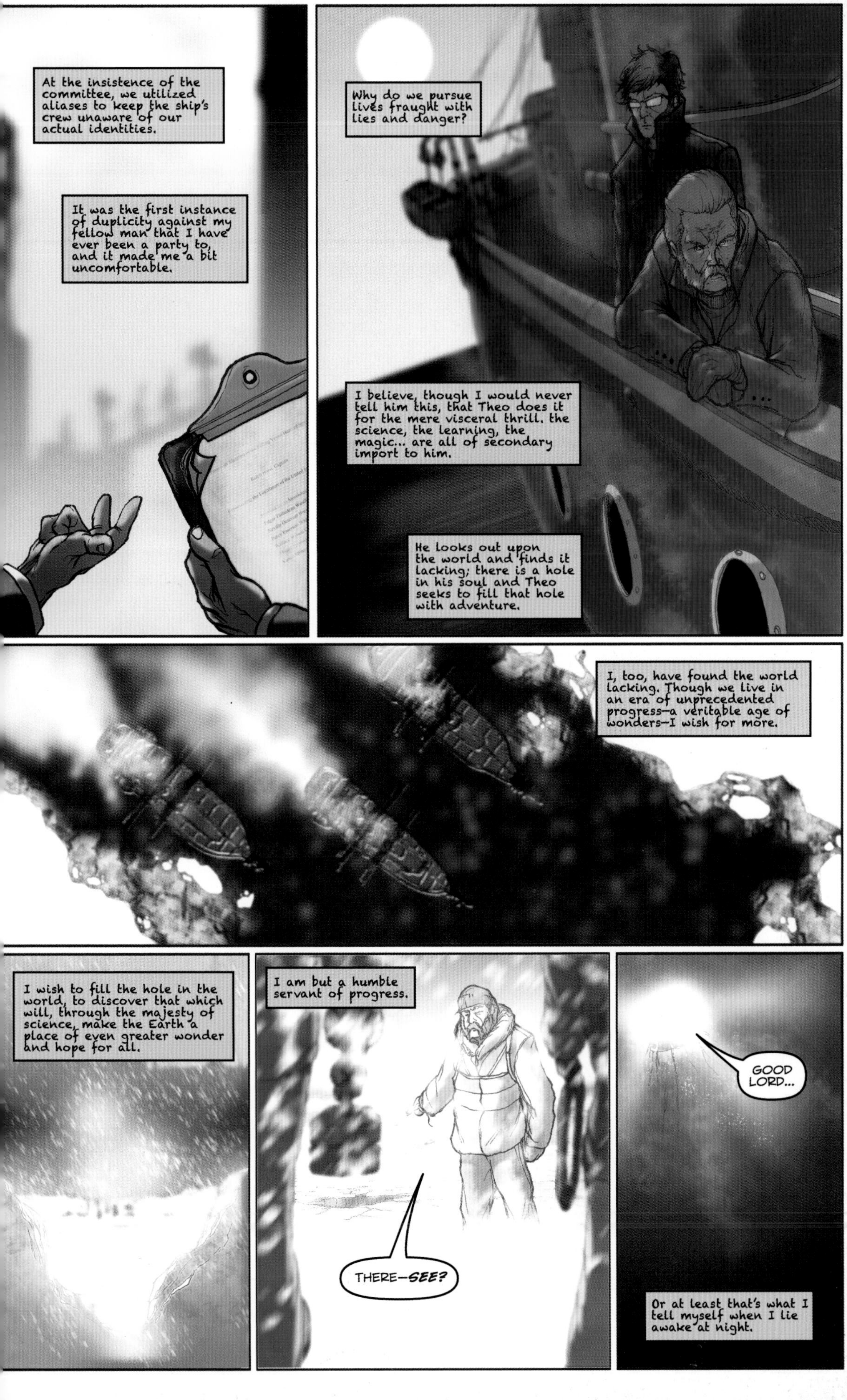
At the insistence of the committee, we utilized aliases to keep the ship's crew unaware of our actual identities.
It was the first instance of duplicity against my fellow man that I have ever been a party to, and it made me a bit uncomfortable.
Why do we pursue lives fraught with lies and danger?
I believe, though I would never tell him this, that Theo does it for the mere visceral thrill. the science, the learning, the magic... are all of secondary import to him.
He looks out upon the world and finds it lacking; there is a hole in his soul and Theo seeks to fill that hole with adventure.
I, too, have found the world lacking. Though we live in an era of unprecedented progress—a veritable age of wonders—I wish for more.
I wish to fill the hole in the world, to discover that which will, through the majesty of science, make the Earth a place of even greater wonder and hope for all.
I am but a humble servant of progress.
THERE—SEE?
GOOD LORD...
Or at least that's what I tell myself when I lie awake at night.

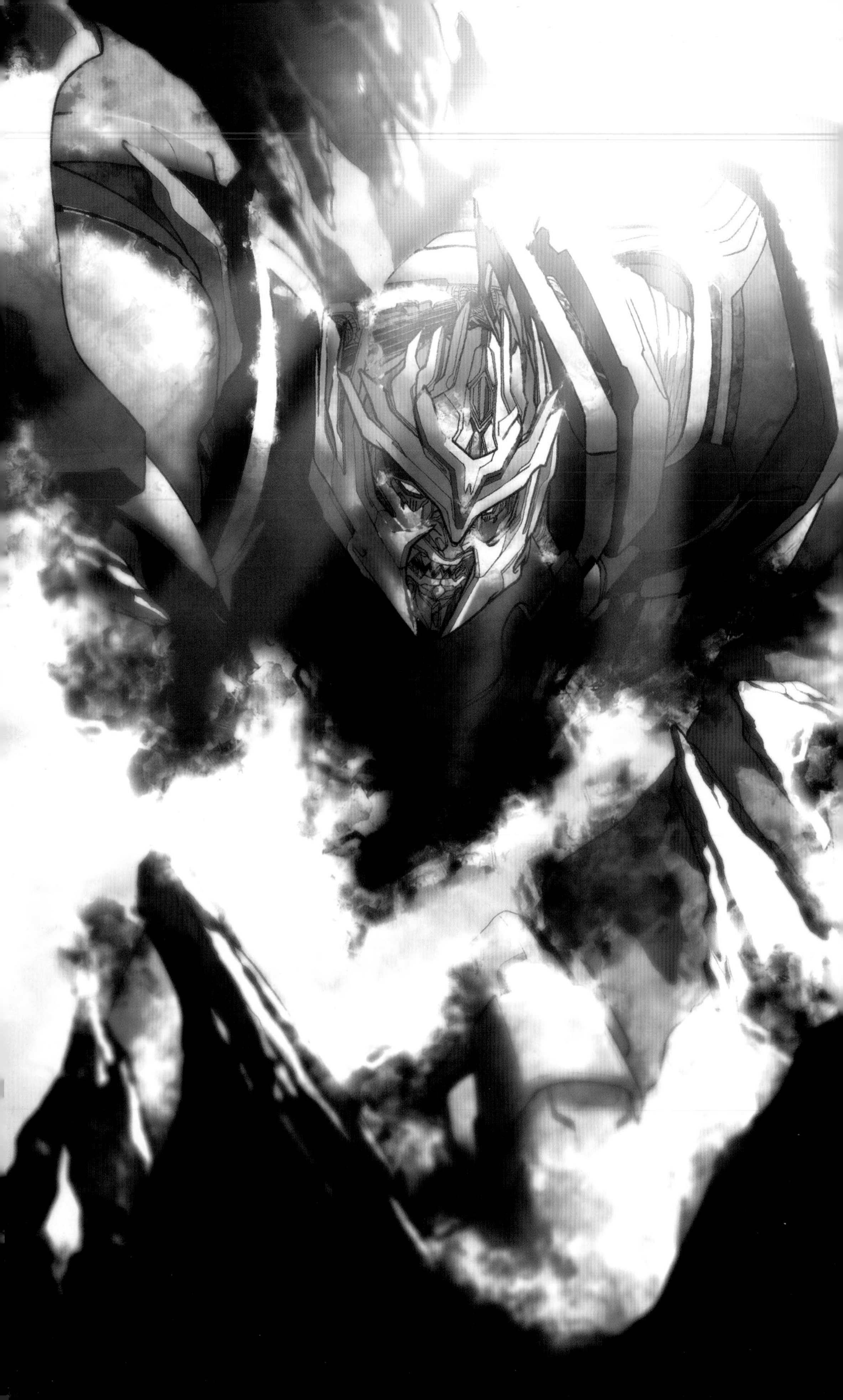

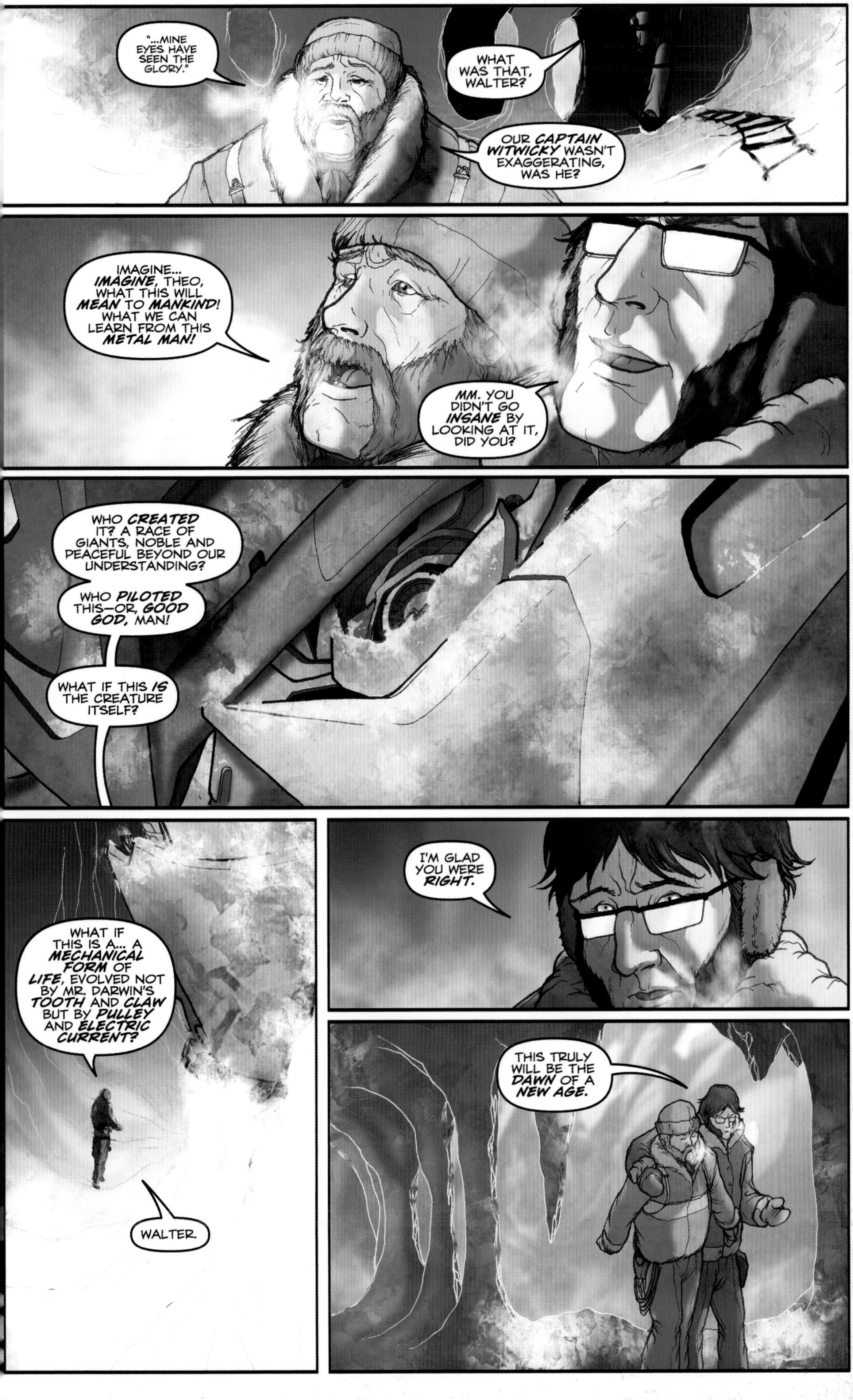
"...MINE EYES HAVE SEEN THE GLORY."
WHAT WAS THAT, WALTER?
OUR CAPTAIN WITWICKY WASN'T EXAGGERATING, WAS HE?
IMAGINE... IMAGINE, THEO, WHAT THIS WILL MEAN TO MANKIND! WHAT WE CAN LEARN FROM THIS METAL MAN!
MM. YOU DIDN'T GO INSANE BY LOOKING AT IT, DID YOU?
WHO CREATED IT? A RACE OF GIANTS, NOBLE AND PEACEFUL BEYOND OUR UNDERSTANDING?
WHO PILOTED THIS—OR, GOOD GOD, MAN!
WHAT IF THIS IS THE CREATURE ITSELF?
WHAT IF THIS IS A... A MECHANICAL FORM OF LIFE, EVOLVED NOT BY MR. DARWIN'S TOOTH AND CLAW BUT BY PULLEY AND ELECTRIC CURRENT?
WALTER.
I'M GLAD YOU WERE RIGHT.
THIS TRULY WILL BE THE DAWN OF A NEW AGE.

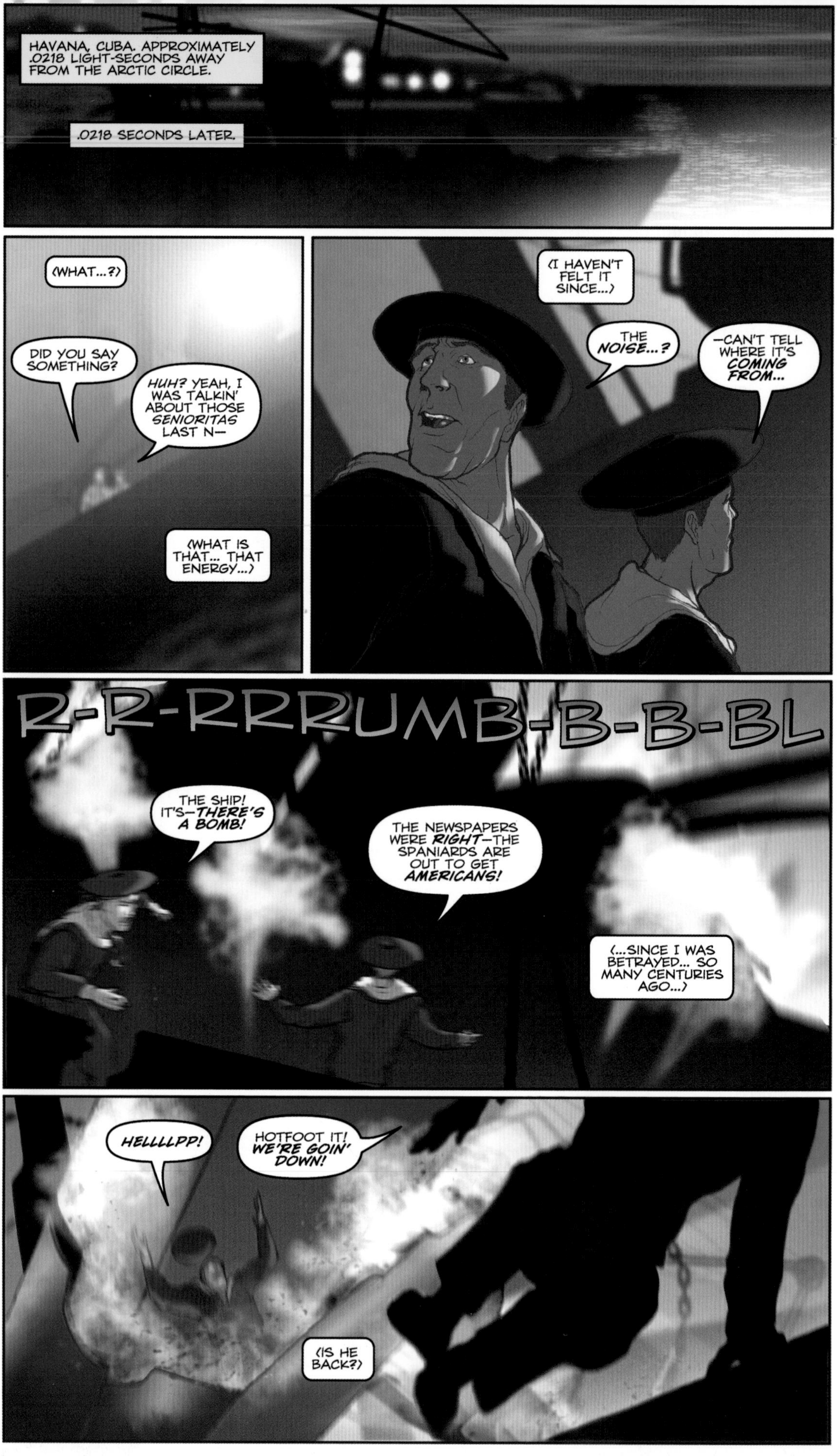
HAVANA, CUBA. APPROXIMATELY .0218 LIGHT-SECONDS AWAY FROM THE ARCTIC CIRCLE.
.0218 SECONDS LATER.
(WHAT...?)
DID YOU SAY SOMETHING?
HUH? YEAH, I WAS TALKIN' ABOUT THOSE SENIORITAS LAST N—
(WHAT IS THAT... THAT ENERGY...)
(I HAVEN'T FELT IT SINCE...)
THE NOISE...?
—CAN'T TELL WHERE IT'S COMING FROM...
R-R-RRRUMB-B-B-BL
THE SHIP! IT'S—THERE'S A BOMB!
THE NEWSPAPERS WERE RIGHT—THE SPANIARDS ARE OUT TO GET AMERICANS!
(...SINCE I WAS BETRAYED... SO MANY CENTURIES AGO...)
HELLLLPP!
HOTFOOT IT! WE'RE GOIN' DOWN!
(IS HE BACK?)

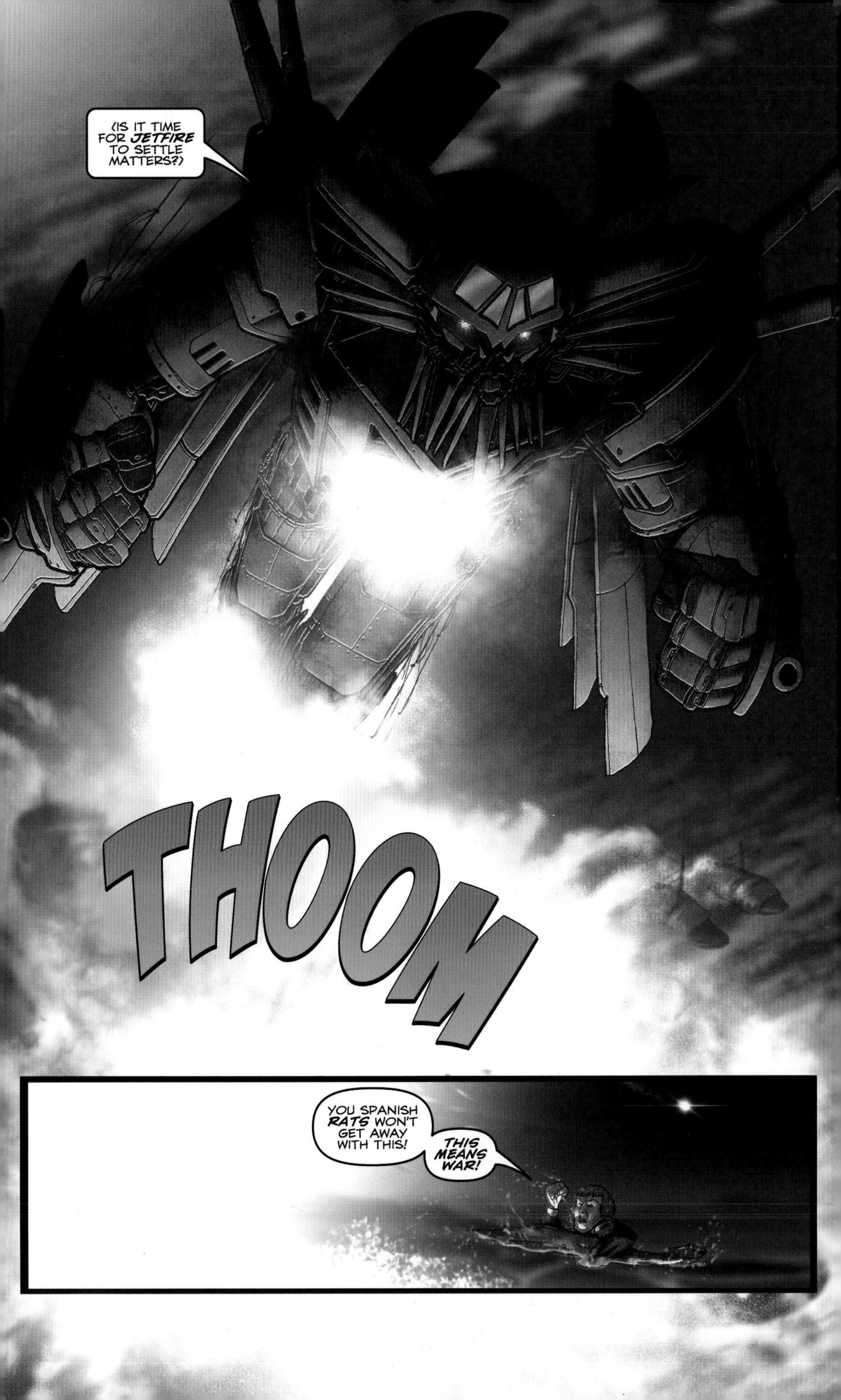
(IS IT TIME FOR JETFIRE TO SETTLE MATTERS?)
THOOM
YOU SPANISH RATS WON'T GET AWAY WITH THIS!
THIS MEANS WAR!

THAT *THING* TURNED MY CAPTAIN *CRAZY*.

YEAH... IT'S *SOMETHIN'* ALL RIGHT, DANCO.

HMPH. IT AIN'T *SOMETHIN'* TO BE *STUDIED* AN' *BROUGHT* HOME.

IT'S *SOMETHIN'* WE OUGHTA *DESTROY*. BEFORE IT DESTROYS *US*.

QUITE A *MOTLEY CREW* WE'VE ASSEMBLED HERE...

...DO YOU THINK THEY'LL BE ABLE TO *FREE* THE ICE MAN? I'D HATE TO SPEND THE REST OF MY DAYS IN THE DAMNED *NORTH POLE*.

I CAN'T BELIEVE HOW *CALMLY* YOU'RE TAKING THIS... IT'S A *MACHINE* FROM *ANOTHER WORLD*, THEO!

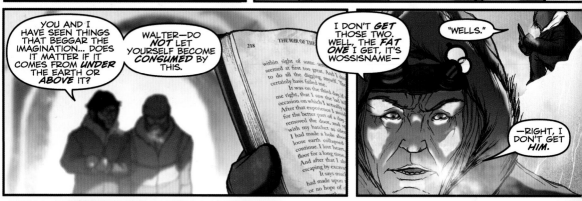

YOU AND I HAVE SEEN THINGS THAT BEGGAR THE IMAGINATION... DOES IT MATTER IF IT COMES FROM *UNDER* THE EARTH OR *ABOVE* IT?

WALTER—DO *NOT* LET YOURSELF BECOME *CONSUMED* BY THIS.

218   THE WAR OF THE

within sight of some sc... seemed at first too great. And I dug to do all the digging myself. T... certainly have failed me. T...

It was on the third day, if... me right, that I saw the lad y... occasion on which I actually y... After that experience I wo... for the better part of a day... removed the door, and a... with my hatchet as slow... I had made a hole abo... loose earth collapsed... continue. I lost hearts floor for a long time... And after that I al... escaping by excava...

It says mu... had made upon... or no hope of ...

I DON'T *GET* THOSE TWO. WELL, THE *FAT ONE* I GET, IT'S WOSSISNAME—

"WELLS."

—RIGHT, I DON'T GET *HIM*.

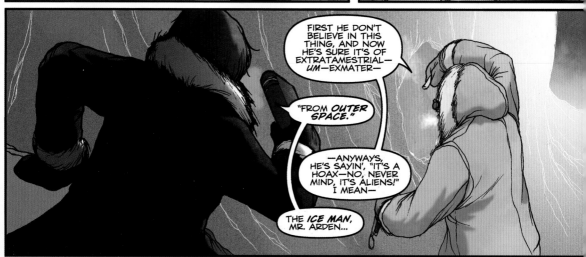

FIRST HE DON'T BELIEVE IN THIS THING, AND NOW HE'S SURE IT'S OF EXTRATAMESTRIAL— UM—EXMATER—

"FROM *OUTER SPACE*."

—ANYWAYS, HE'S SAYIN', "IT'S A HOAX—NO, NEVER MIND, IT'S ALIENS!" I MEAN—

THE *ICE MAN*, MR. ARDEN...

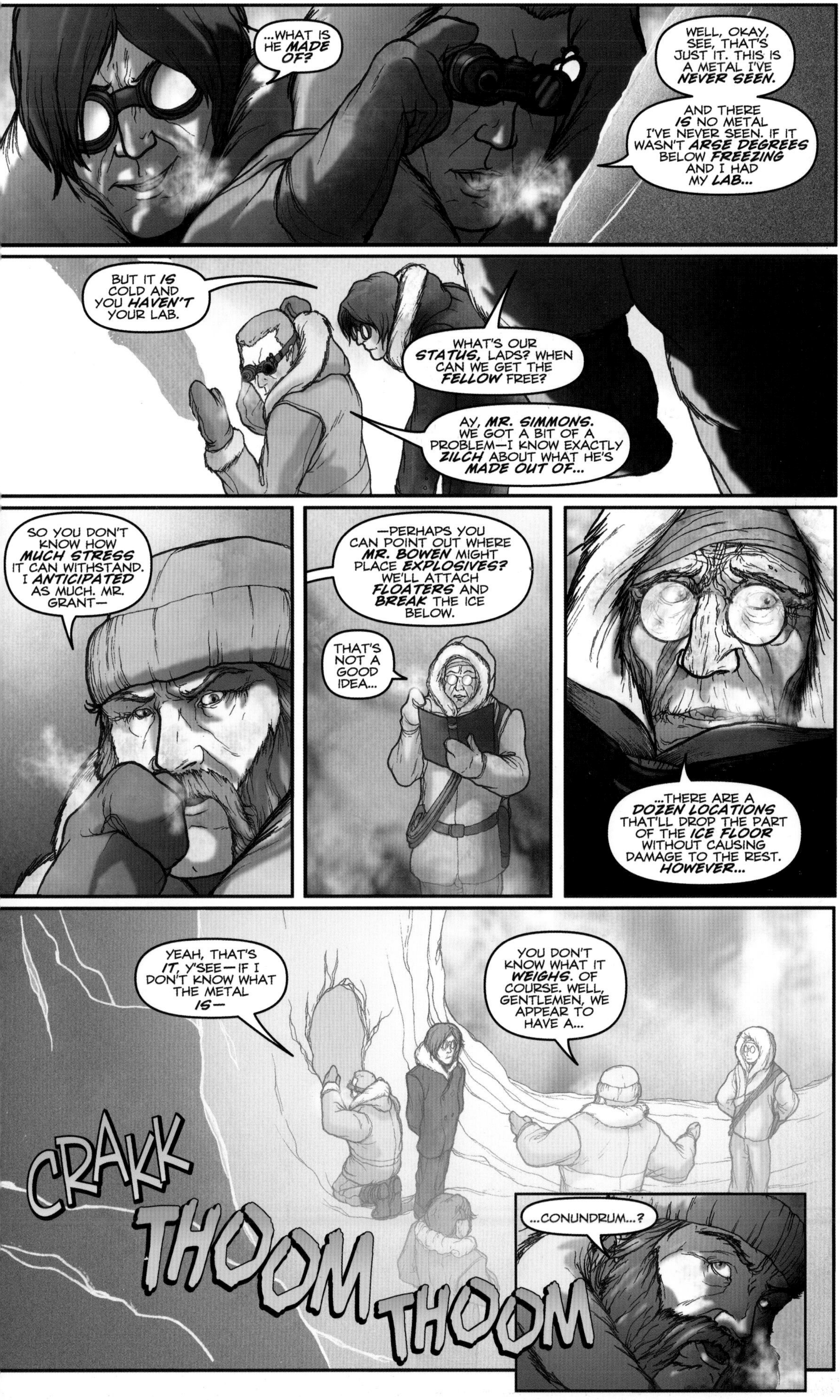
...WHAT IS HE MADE OF?
WELL, OKAY, SEE, THAT'S JUST IT. THIS IS A METAL I'VE NEVER SEEN.
AND THERE IS NO METAL I'VE NEVER SEEN. IF IT WASN'T ARSE DEGREES BELOW FREEZING AND I HAD MY LAB...
BUT IT IS COLD AND YOU HAVEN'T YOUR LAB.
WHAT'S OUR STATUS, LADS? WHEN CAN WE GET THE FELLOW FREE?
AY, MR. SIMMONS. WE GOT A BIT OF A PROBLEM—I KNOW EXACTLY ZILCH ABOUT WHAT HE'S MADE OUT OF...
SO YOU DON'T KNOW HOW MUCH STRESS IT CAN WITHSTAND. I ANTICIPATED AS MUCH. MR. GRANT—
—PERHAPS YOU CAN POINT OUT WHERE MR. BOWEN MIGHT PLACE EXPLOSIVES? WE'LL ATTACH FLOATERS AND BREAK THE ICE BELOW.
THAT'S NOT A GOOD IDEA...
...THERE ARE A DOZEN LOCATIONS THAT'LL DROP THE PART OF THE ICE FLOOR WITHOUT CAUSING DAMAGE TO THE REST. HOWEVER...
YEAH, THAT'S IT, Y'SEE—IF I DON'T KNOW WHAT THE METAL IS—
YOU DON'T KNOW WHAT IT WEIGHS. OF COURSE. WELL, GENTLEMEN, WE APPEAR TO HAVE A...
CRAKK
THOOM
THOOM
...CONUNDRUM...?

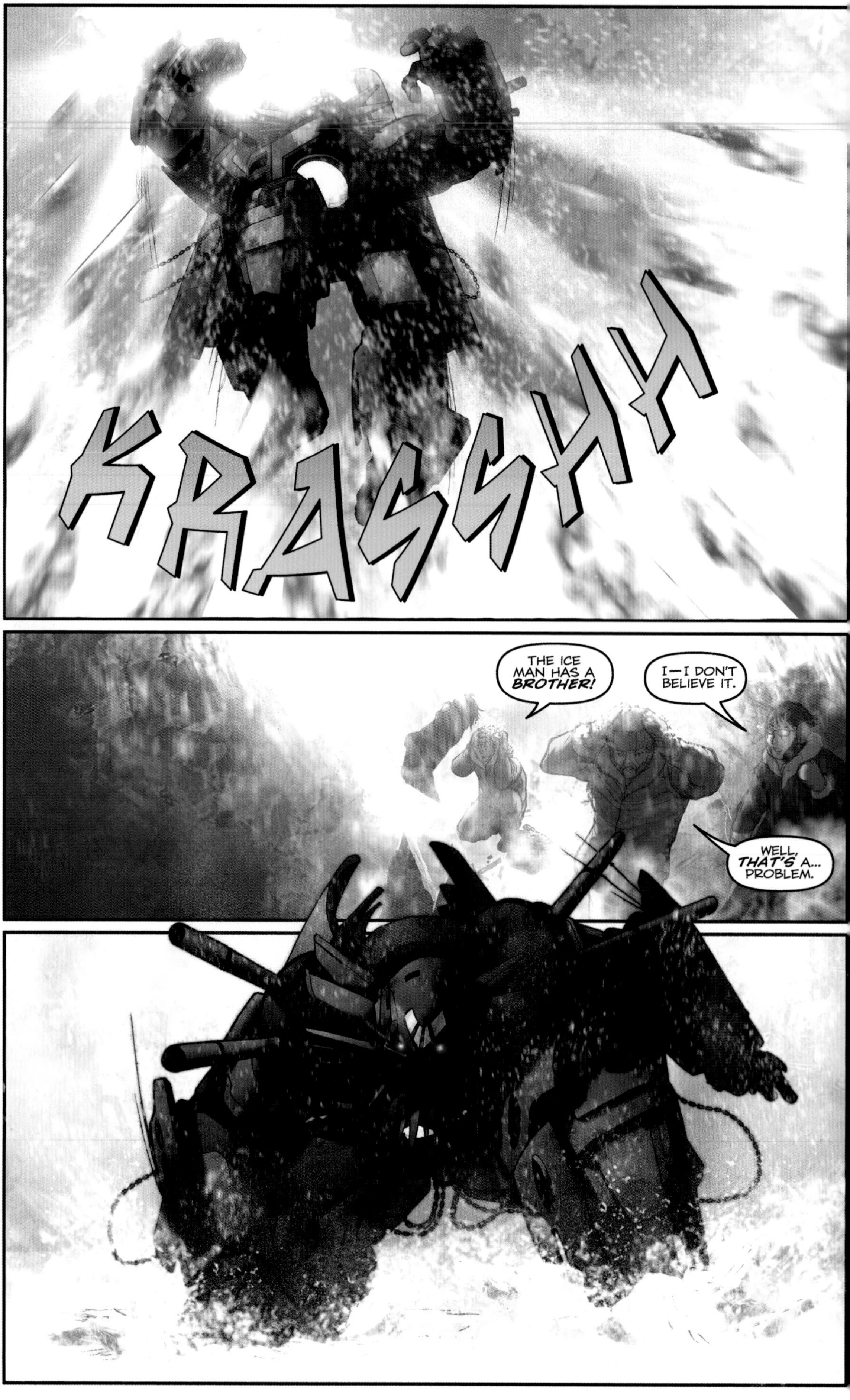
KRASSHH
THE ICE MAN HAS A *BROTHER!*
I—I DON'T BELIEVE IT.
WELL, *THAT'S* A... PROBLEM.

MY GOD—IT'S—IT'S *UNHOLY*...

UH... WHAT *NOW*, BOSS?

⟨YOU. YOU HAVE *AWAKENED*.⟩

⟨Y-YES...⟩

OI! THAT NOISE—*WHAT IS IT!?*

⟨YOU WEAR THE MARKINGS OF THE *DECEPTICONS*.⟩

IT'S TALKING.

HM. I SUPPOSE YOU SHOULD'VE EMPLOYED A CLEVER *LINGUIST* RATHER THAN A *USELESS METALLURGIST*.

HEY! WATCH WHO YOU'RE CALLIN' "CLEVER"!

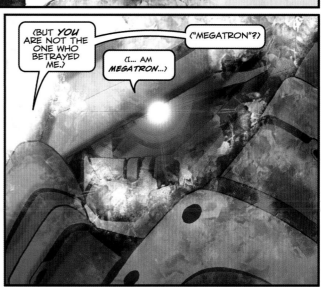

⟨BUT *YOU* ARE NOT THE ONE WHO BETRAYED ME.⟩

⟨"MEGATRON"?⟩

⟨I... AM *MEGATRON*...⟩

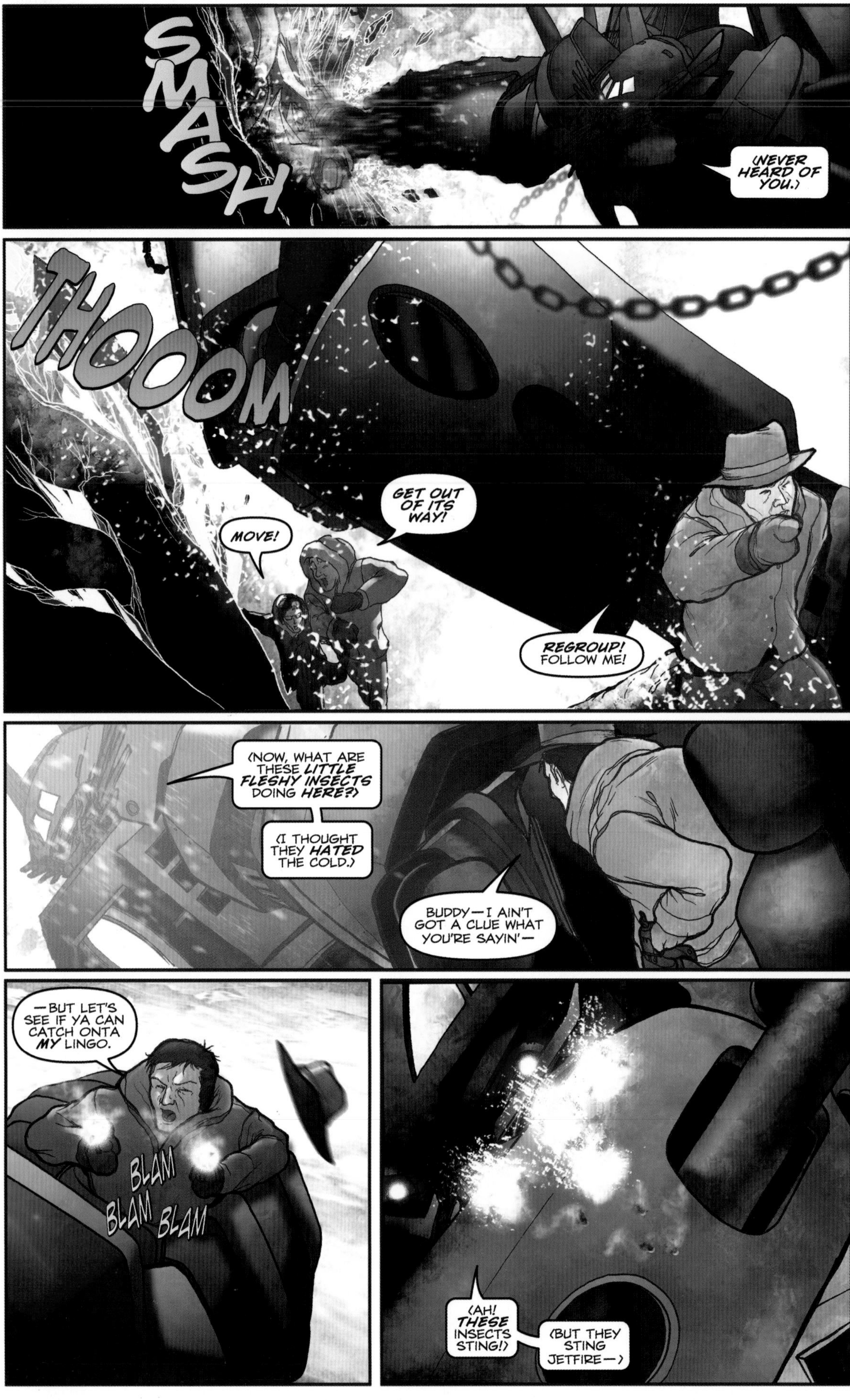

SMASH
⟨NEVER HEARD OF YOU.⟩
THOOOM
GET OUT OF ITS WAY!
MOVE!
REGROUP! FOLLOW ME!
⟨NOW, WHAT ARE THESE LITTLE FLESHY INSECTS DOING HERE?⟩
⟨I THOUGHT THEY HATED THE COLD.⟩
BUDDY—I AIN'T GOT A CLUE WHAT YOU'RE SAYIN'—
—BUT LET'S SEE IF YA CAN CATCH ONTA MY LINGO.
BLAM BLAM BLAM BLAM
⟨AH! THESE INSECTS STING!⟩
⟨BUT THEY STING JETFIRE—⟩

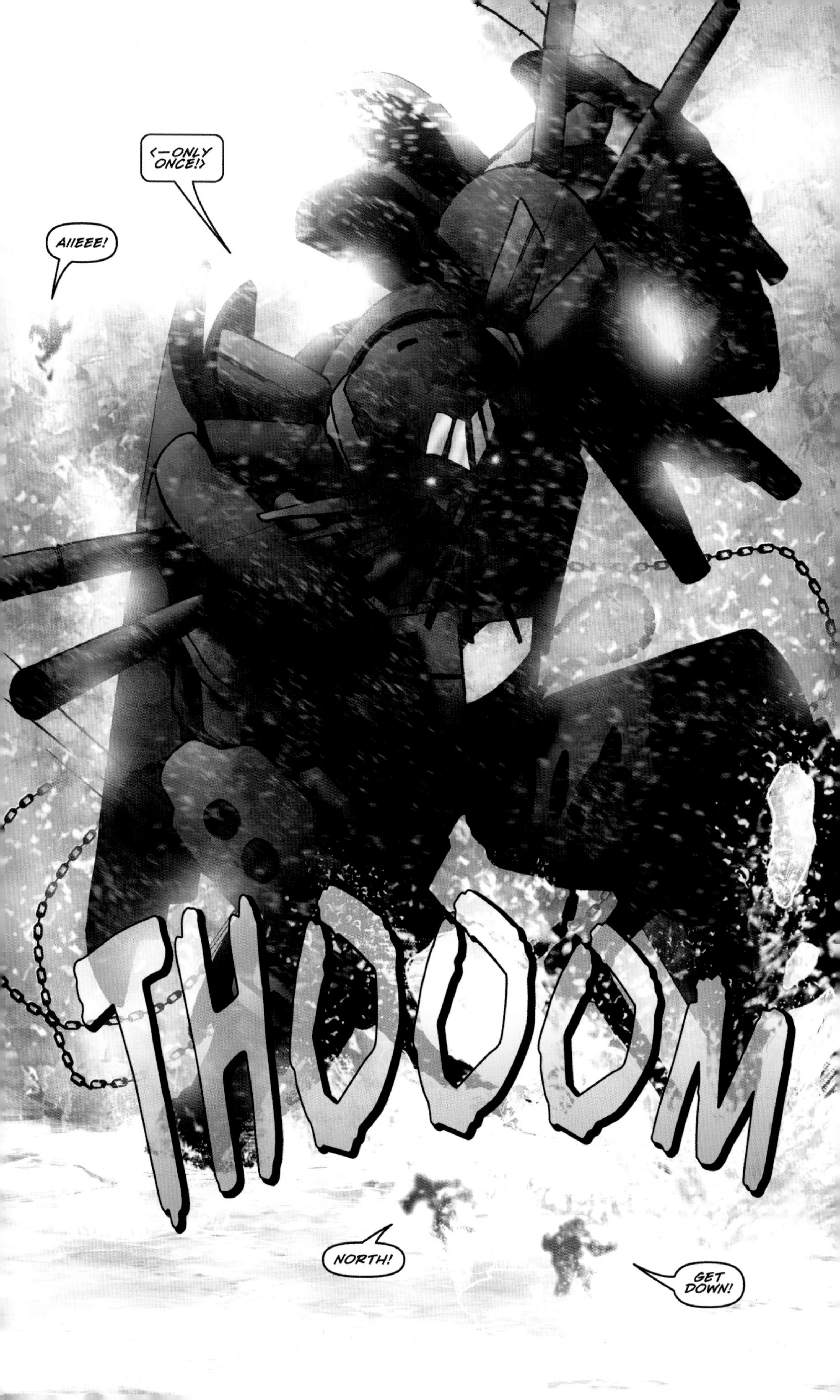

<—ONLY ONCE!>
AIIEEE!
THOOOM!
NORTH!
GET DOWN!

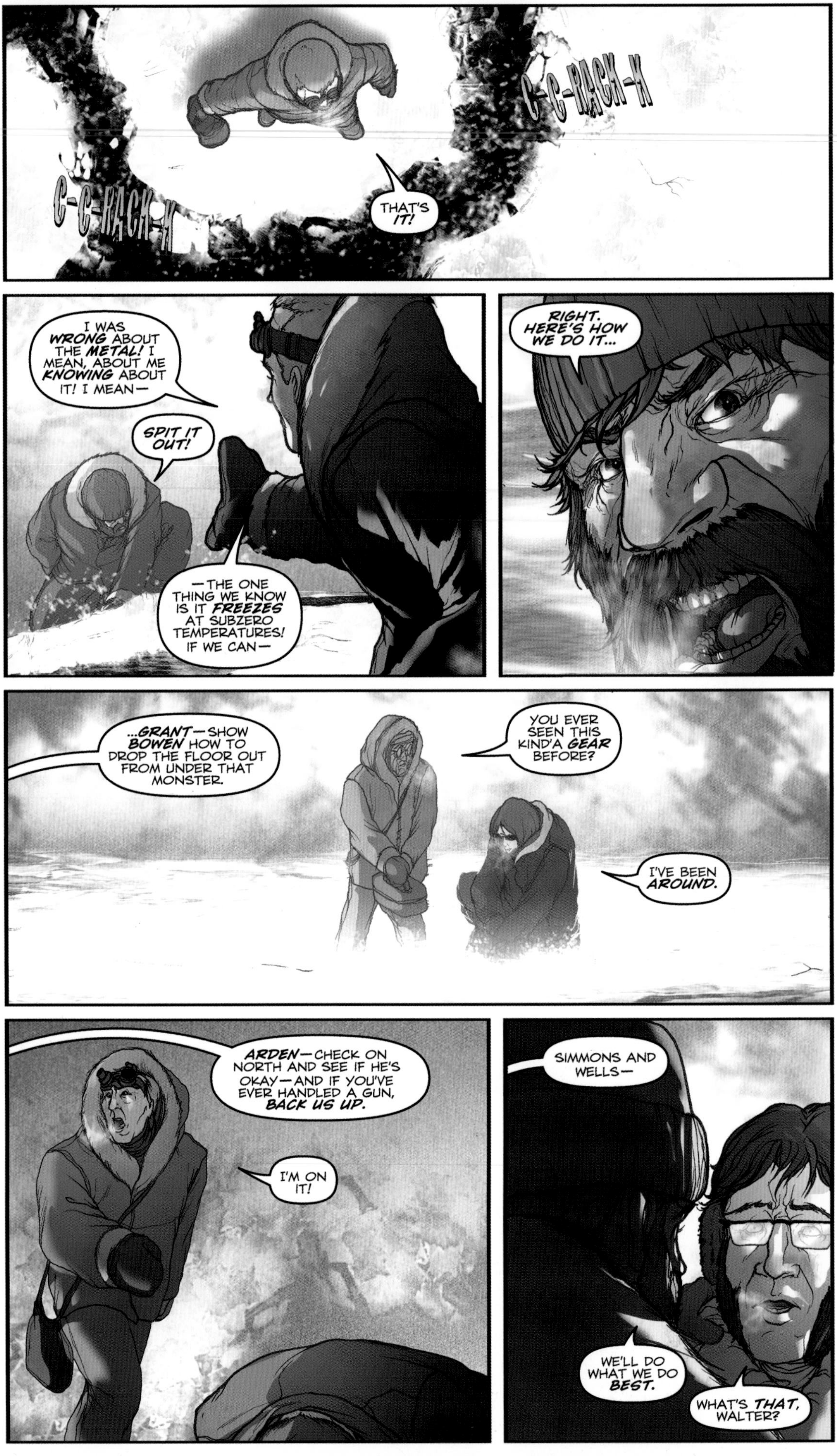
C-C-RACK-K
C-C-RACK-K
THAT'S *IT!*
I WAS ***WRONG*** ABOUT THE ***METAL!*** I MEAN, ABOUT ME ***KNOWING*** ABOUT IT! I MEAN—
SPIT IT OUT!
—THE ONE THING WE KNOW IS IT ***FREEZES*** AT SUBZERO TEMPERATURES! IF WE CAN—
RIGHT. HERE'S HOW WE DO IT...
...***GRANT***—SHOW ***BOWEN*** HOW TO DROP THE FLOOR OUT FROM UNDER THAT MONSTER.
YOU EVER SEEN THIS KIND'A ***GEAR*** BEFORE?
I'VE BEEN ***AROUND.***
ARDEN—CHECK ON NORTH AND SEE IF HE'S OKAY—AND IF YOU'VE EVER HANDLED A GUN, ***BACK US UP.***
I'M ON IT!
SIMMONS AND WELLS—
WE'LL DO WHAT WE DO ***BEST.***
WHAT'S ***THAT,*** WALTER?

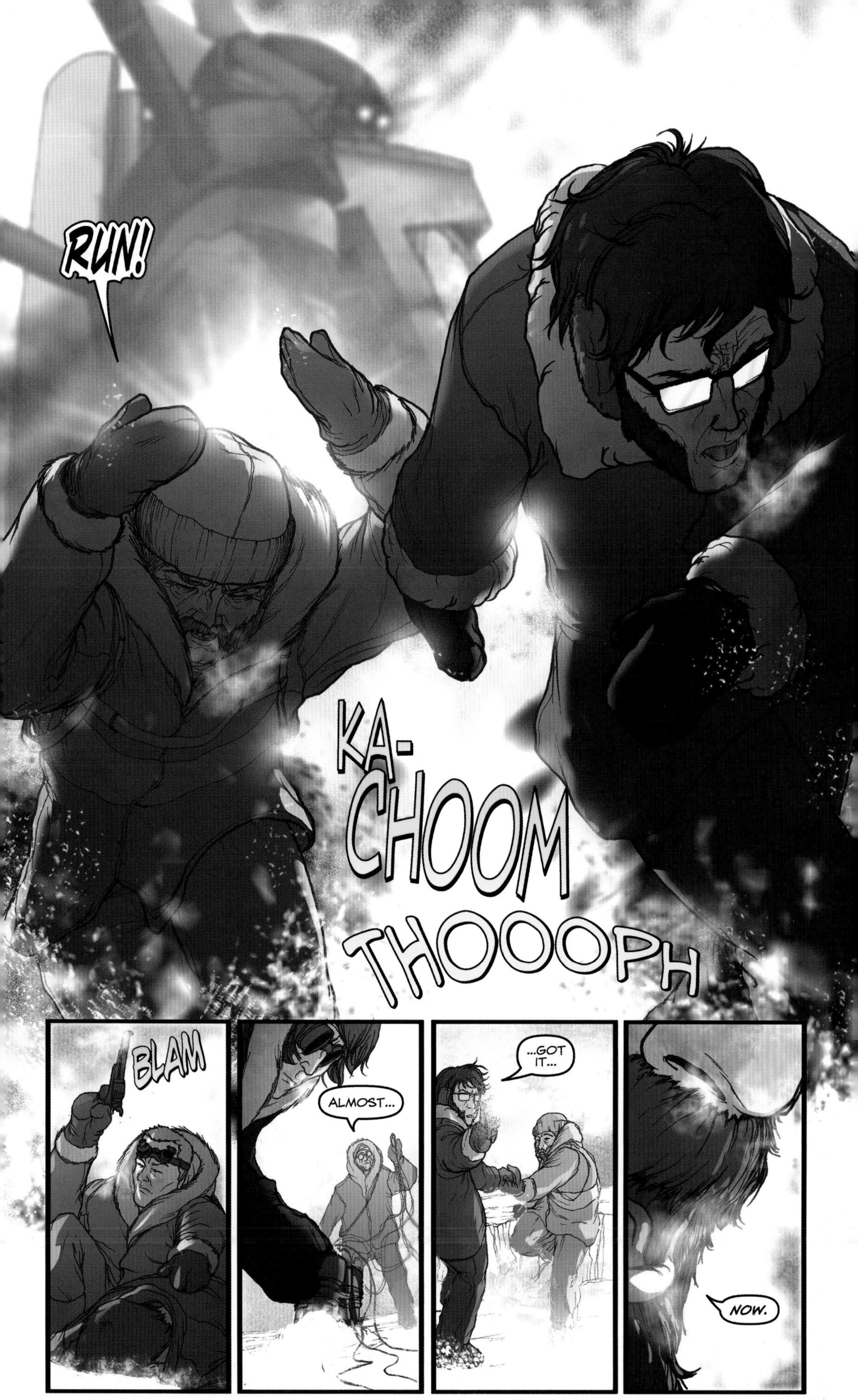
RUN!
KA-CHOOM
THOOOPH
BLAM
ALMOST...
...GOT IT...
NOW.

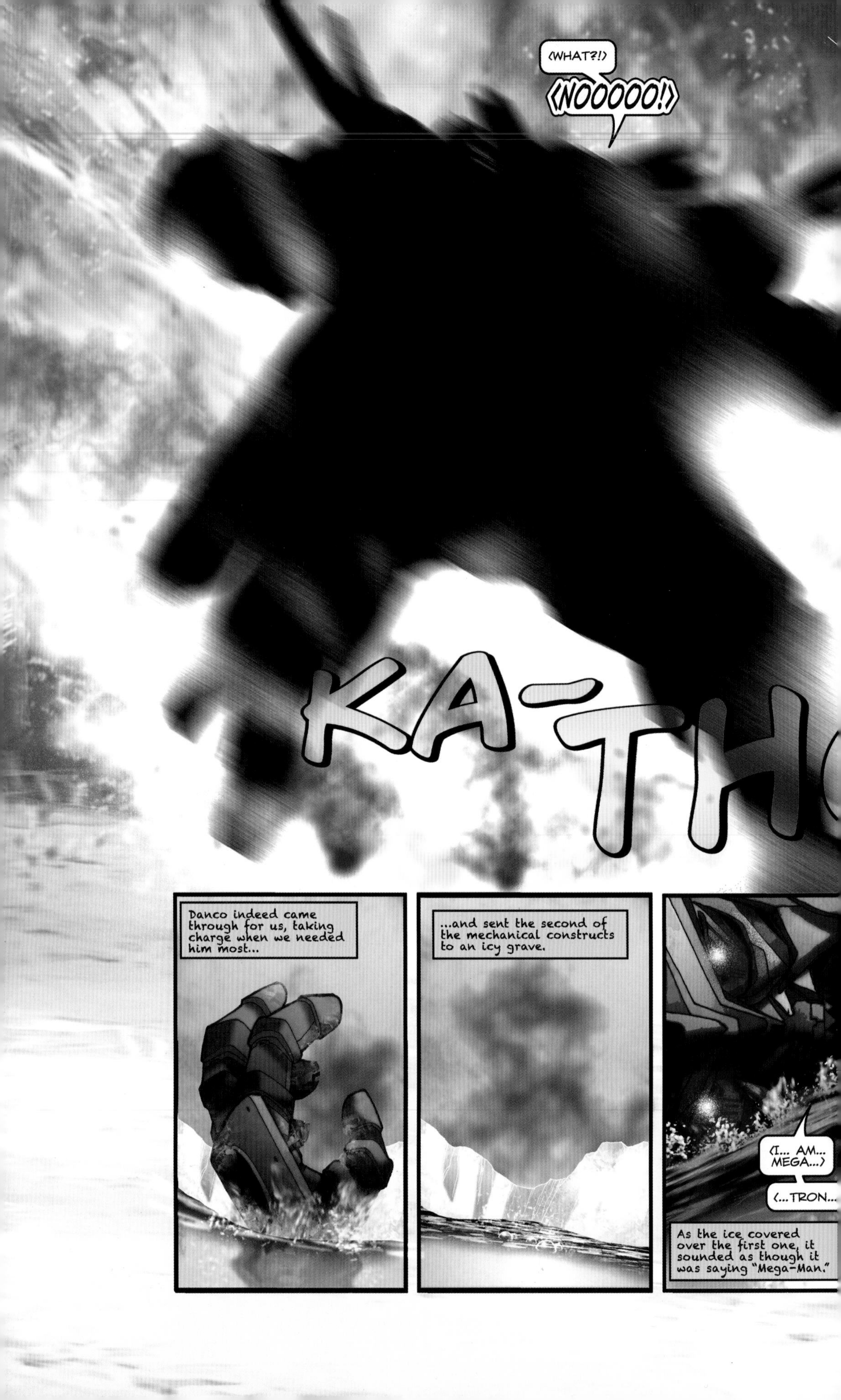

‹WHAT?!›
‹NOOOOO!›
KA-TH
Danco indeed came through for us, taking charge when we needed him most...
...and sent the second of the mechanical constructs to an icy grave.
‹I... AM... MEGA...›
‹...TRON...
As the ice covered over the first one, it sounded as though it was saying "Mega-Man."

DOOM

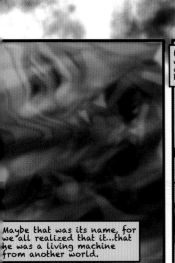

Maybe that was its name, for we all realized that it...that he was a living machine from another world.

Or, in less fantastical terms, a non-biological extraterrestrial.

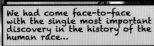

We had come face-to-face with the single most important discovery in the history of the human race...

...and we had not all lived to tell the tale.

YOU ASKED THAT I NOT LET THIS *CONSUME ME*, THEO?

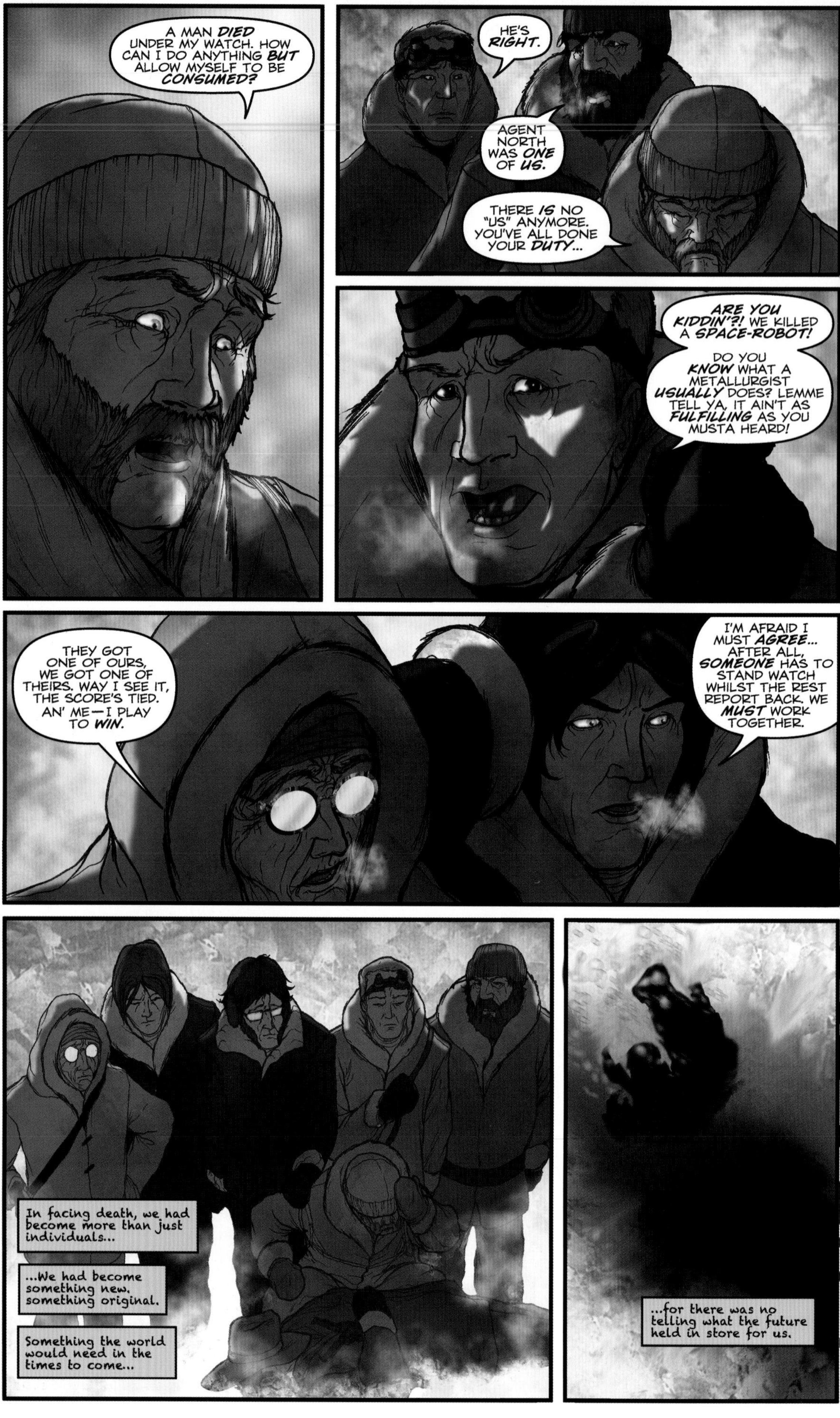
A MAN DIED UNDER MY WATCH. HOW CAN I DO ANYTHING BUT ALLOW MYSELF TO BE CONSUMED?
HE'S RIGHT.
AGENT NORTH WAS ONE OF US.
THERE IS NO "US" ANYMORE. YOU'VE ALL DONE YOUR DUTY...
ARE YOU KIDDIN'?! WE KILLED A SPACE-ROBOT!
DO YOU KNOW WHAT A METALLURGIST USUALLY DOES? LEMME TELL YA, IT AIN'T AS FULFILLING AS YOU MUSTA HEARD!
THEY GOT ONE OF OURS, WE GOT ONE OF THEIRS. WAY I SEE IT, THE SCORE'S TIED. AN' ME—I PLAY TO WIN.
I'M AFRAID I MUST AGREE... AFTER ALL, SOMEONE HAS TO STAND WATCH WHILST THE REST REPORT BACK. WE MUST WORK TOGETHER.
In facing death, we had become more than just individuals...
...We had become something new. something original.
Something the world would need in the times to come...
...for there was no telling what the future held in store for us.

THE MIDDLE OF NOWHERE, NEVADA. SUNDAY, APRIL 6, 1913.
2
MOMMY— WILL DADDY LIKE MY PICTURE?

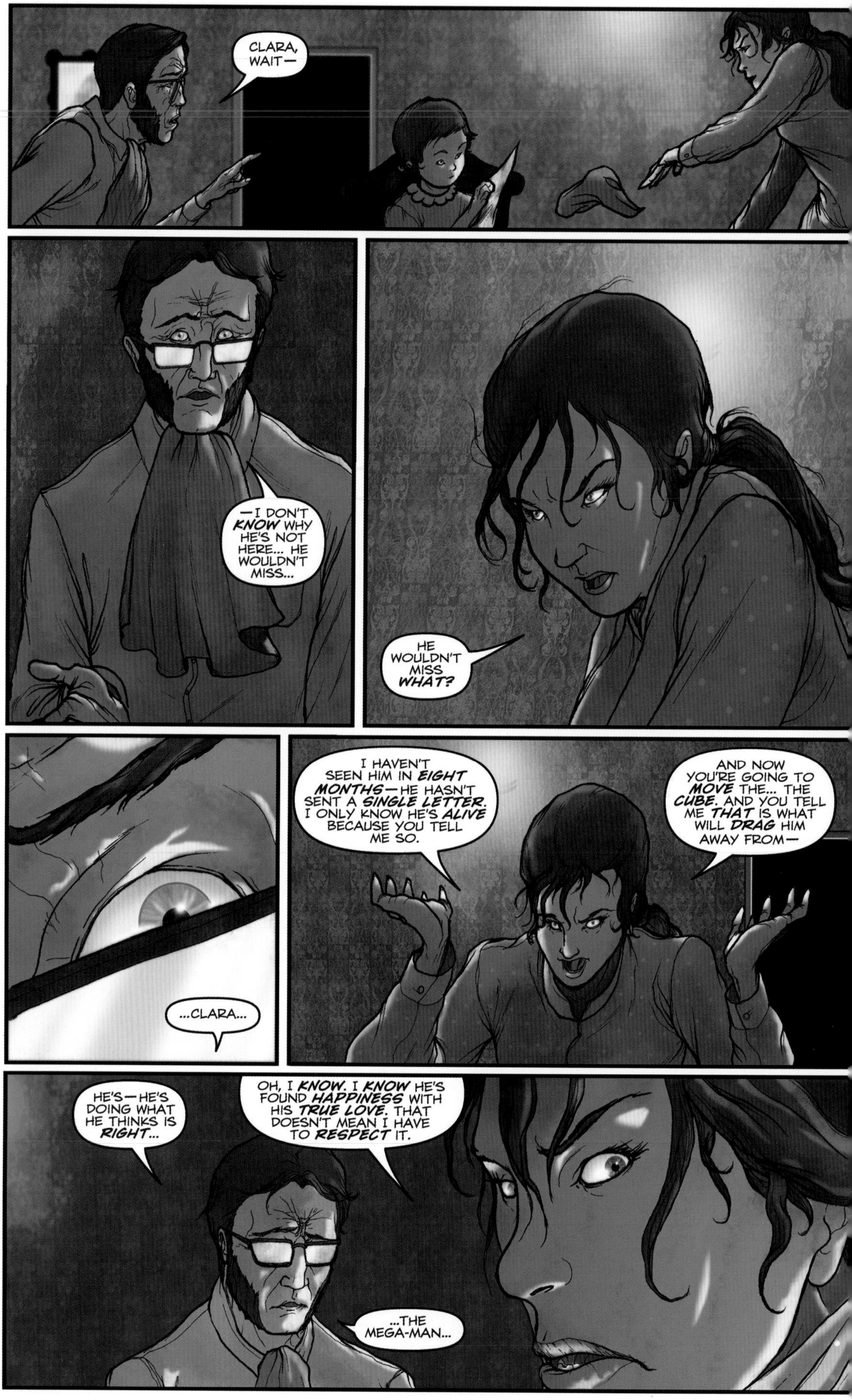
CLARA, WAIT—
—I DON'T KNOW WHY HE'S NOT HERE... HE WOULDN'T MISS...
HE WOULDN'T MISS WHAT?
...CLARA...
I HAVEN'T SEEN HIM IN EIGHT MONTHS—HE HASN'T SENT A SINGLE LETTER. I ONLY KNOW HE'S ALIVE BECAUSE YOU TELL ME SO.
AND NOW YOU'RE GOING TO MOVE THE... THE CUBE. AND YOU TELL ME THAT IS WHAT WILL DRAG HIM AWAY FROM—
HE'S—HE'S DOING WHAT HE THINKS IS RIGHT...
OH, I KNOW. I KNOW HE'S FOUND HAPPINESS WITH HIS TRUE LOVE. THAT DOESN'T MEAN I HAVE TO RESPECT IT.
...THE MEGA-MAN...

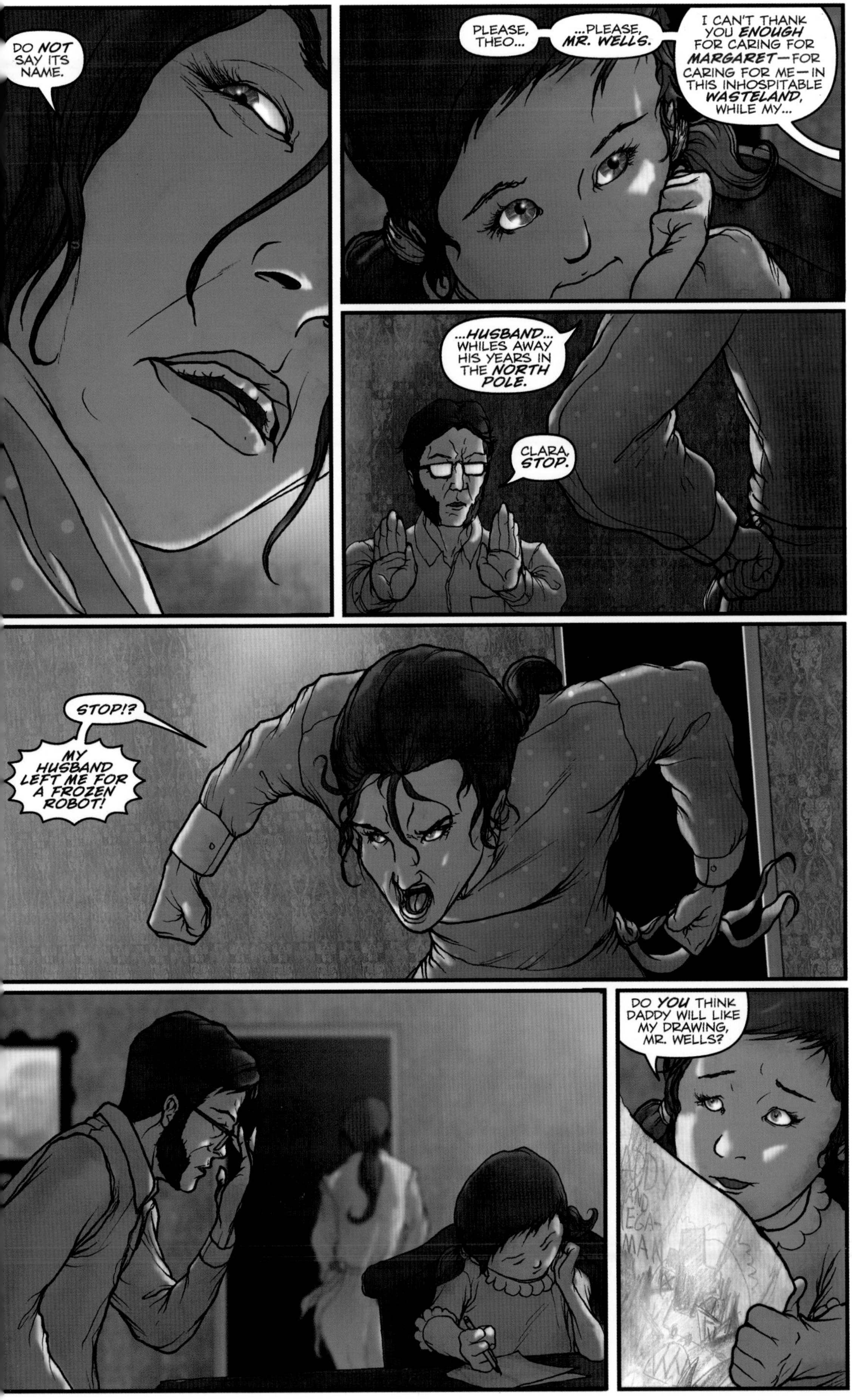
DO NOT SAY ITS NAME.
PLEASE, THEO...
...PLEASE, MR. WELLS.
I CAN'T THANK YOU ENOUGH FOR CARING FOR MARGARET—FOR CARING FOR ME—IN THIS INHOSPITABLE WASTELAND, WHILE MY...
...HUSBAND... WHILES AWAY HIS YEARS IN THE NORTH POLE.
CLARA, STOP.
STOP!?
MY HUSBAND LEFT ME FOR A FROZEN ROBOT!
DO YOU THINK DADDY WILL LIKE MY DRAWING, MR. WELLS?

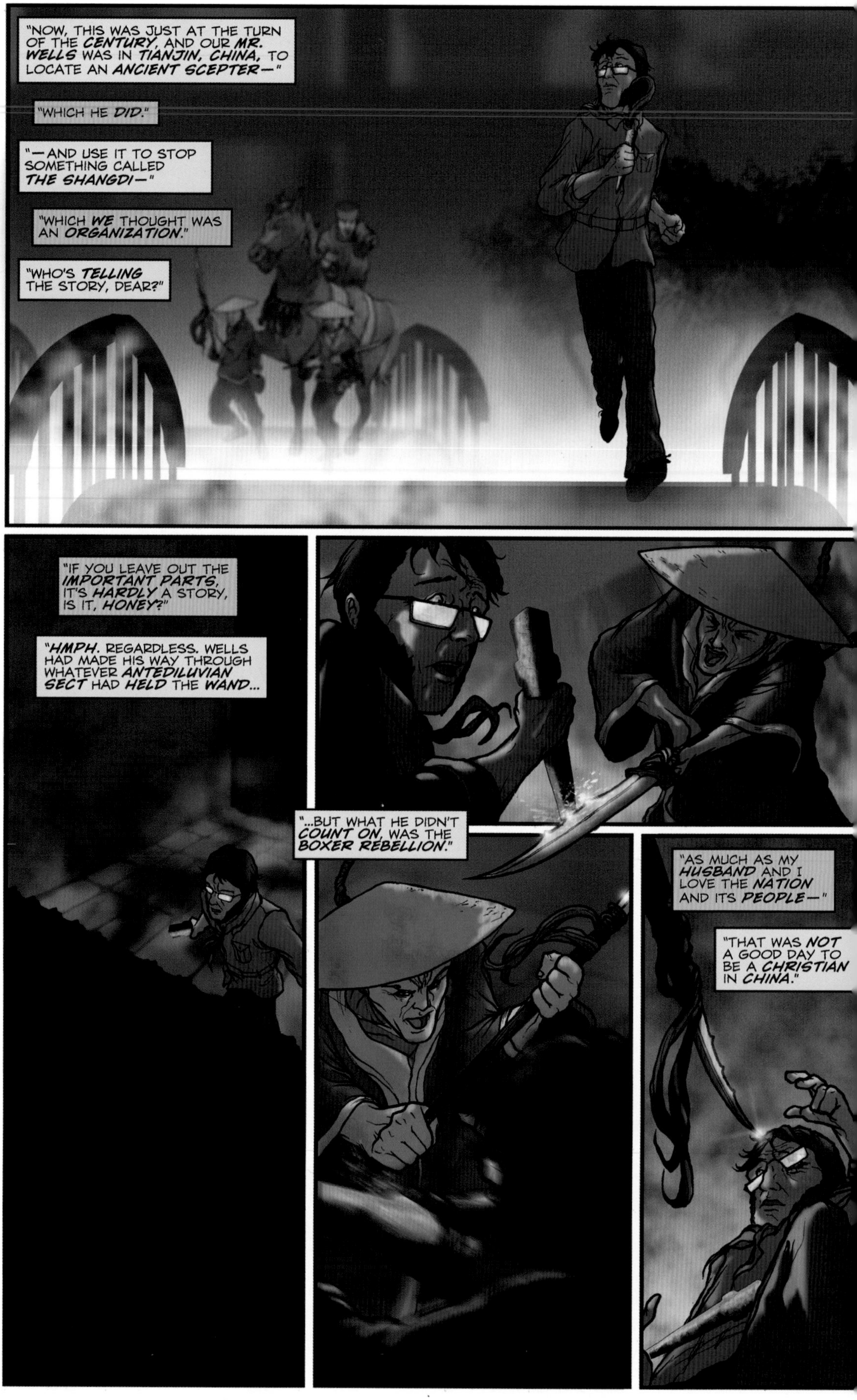
"NOW, THIS WAS JUST AT THE TURN OF THE CENTURY, AND OUR MR. WELLS WAS IN TIANJIN, CHINA, TO LOCATE AN ANCIENT SCEPTER—"
"WHICH HE DID."
"—AND USE IT TO STOP SOMETHING CALLED THE SHANGDI—"
"WHICH WE THOUGHT WAS AN ORGANIZATION."
"WHO'S TELLING THE STORY, DEAR?"
"IF YOU LEAVE OUT THE IMPORTANT PARTS, IT'S HARDLY A STORY, IS IT, HONEY?"
"HMPH. REGARDLESS. WELLS HAD MADE HIS WAY THROUGH WHATEVER ANTEDILUVIAN SECT HAD HELD THE WAND...
"...BUT WHAT HE DIDN'T COUNT ON, WAS THE BOXER REBELLION."
"AS MUCH AS MY HUSBAND AND I LOVE THE NATION AND ITS PEOPLE—"
"THAT WAS NOT A GOOD DAY TO BE A CHRISTIAN IN CHINA."

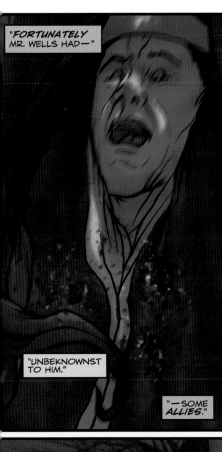

"FORTUNATELY MR. WELLS HAD—"

"UNBEKNOWNST TO HIM."

"—SOME ALLIES."

"IF MY WIFE HADN'T BEEN WATCHING THE *NORTH WALL* AT THAT MOMENT..."

"HE WOULD HAVE BEEN MR. QUITE-*UN*WELLS."

"...HARUMPH. *PLEASE*, LOU. *SPARE* US THE *PUNNING*."

"*HERBERT* AND I HAD FOUND OURSELVES *TRAPPED* UPON THE *OUTBREAK* OF THE *REBELLION*—"

"BEHIND *ENEMY LINES*, AS IT WERE."

"—AND DECIDED TO MAKE THE *MOST* OF A *BAD SITUATION*, USING OUR *POSITION* TO DELIVER *INTELLIGENCE* TO *AMERICAN FORCES*."

"I DO BELIEVE MR. WELLS WAS RATHER *TAKEN* WITH OUR LITTLE *OPERATION*."

"SO, WHEN HIS *ORGANIZATION* LOCATED THE *CUBE* IN THE *COLORADO RIVER*..."

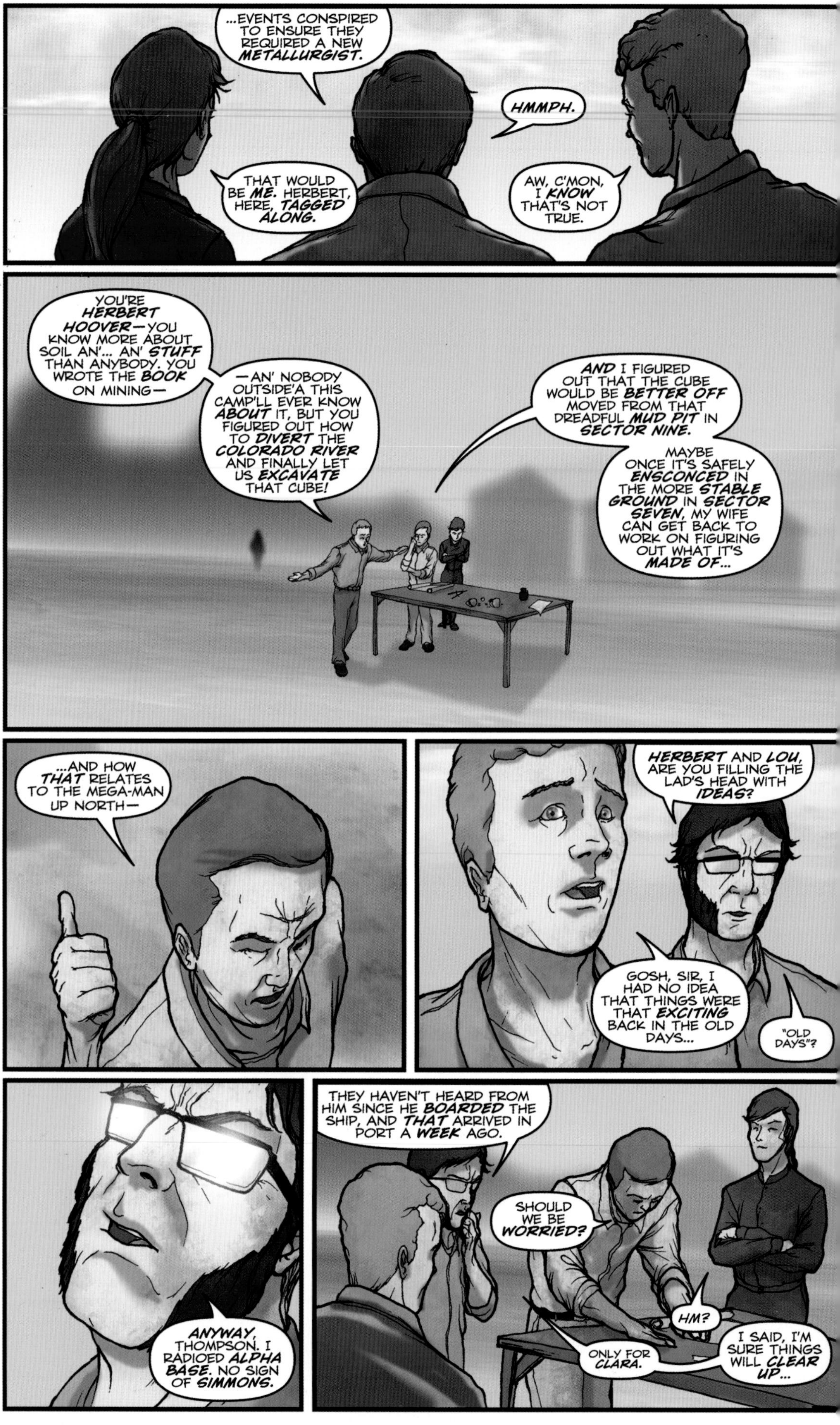
...EVENTS CONSPIRED TO ENSURE THEY REQUIRED A NEW METALLURGIST.
HMMPH.
THAT WOULD BE ME. HERBERT, HERE, TAGGED ALONG.
AW, C'MON, I KNOW THAT'S NOT TRUE.
YOU'RE HERBERT HOOVER—YOU KNOW MORE ABOUT SOIL AN'... AN' STUFF THAN ANYBODY. YOU WROTE THE BOOK ON MINING—
—AN' NOBODY OUTSIDE'A THIS CAMP'LL EVER KNOW ABOUT IT, BUT YOU FIGURED OUT HOW TO DIVERT THE COLORADO RIVER AND FINALLY LET US EXCAVATE THAT CUBE!
AND I FIGURED OUT THAT THE CUBE WOULD BE BETTER OFF MOVED FROM THAT DREADFUL MUD PIT IN SECTOR NINE.
MAYBE ONCE IT'S SAFELY ENSCONCED IN THE MORE STABLE GROUND IN SECTOR SEVEN, MY WIFE CAN GET BACK TO WORK ON FIGURING OUT WHAT IT'S MADE OF...
...AND HOW THAT RELATES TO THE MEGA-MAN UP NORTH—
HERBERT AND LOU, ARE YOU FILLING THE LAD'S HEAD WITH IDEAS?
GOSH, SIR, I HAD NO IDEA THAT THINGS WERE THAT EXCITING BACK IN THE OLD DAYS...
"OLD DAYS"?
ANYWAY, THOMPSON. I RADIOED ALPHA BASE. NO SIGN OF SIMMONS.
THEY HAVEN'T HEARD FROM HIM SINCE HE BOARDED THE SHIP, AND THAT ARRIVED IN PORT A WEEK AGO.
SHOULD WE BE WORRIED?
ONLY FOR CLARA.
HM?
I SAID, I'M SURE THINGS WILL CLEAR UP...

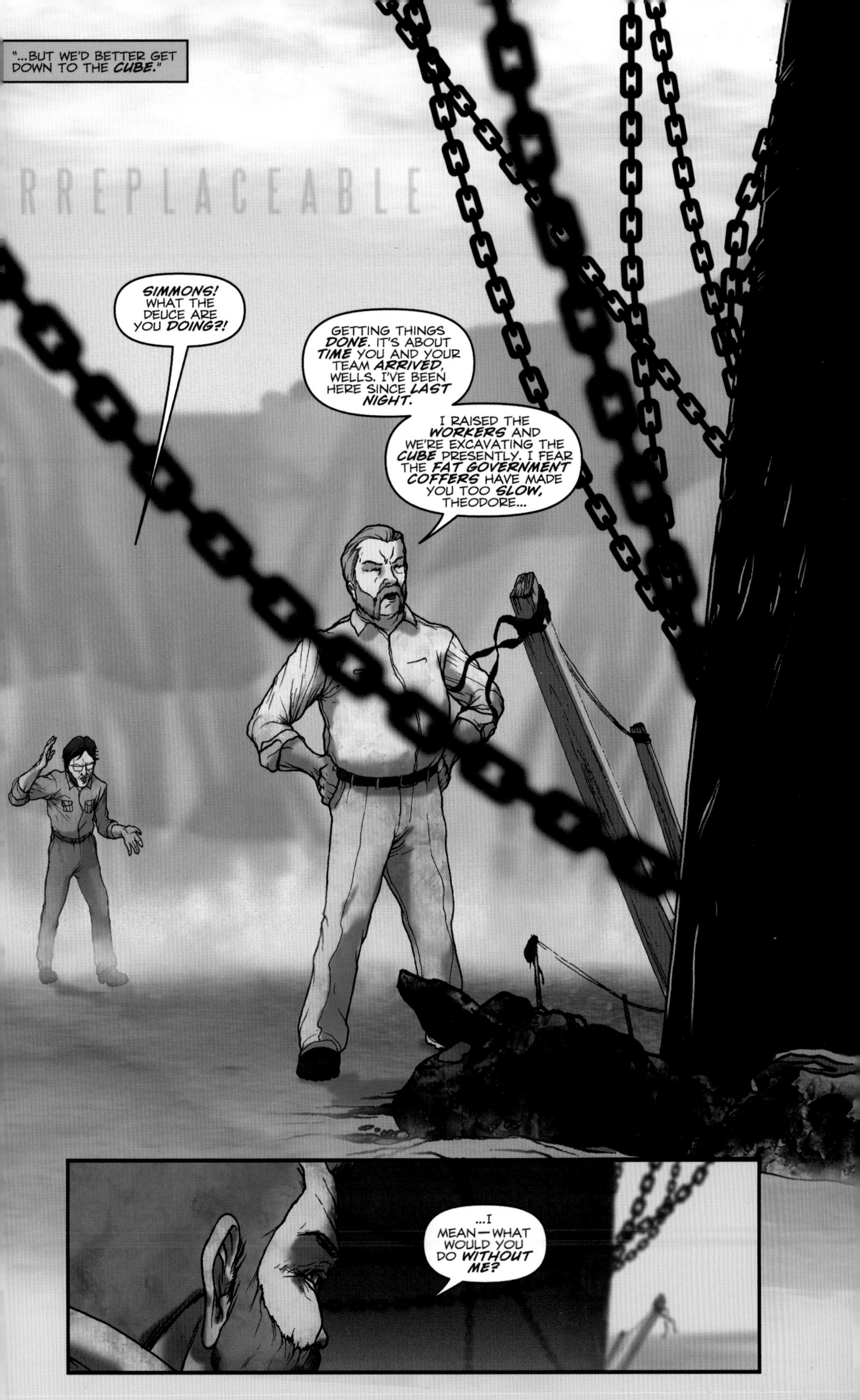
"...BUT WE'D BETTER GET DOWN TO THE CUBE."
RREPLACEABLE
SIMMONS! WHAT THE DEUCE ARE YOU DOING?!
GETTING THINGS DONE. IT'S ABOUT TIME YOU AND YOUR TEAM ARRIVED, WELLS. I'VE BEEN HERE SINCE LAST NIGHT.
I RAISED THE WORKERS AND WE'RE EXCAVATING THE CUBE PRESENTLY. I FEAR THE FAT GOVERNMENT COFFERS HAVE MADE YOU TOO SLOW, THEODORE...
...I MEAN—WHAT WOULD YOU DO WITHOUT ME?

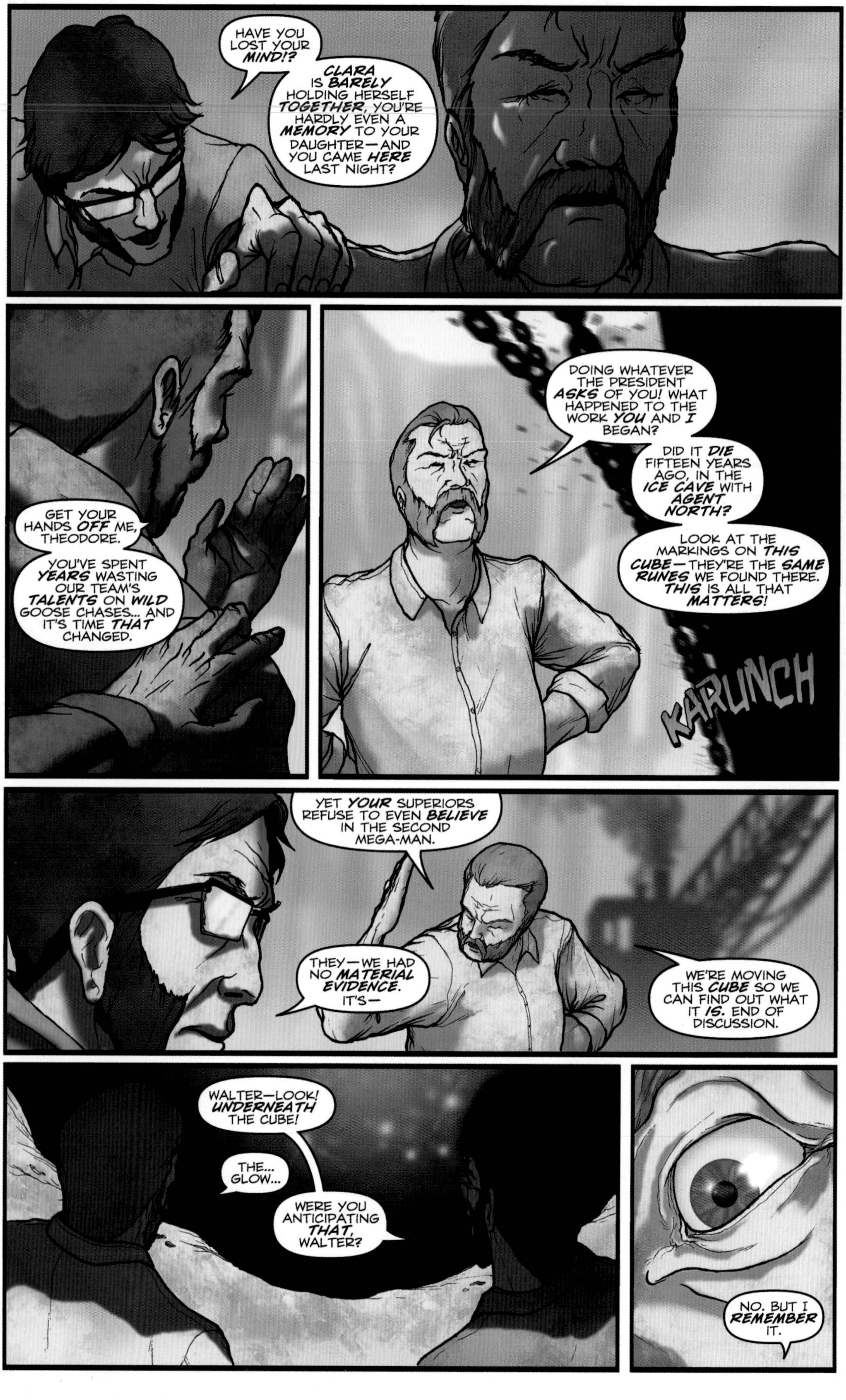
HAVE YOU LOST YOUR MIND!?
CLARA IS BARELY HOLDING HERSELF TOGETHER, YOU'RE HARDLY EVEN A MEMORY TO YOUR DAUGHTER—AND YOU CAME HERE LAST NIGHT?
GET YOUR HANDS OFF ME, THEODORE.
YOU'VE SPENT YEARS WASTING OUR TEAM'S TALENTS ON WILD GOOSE CHASES... AND IT'S TIME THAT CHANGED.
DOING WHATEVER THE PRESIDENT ASKS OF YOU! WHAT HAPPENED TO THE WORK YOU AND I BEGAN?
DID IT DIE FIFTEEN YEARS AGO, IN THE ICE CAVE WITH AGENT NORTH?
LOOK AT THE MARKINGS ON THIS CUBE—THEY'RE THE SAME RUNES WE FOUND THERE. THIS IS ALL THAT MATTERS!
KARUNCH
YET YOUR SUPERIORS REFUSE TO EVEN BELIEVE IN THE SECOND MEGA-MAN.
THEY—WE HAD NO MATERIAL EVIDENCE. IT'S—
WE'RE MOVING THIS CUBE SO WE CAN FIND OUT WHAT IT IS. END OF DISCUSSION.
WALTER—LOOK! UNDERNEATH THE CUBE!
THE... GLOW...
WERE YOU ANTICIPATING THAT, WALTER?
NO. BUT I REMEMBER IT.

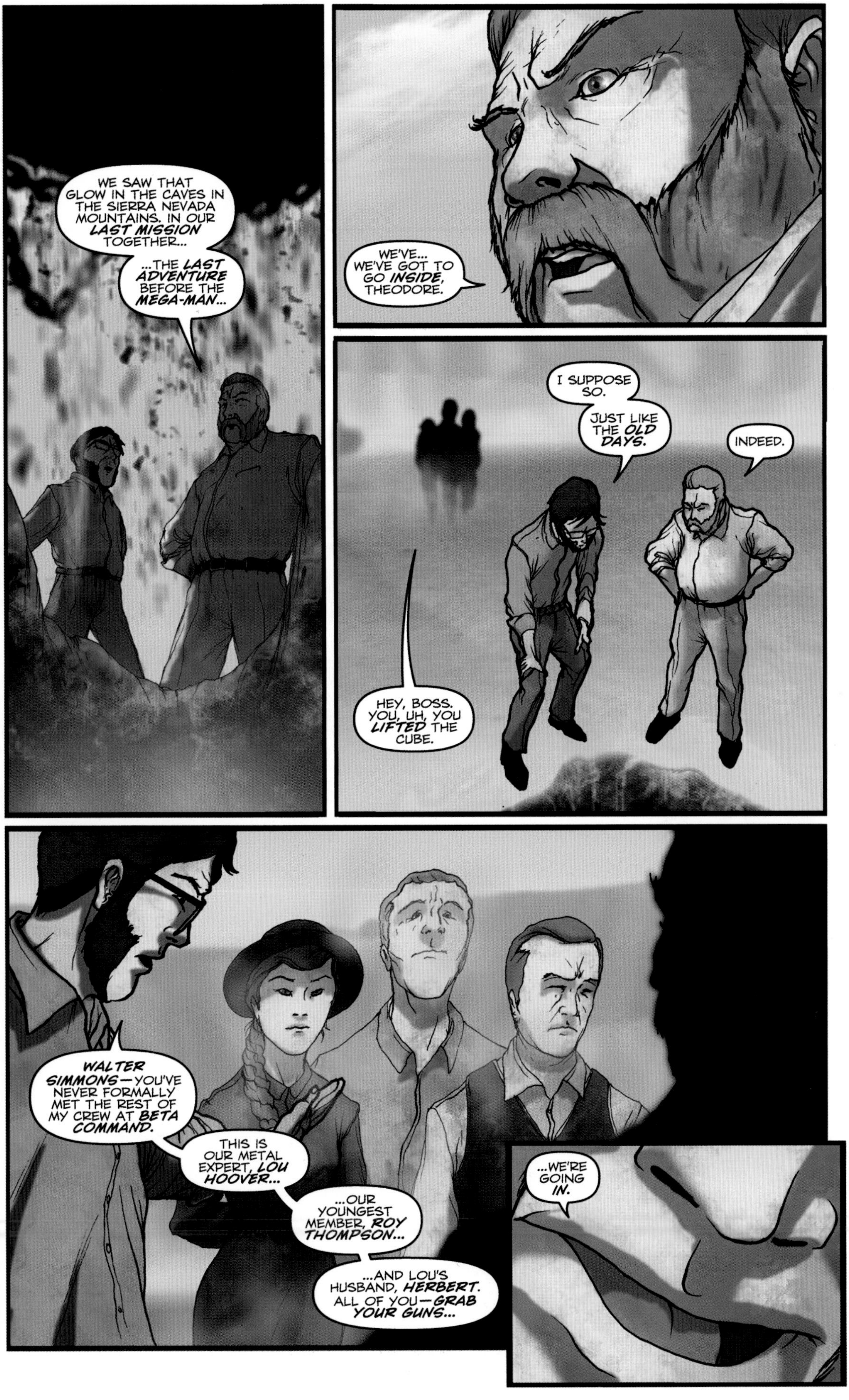
WE SAW THAT GLOW IN THE CAVES IN THE SIERRA NEVADA MOUNTAINS. IN OUR LAST MISSION TOGETHER...
...THE LAST ADVENTURE BEFORE THE MEGA-MAN...
WE'VE... WE'VE GOT TO GO INSIDE, THEODORE.
HEY, BOSS. YOU, UH, YOU LIFTED THE CUBE.
I SUPPOSE SO.
JUST LIKE THE OLD DAYS.
INDEED.
WALTER SIMMONS—YOU'VE NEVER FORMALLY MET THE REST OF MY CREW AT BETA COMMAND.
THIS IS OUR METAL EXPERT, LOU HOOVER...
...OUR YOUNGEST MEMBER, ROY THOMPSON...
...AND LOU'S HUSBAND, HERBERT. ALL OF YOU—GRAB YOUR GUNS...
...WE'RE GOING IN.

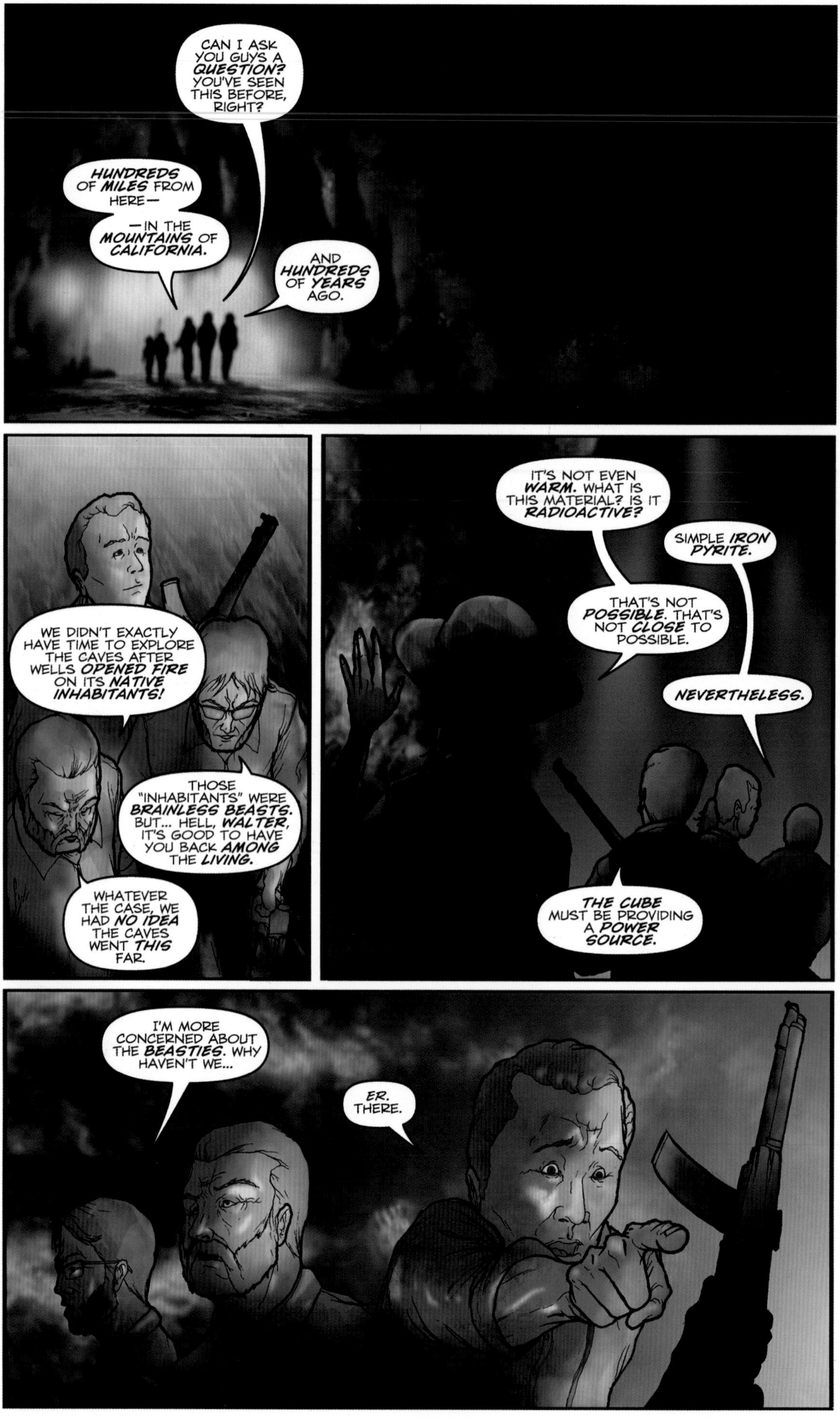
CAN I ASK YOU GUYS A QUESTION? YOU'VE SEEN THIS BEFORE, RIGHT?
HUNDREDS OF MILES FROM HERE—
—IN THE MOUNTAINS OF CALIFORNIA.
AND HUNDREDS OF YEARS AGO.
WE DIDN'T EXACTLY HAVE TIME TO EXPLORE THE CAVES AFTER WELLS OPENED FIRE ON ITS NATIVE INHABITANTS!
THOSE "INHABITANTS" WERE BRAINLESS BEASTS. BUT... HELL, WALTER, IT'S GOOD TO HAVE YOU BACK AMONG THE LIVING.
WHATEVER THE CASE, WE HAD NO IDEA THE CAVES WENT THIS FAR.
IT'S NOT EVEN WARM. WHAT IS THIS MATERIAL? IS IT RADIOACTIVE?
SIMPLE IRON PYRITE.
THAT'S NOT POSSIBLE. THAT'S NOT CLOSE TO POSSIBLE.
NEVERTHELESS.
THE CUBE MUST BE PROVIDING A POWER SOURCE.
I'M MORE CONCERNED ABOUT THE BEASTIES. WHY HAVEN'T WE...
ER. THERE.

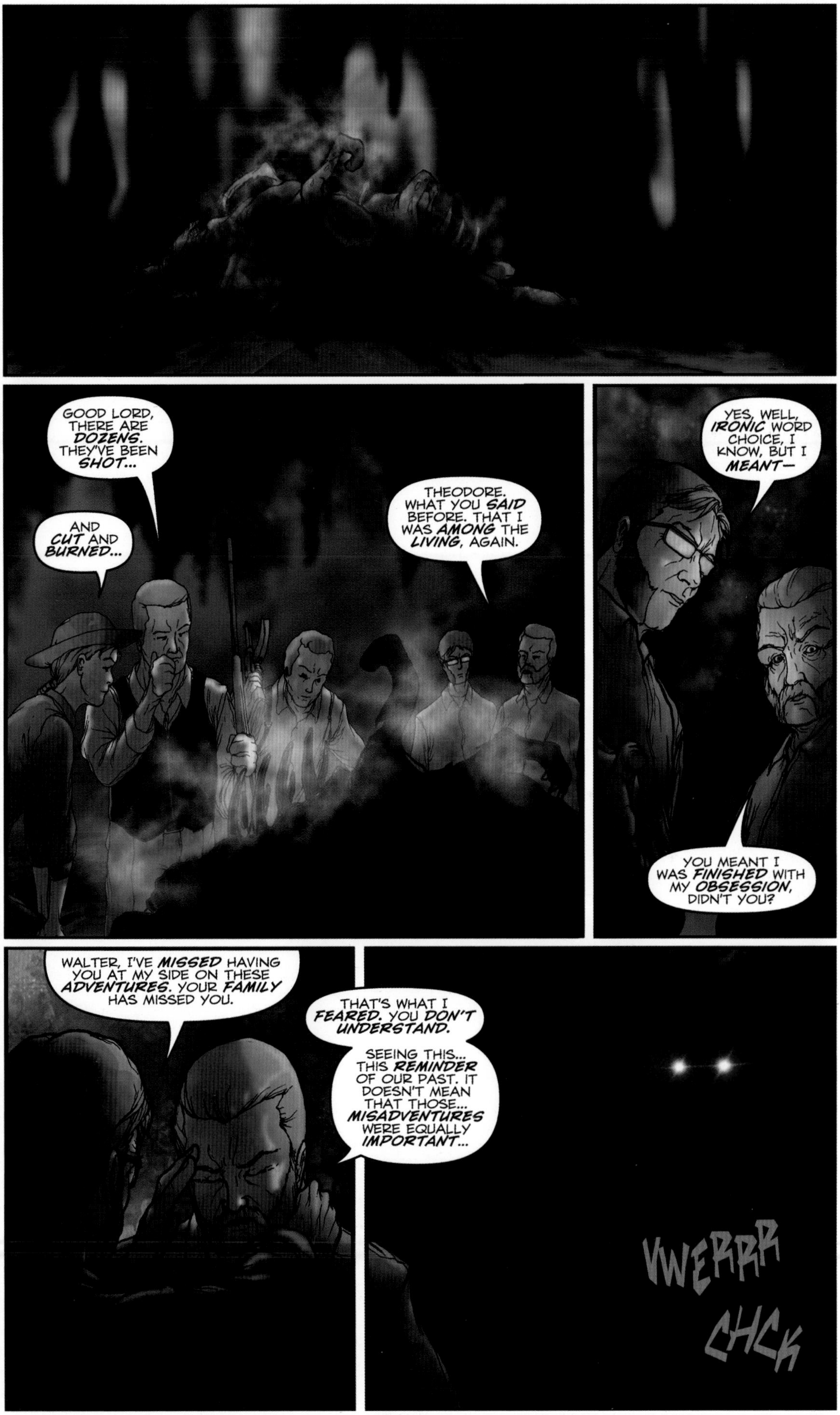

GOOD LORD, THERE ARE DOZENS. THEY'VE BEEN SHOT...
AND CUT AND BURNED...
THEODORE. WHAT YOU SAID BEFORE. THAT I WAS AMONG THE LIVING, AGAIN.
YES, WELL, IRONIC WORD CHOICE, I KNOW, BUT I MEANT—
YOU MEANT I WAS FINISHED WITH MY OBSESSION, DIDN'T YOU?
WALTER, I'VE MISSED HAVING YOU AT MY SIDE ON THESE ADVENTURES. YOUR FAMILY HAS MISSED YOU.
THAT'S WHAT I FEARED. YOU DON'T UNDERSTAND.
SEEING THIS... THIS REMINDER OF OUR PAST. IT DOESN'T MEAN THAT THOSE... MISADVENTURES WERE EQUALLY IMPORTANT...
VWERRR
CHCK

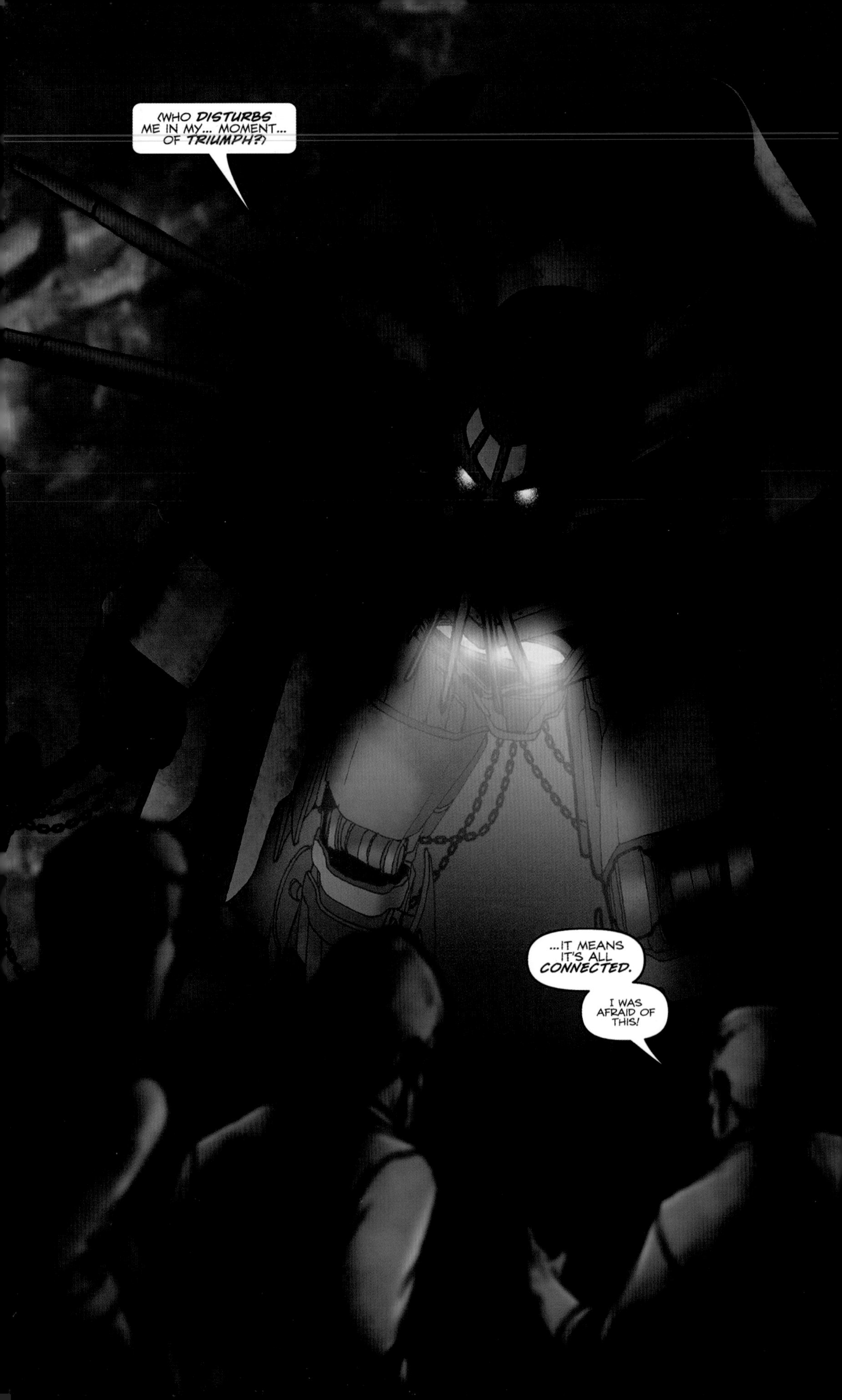
(WHO DISTURBS ME IN MY... MOMENT... OF TRIUMPH?)
...IT MEANS IT'S ALL CONNECTED.
I WAS AFRAID OF THIS!

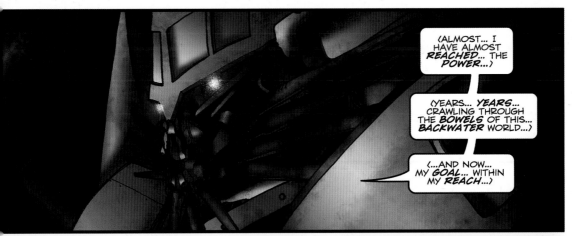

(ALMOST... I HAVE ALMOST *REACHED*... THE *POWER*...)

(YEARS... *YEARS*... CRAWLING THROUGH THE *BOWELS* OF THIS... *BACKWATER* WORLD...)

(....AND NOW... MY *GOAL*... WITHIN MY *REACH*...)

(...YOU... THE SAME *FLESHY INSECTS* THAT... *CONDEMNED* ME TO THIS *HELL*...)

WHAT—WHAT *IS* IT—?

WALTER, THAT'S... THAT'S THE *SAME ONE!* THE SECOND *MEGA-MAN* THAT KILLED *AGENT NORTH!*

I BELIEVE *SO*, AND I BELIEVE—

IT *RECOGNIZES* US!

(...YOU BLOCK *JETFIRE'S* PATH *AGAIN!*)

BLAM

BLAM

ARE YOU *MAD*, WOMAN?

RUN!

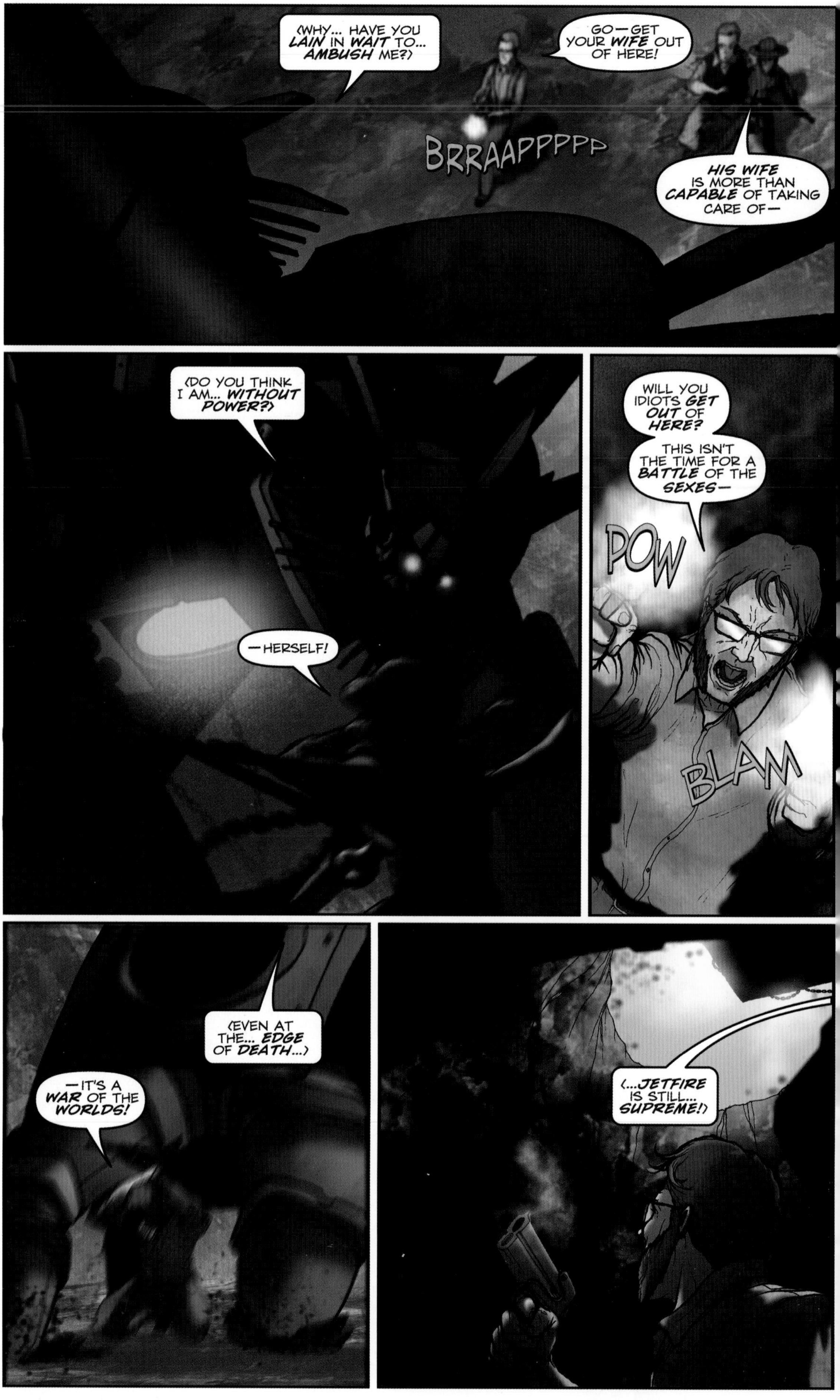

(WHY... HAVE YOU LAIN IN WAIT TO... AMBUSH ME?)
GO—GET YOUR WIFE OUT OF HERE!
BRRAAPPPPP
HIS WIFE IS MORE THAN CAPABLE OF TAKING CARE OF—
(DO YOU THINK I AM... WITHOUT POWER?)
—HERSELF!
WILL YOU IDIOTS GET OUT OF HERE?
THIS ISN'T THE TIME FOR A BATTLE OF THE SEXES—
POW
BLAM
(EVEN AT THE... EDGE OF DEATH...)
—IT'S A WAR OF THE WORLDS!
(...JETFIRE IS STILL... SUPREME!)

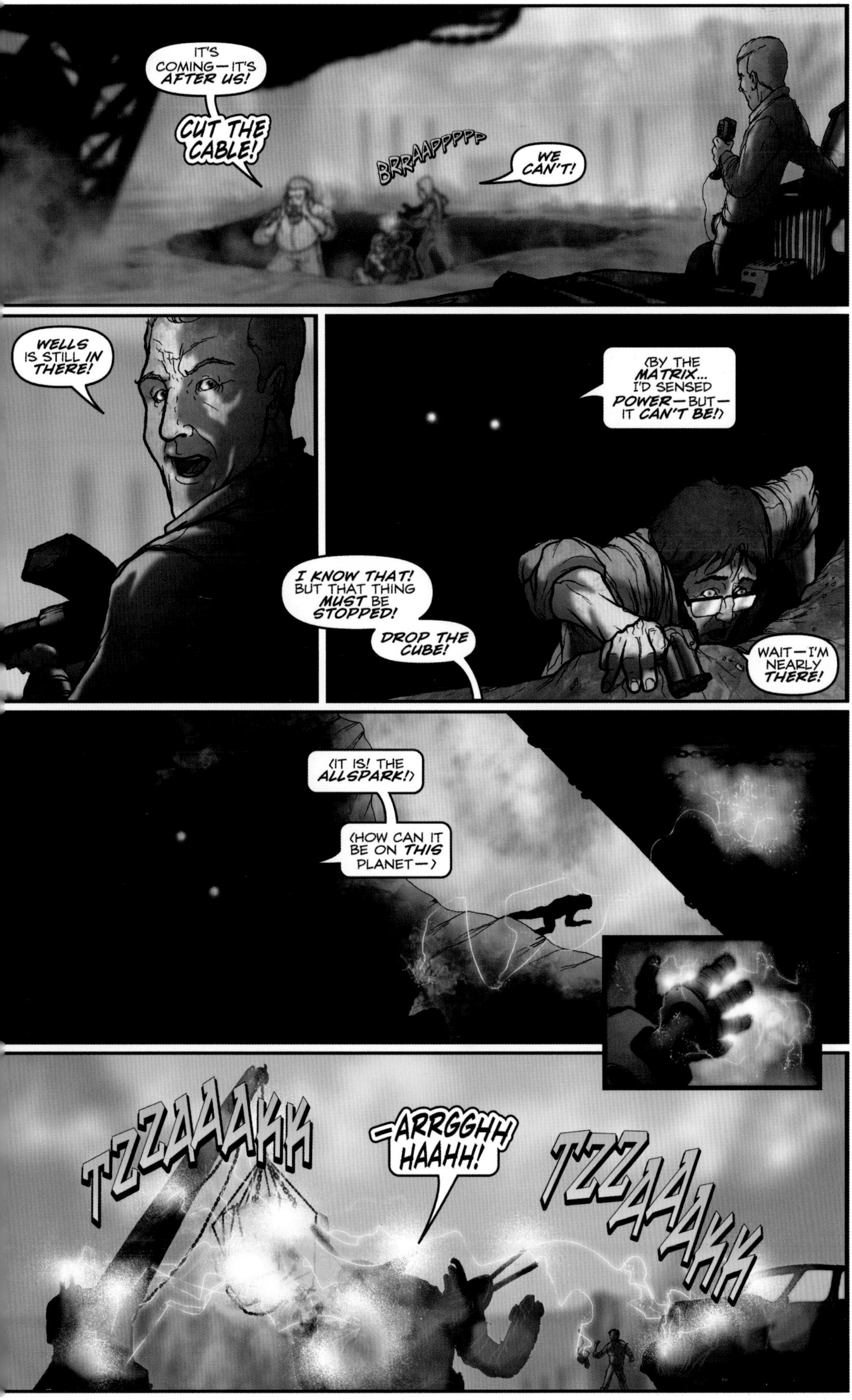

IT'S COMING—IT'S AFTER US!
CUT THE CABLE!
BRRAAPPPPP
WE CAN'T!
WELLS IS STILL IN THERE!
‹BY THE MATRIX... I'D SENSED POWER—BUT—IT CAN'T BE!›
I KNOW THAT! BUT THAT THING MUST BE STOPPED!
DROP THE CUBE!
WAIT—I'M NEARLY THERE!
‹IT IS! THE ALLSPARK!›
‹HOW CAN IT BE ON THIS PLANET—›
TZZAAAKK
—ARRGGHH HAAHH!
TZZAAAKK

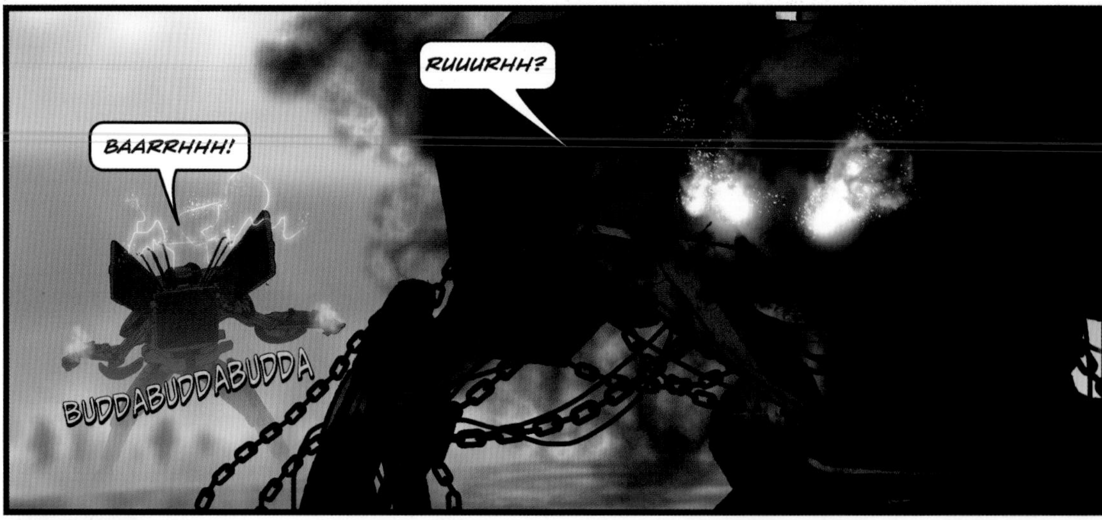
RUUURHH?
BAARRHHH!
BUDDABUDDABUDDA

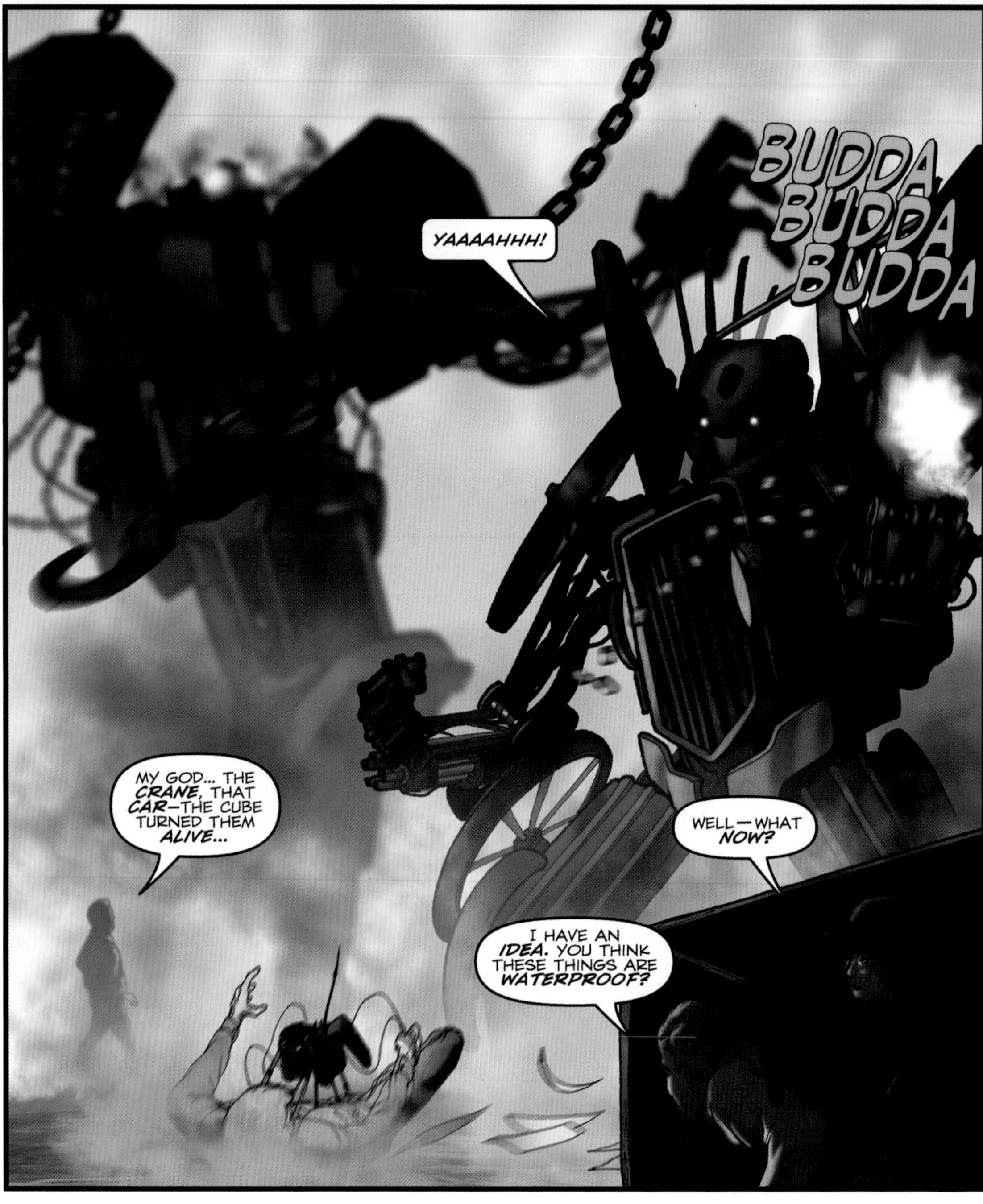
BUDDA BUDDA BUDDA
YAAAAHHH!
MY GOD... THE CRANE, THAT CAR—THE CUBE TURNED THEM ALIVE...
WELL—WHAT NOW?
I HAVE AN IDEA. YOU THINK THESE THINGS ARE WATERPROOF?

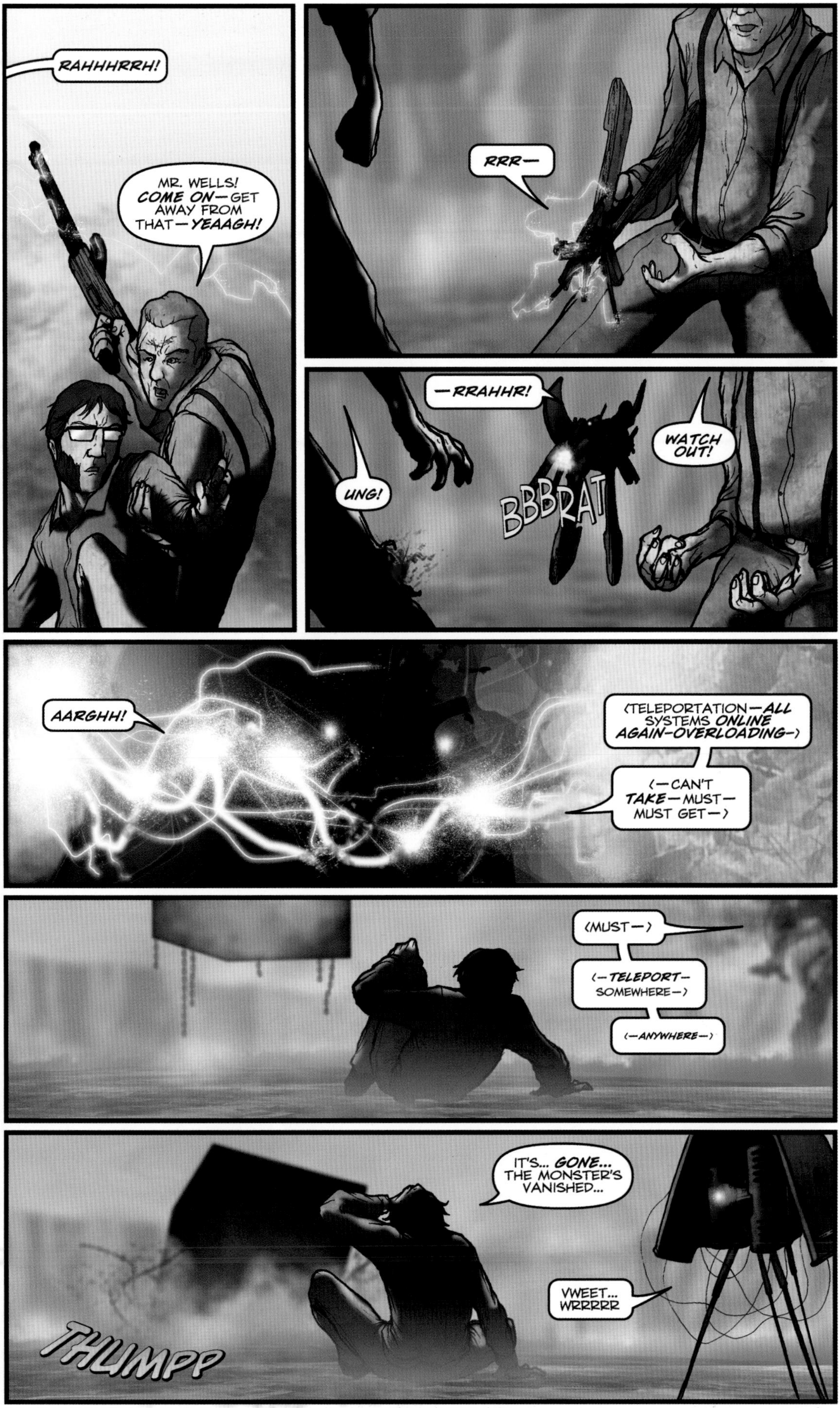
RAHHHRRH!
MR. WELLS! COME ON—GET AWAY FROM THAT—YEAAGH!
RRR—
—RRAHHR!
UNG!
WATCH OUT!
BBBRAT
AARGHH!
⟨TELEPORTATION—ALL SYSTEMS ONLINE AGAIN-OVERLOADING-⟩
⟨—CAN'T TAKE—MUST— MUST GET—⟩
⟨MUST—⟩
⟨—TELEPORT— SOMEWHERE—⟩
⟨—ANYWHERE—⟩
IT'S... GONE... THE MONSTER'S VANISHED...
VWEET... WRRRRR
THUMPP

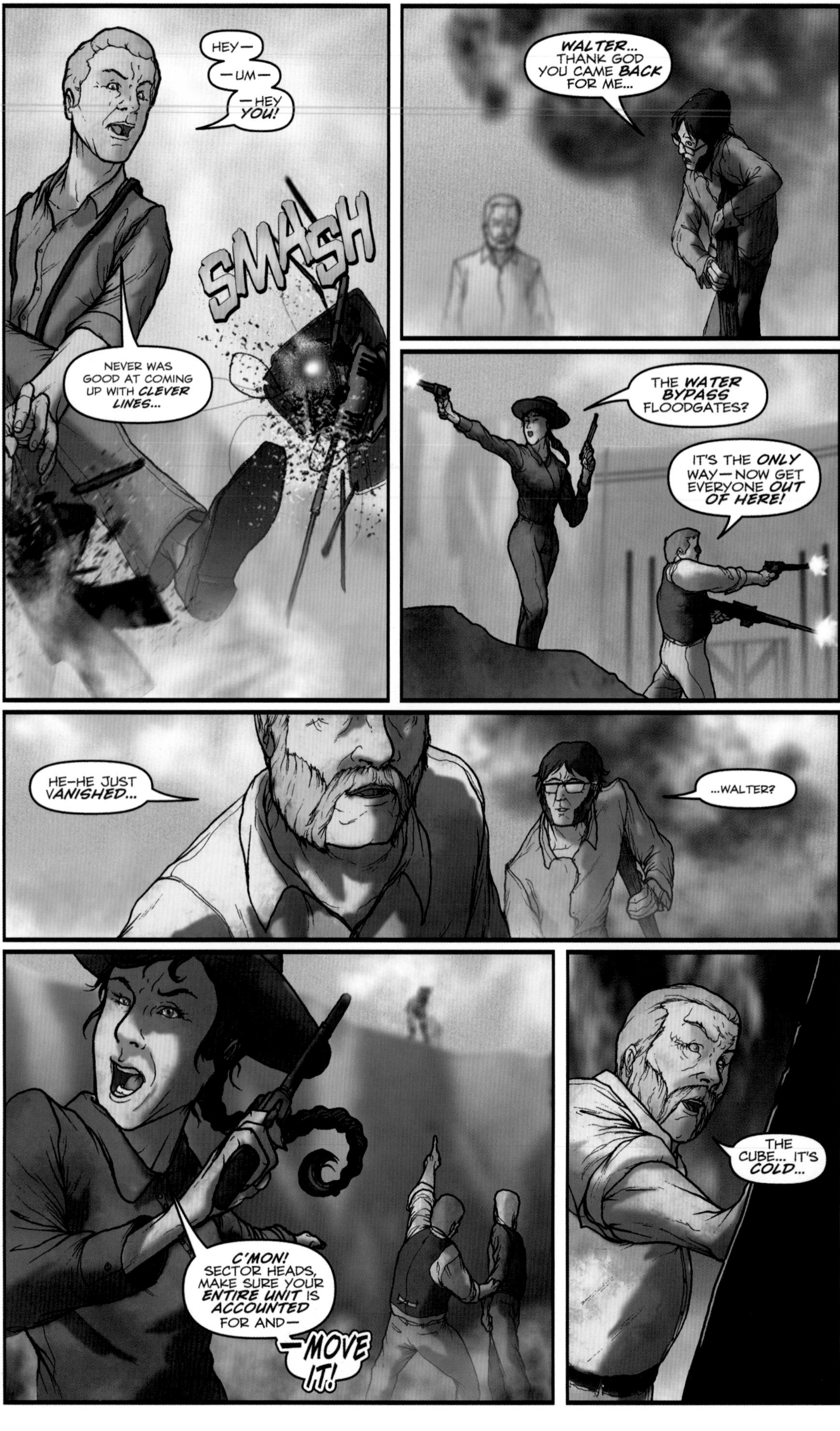

HEY—
—UM—
—HEY YOU!
SMASH
NEVER WAS GOOD AT COMING UP WITH CLEVER LINES...
WALTER... THANK GOD YOU CAME BACK FOR ME...
THE WATER BYPASS FLOODGATES?
IT'S THE ONLY WAY—NOW GET EVERYONE OUT OF HERE!
HE—HE JUST VANISHED...
...WALTER?
C'MON! SECTOR HEADS, MAKE SURE YOUR ENTIRE UNIT IS ACCOUNTED FOR AND—
—MOVE IT!
THE CUBE... IT'S COLD...

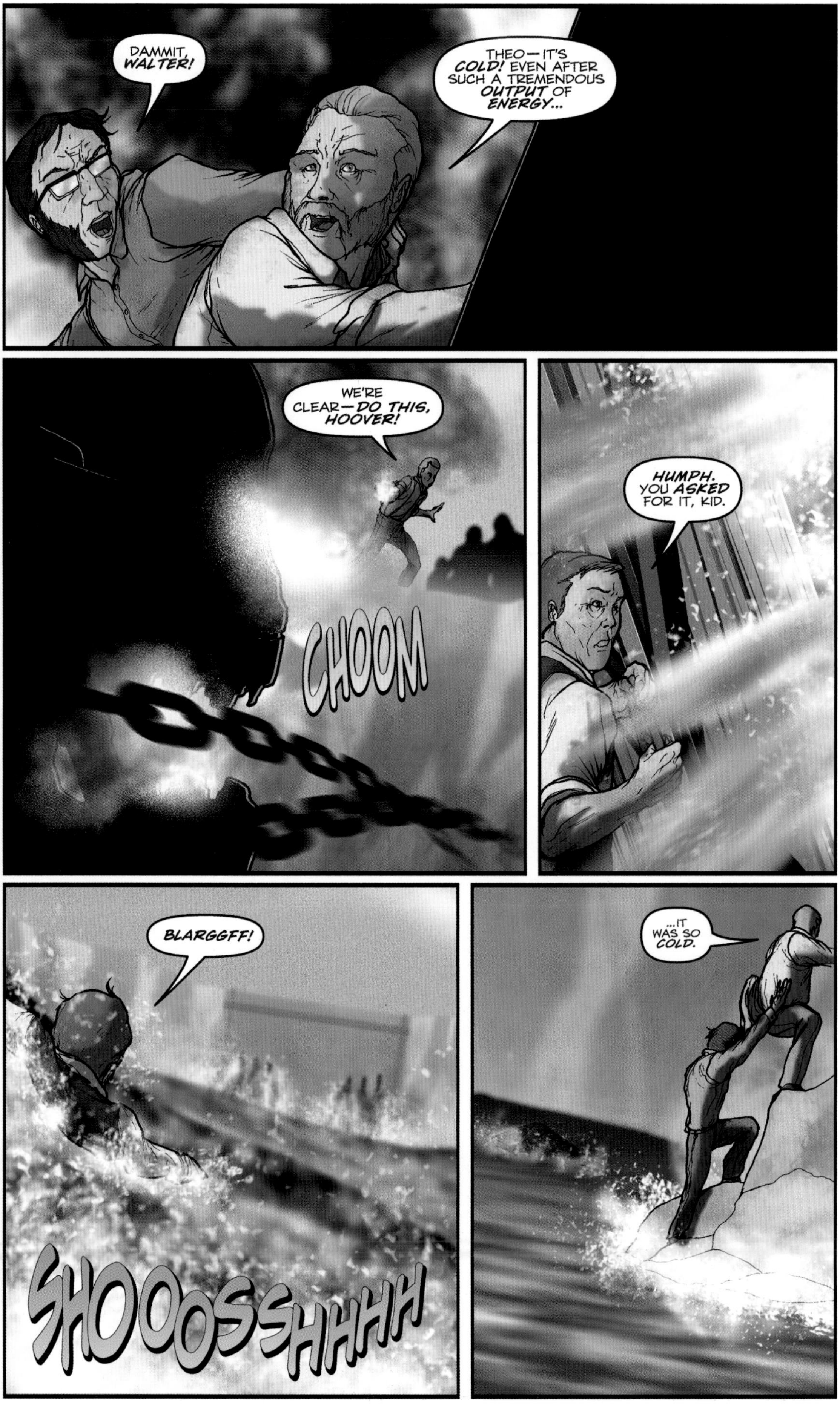
DAMMIT, WALTER!
THEO—IT'S COLD! EVEN AFTER SUCH A TREMENDOUS OUTPUT OF ENERGY...
WE'RE CLEAR—DO THIS, HOOVER!
CHOOM
HUMPH. YOU ASKED FOR IT, KID.
BLARGGFF!
SHOOOSSHHHH
...IT WAS SO COLD.

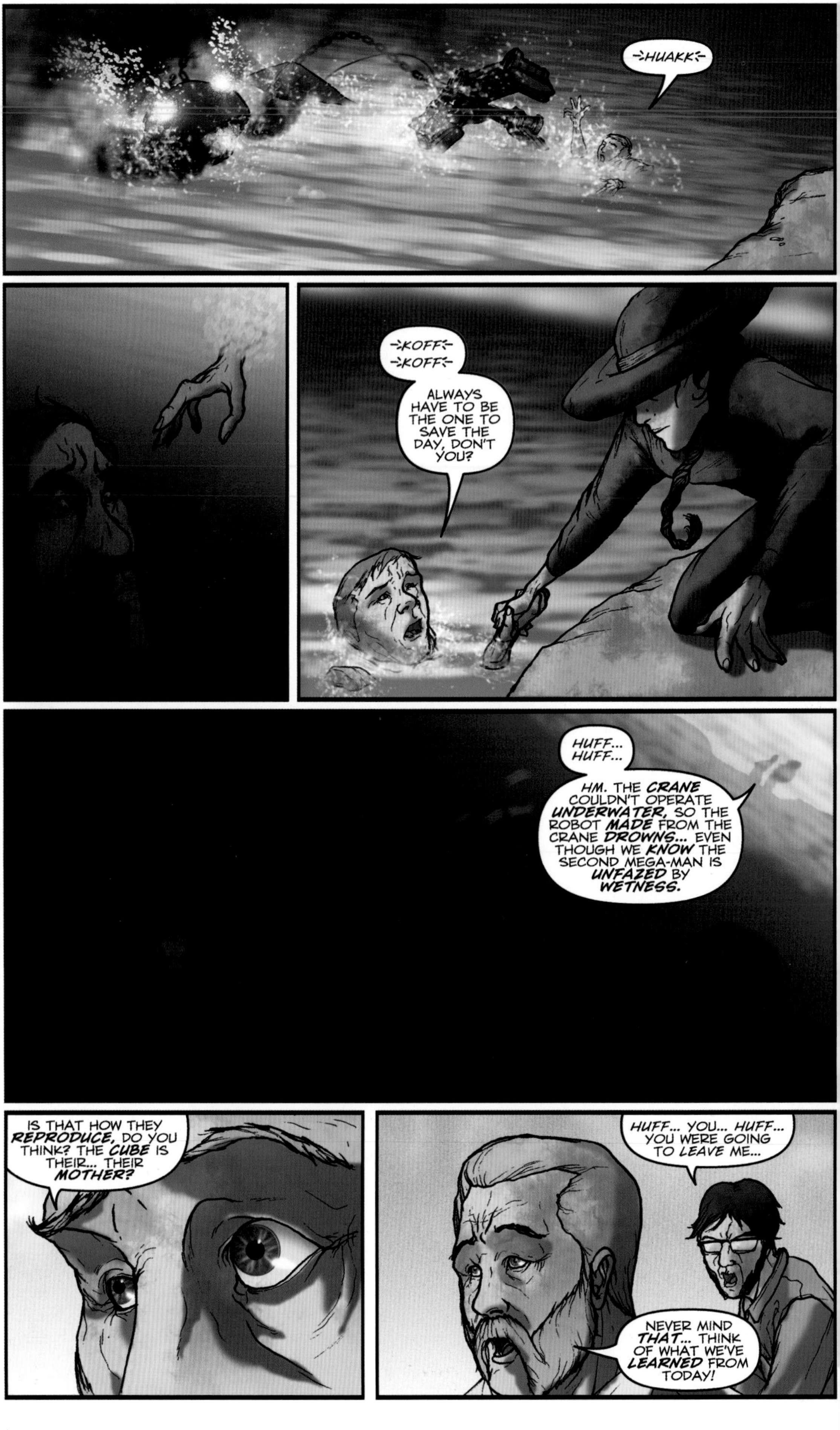

-HUAKK-
-KOFF- -KOFF-
ALWAYS HAVE TO BE THE ONE TO SAVE THE DAY, DON'T YOU?
HUFF... HUFF...
HM. THE CRANE COULDN'T OPERATE UNDERWATER, SO THE ROBOT MADE FROM THE CRANE DROWNS... EVEN THOUGH WE KNOW THE SECOND MEGA-MAN IS UNFAZED BY WETNESS.
IS THAT HOW THEY REPRODUCE, DO YOU THINK? THE CUBE IS THEIR... THEIR MOTHER?
HUFF... YOU... HUFF... YOU WERE GOING TO LEAVE ME...
NEVER MIND THAT... THINK OF WHAT WE'VE LEARNED FROM TODAY!

HUFF... I *AM.*

THIS WILL SET US BACK A NUMBER OF *MONTHS...* YEARS, PERHAPS.

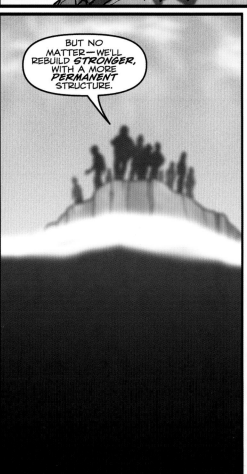

BUT NO MATTER—WE'LL REBUILD *STRONGER,* WITH A MORE *PERMANENT* STRUCTURE.

"IT GOES WITHOUT *SAYING* THAT I'LL BE *MOVING* HERE. THE MEGA-MAN CAN TAKE CARE OF *HIMSELF...*

"...THIS... THE *CUBE...*

"...*THIS* HOLDS THE *KEY* TO THE *FUTURE...*"

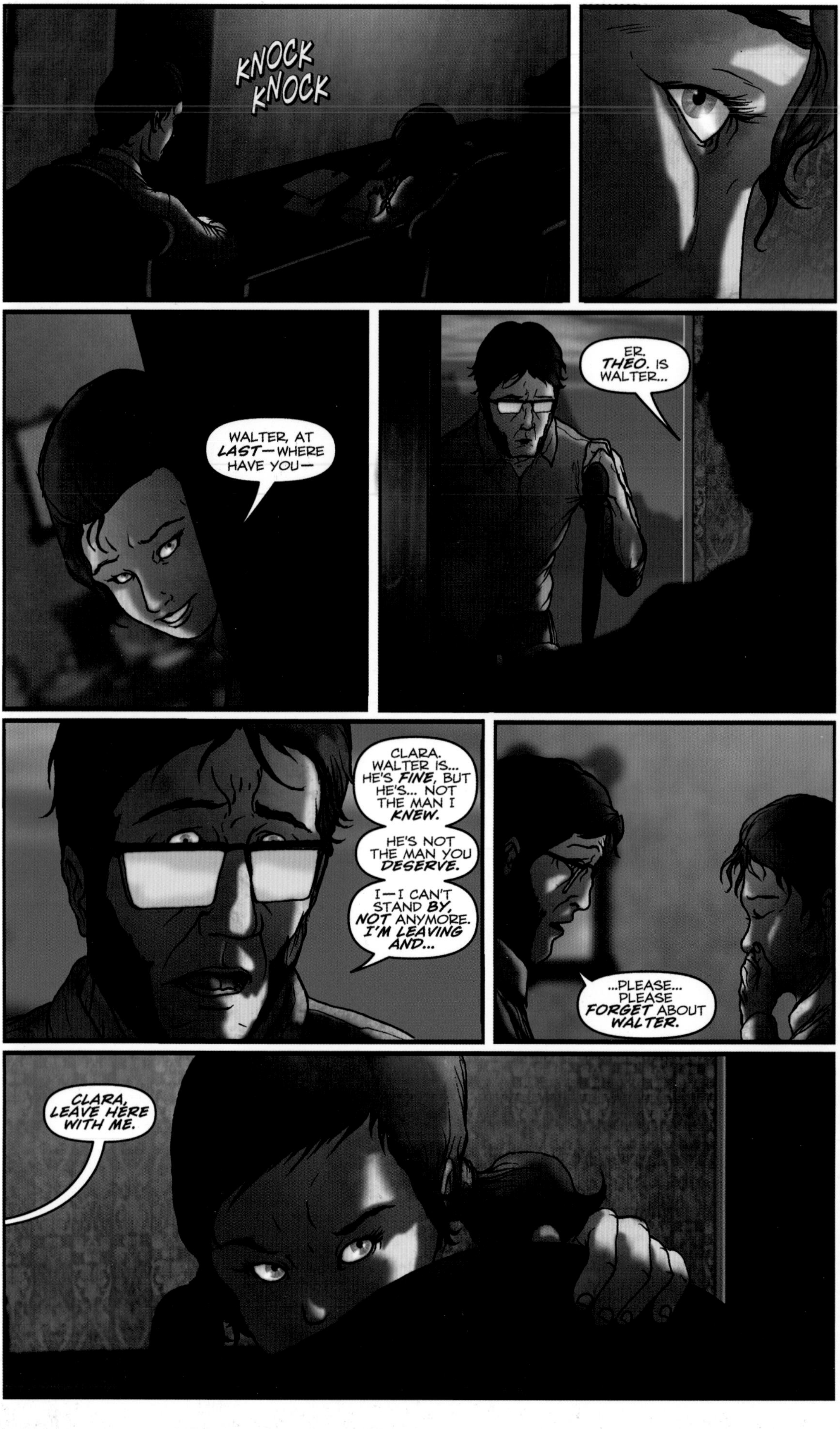
KNOCK KNOCK
WALTER, AT LAST—WHERE HAVE YOU—
ER. THEO. IS WALTER...
CLARA. WALTER IS... HE'S FINE, BUT HE'S... NOT THE MAN I KNEW.
HE'S NOT THE MAN YOU DESERVE.
I—I CAN'T STAND BY, NOT ANYMORE. I'M LEAVING AND...
...PLEASE... PLEASE FORGET ABOUT WALTER.
CLARA, LEAVE HERE WITH ME.

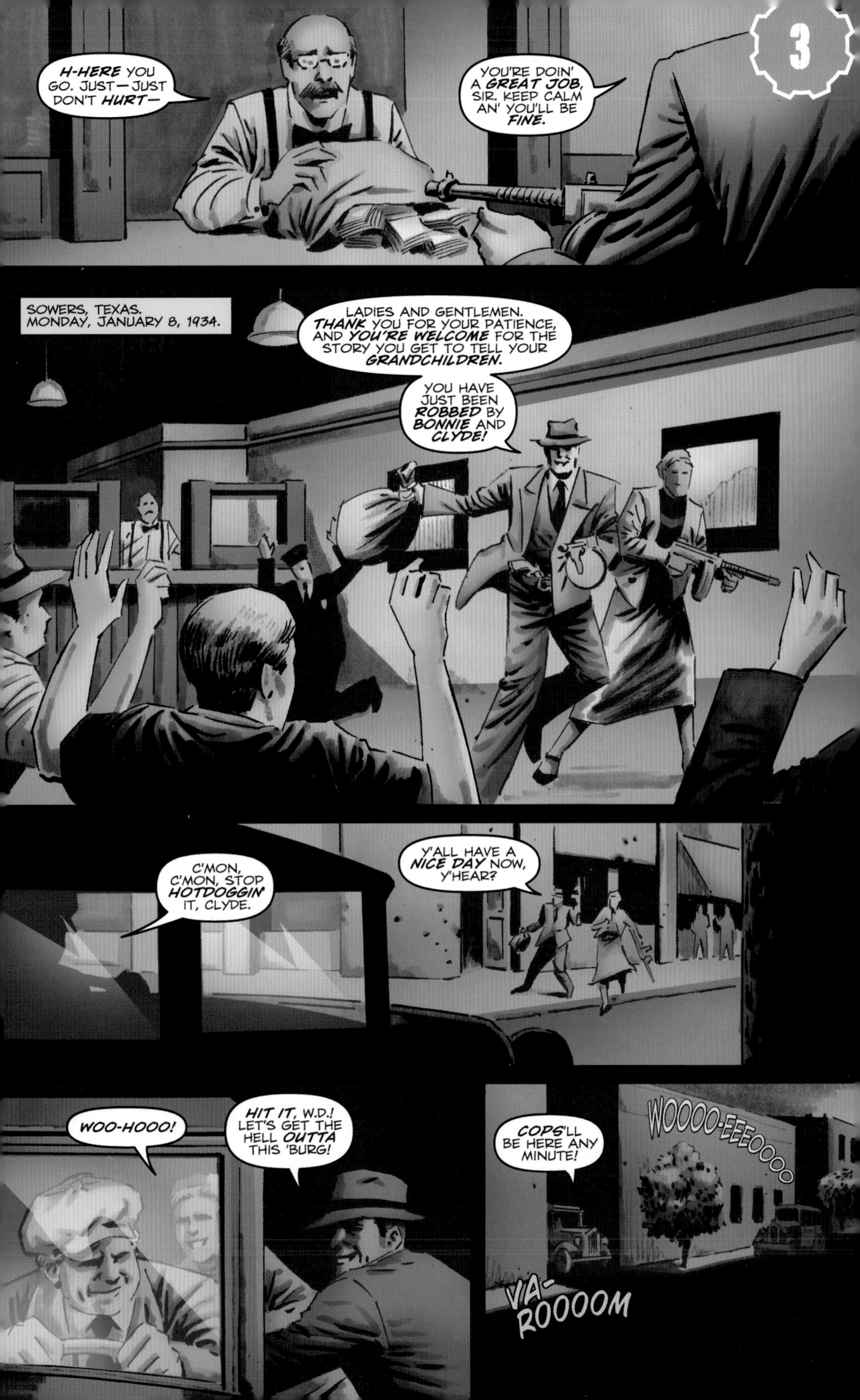
H-HERE YOU GO. JUST—JUST DON'T HURT—
YOU'RE DOIN' A GREAT JOB, SIR. KEEP CALM AN' YOU'LL BE FINE.
SOWERS, TEXAS. MONDAY, JANUARY 8, 1934.
LADIES AND GENTLEMEN. THANK YOU FOR YOUR PATIENCE, AND YOU'RE WELCOME FOR THE STORY YOU GET TO TELL YOUR GRANDCHILDREN.
YOU HAVE JUST BEEN ROBBED BY BONNIE AND CLYDE!
C'MON, C'MON, STOP HOTDOGGIN' IT, CLYDE.
Y'ALL HAVE A NICE DAY NOW, Y'HEAR?
WOO-HOOO!
HIT IT, W.D.! LET'S GET THE HELL OUTTA THIS 'BURG!
COPS'LL BE HERE ANY MINUTE!
WOOOO-EEEOOOO
VA-ROOOOM

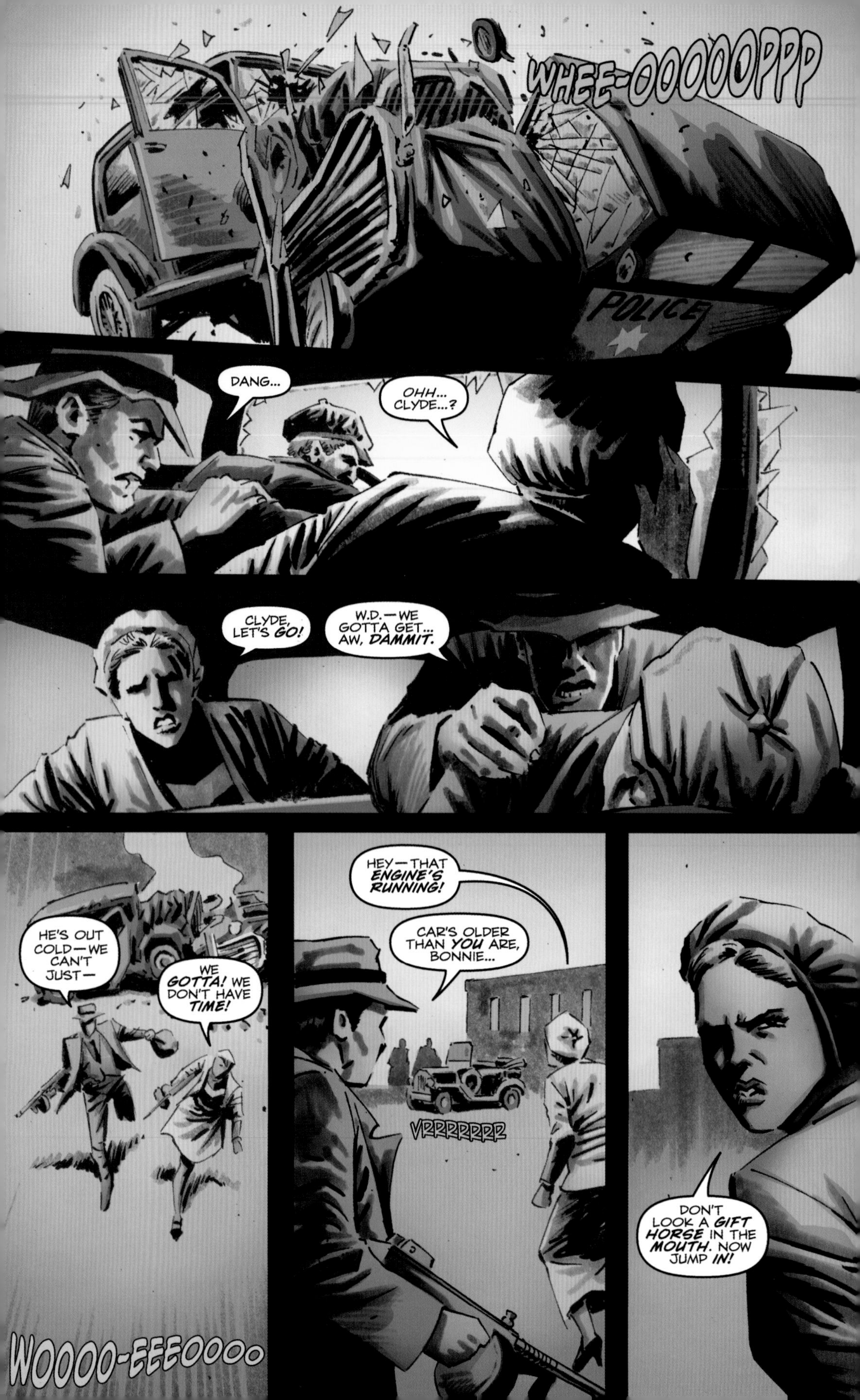
WHEE-OOOOOPPP
POLICE
DANG...
OHH... CLYDE...?
CLYDE, LET'S GO!
W.D.—WE GOTTA GET... AW, DAMMIT.
HE'S OUT COLD—WE CAN'T JUST—
WE GOTTA! WE DON'T HAVE TIME!
WOOOO-EEEOOOo
HEY—THAT ENGINE'S RUNNING!
CAR'S OLDER THAN YOU ARE, BONNIE...
VRRRRRRR
DON'T LOOK A GIFT HORSE IN THE MOUTH. NOW JUMP IN!

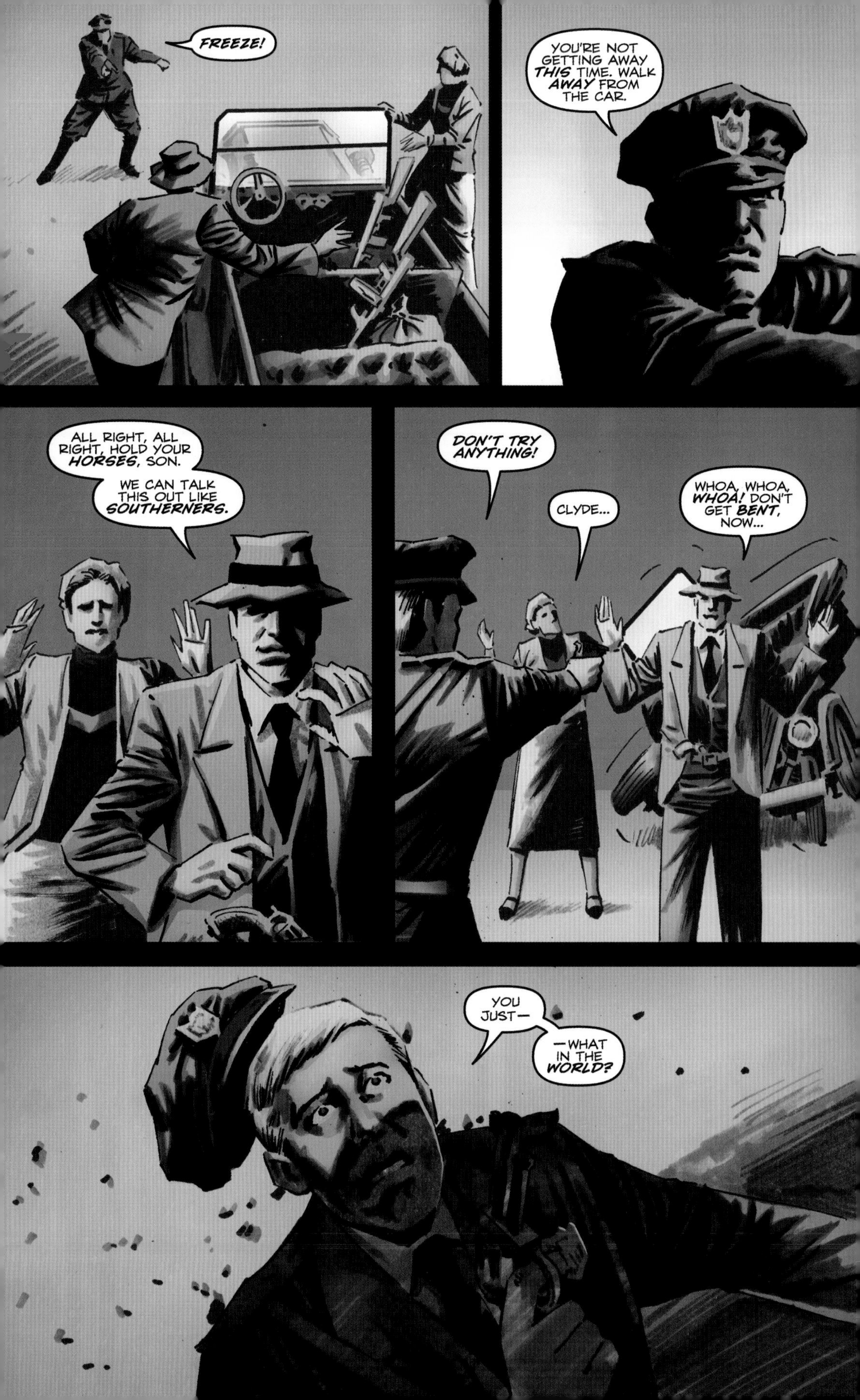
FREEZE!
YOU'RE NOT GETTING AWAY THIS TIME. WALK AWAY FROM THE CAR.
ALL RIGHT, ALL RIGHT, HOLD YOUR HORSES, SON.
WE CAN TALK THIS OUT LIKE SOUTHERNERS.
DON'T TRY ANYTHING!
CLYDE...
WHOA, WHOA, WHOA! DON'T GET BENT, NOW...
YOU JUST—
—WHAT IN THE WORLD?

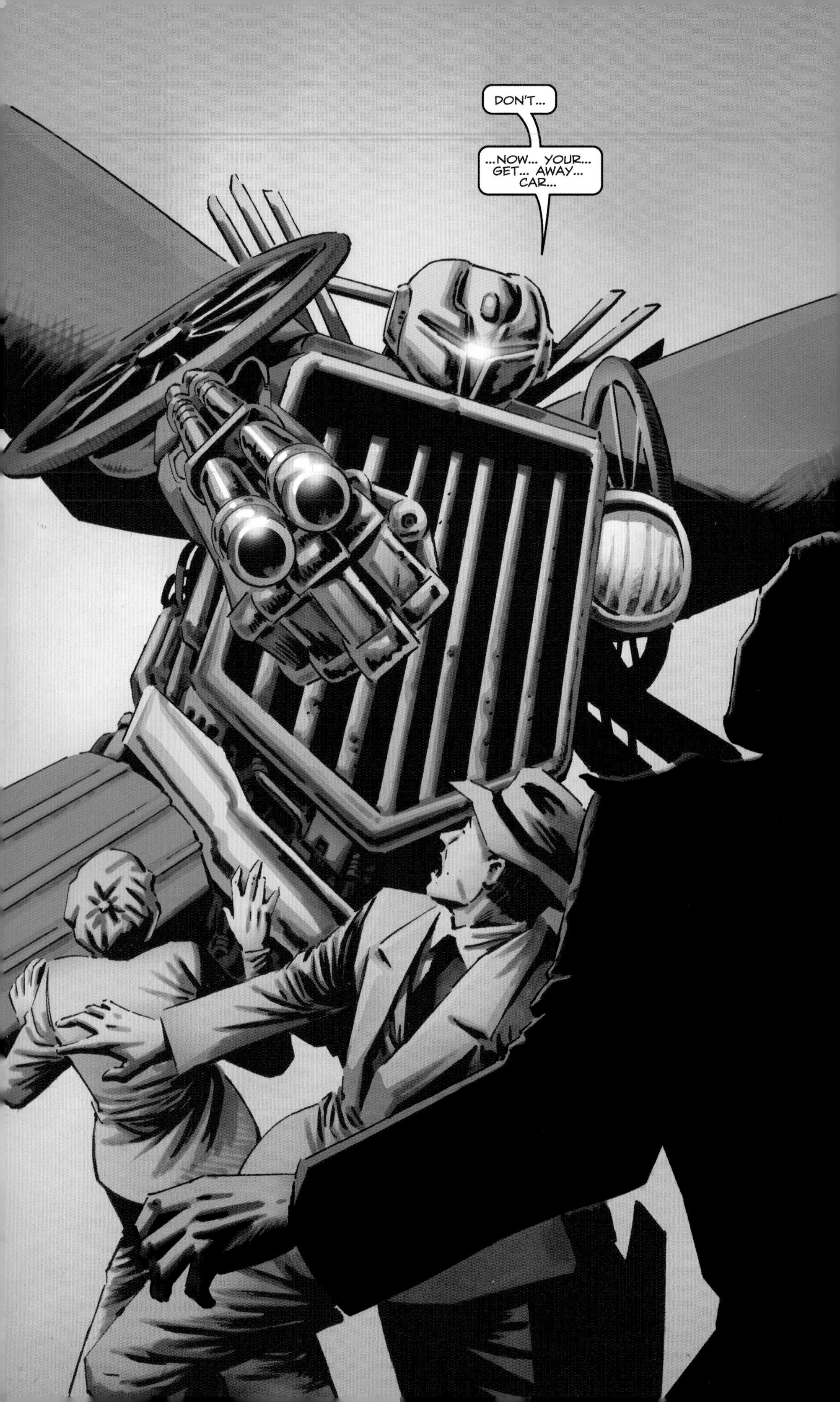
DON'T...
...NOW... YOUR... GET... AWAY... CAR...

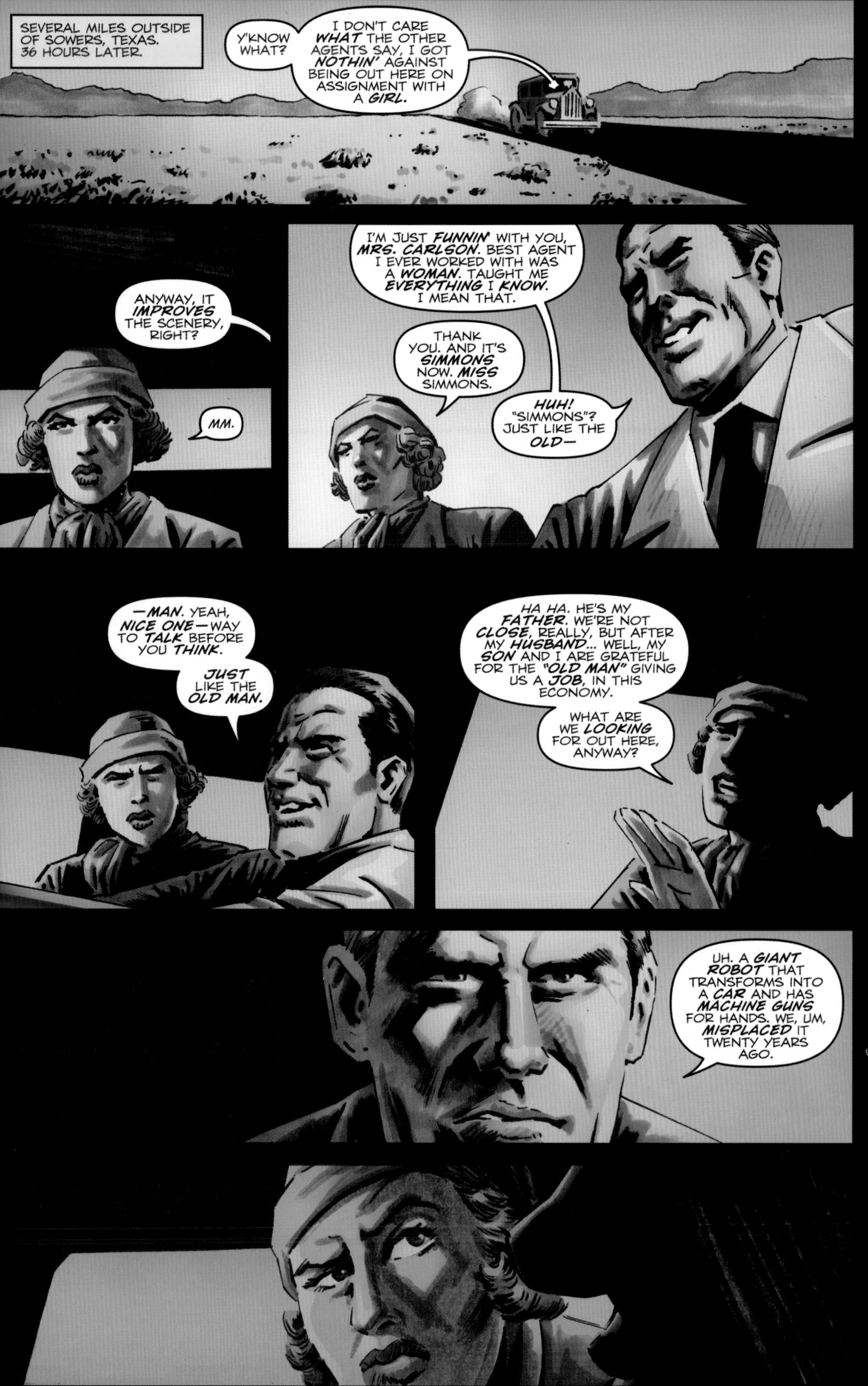
SEVERAL MILES OUTSIDE OF SOWERS, TEXAS. 36 HOURS LATER.
Y'KNOW WHAT?
I DON'T CARE WHAT THE OTHER AGENTS SAY, I GOT NOTHIN' AGAINST BEING OUT HERE ON ASSIGNMENT WITH A GIRL.
ANYWAY, IT IMPROVES THE SCENERY, RIGHT?
MM.
I'M JUST FUNNIN' WITH YOU, MRS. CARLSON. BEST AGENT I EVER WORKED WITH WAS A WOMAN. TAUGHT ME EVERYTHING I KNOW. I MEAN THAT.
THANK YOU. AND IT'S SIMMONS NOW. MISS SIMMONS.
HUH! "SIMMONS"? JUST LIKE THE OLD—
—MAN. YEAH, NICE ONE—WAY TO TALK BEFORE YOU THINK.
JUST LIKE THE OLD MAN.
HA HA. HE'S MY FATHER. WE'RE NOT CLOSE, REALLY, BUT AFTER MY HUSBAND... WELL, MY SON AND I ARE GRATEFUL FOR THE "OLD MAN" GIVING US A JOB, IN THIS ECONOMY.
WHAT ARE WE LOOKING FOR OUT HERE, ANYWAY?
UH. A GIANT ROBOT THAT TRANSFORMS INTO A CAR AND HAS MACHINE GUNS FOR HANDS. WE, UM, MISPLACED IT TWENTY YEARS AGO.

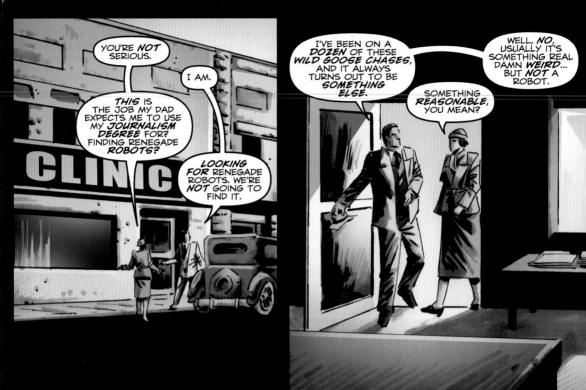

YOU'RE **NOT** SERIOUS.

I AM.

THIS IS THE JOB MY DAD EXPECTS ME TO USE MY **JOURNALISM DEGREE** FOR? FINDING RENEGADE **ROBOTS**?

LOOKING FOR RENEGADE ROBOTS. WE'RE **NOT** GOING TO FIND IT.

I'VE BEEN ON A **DOZEN** OF THESE **WILD GOOSE CHASES**, AND IT ALWAYS TURNS OUT TO BE **SOMETHING ELSE**.

WELL, **NO**, USUALLY IT'S SOMETHING REAL DAMN **WEIRD**... BUT **NOT** A ROBOT.

SOMETHING **REASONABLE**, YOU MEAN?

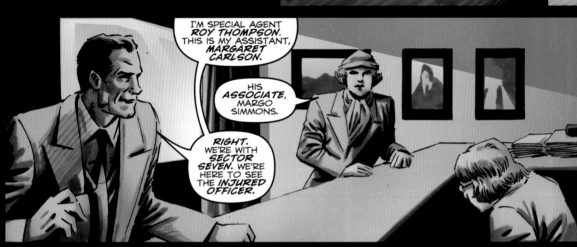

I'M SPECIAL AGENT **ROY THOMPSON**. THIS IS MY ASSISTANT, **MARGARET CARLSON**.

HIS **ASSOCIATE**, MARGO SIMMONS.

RIGHT. WE'RE WITH **SECTOR SEVEN**. WE'RE HERE TO SEE THE **INJURED OFFICER**.

YEAH—I WAS TOLD SOMEBODY'D BE COMING. AIN'T NEVER HEARD O' NO "**SECTOR SEVEN**."

NO, MA'AM—AND WE'D BE **OBLIGED** IF YOU WENT AHEAD AND **FORGOT** THAT YOU DID, TODAY.

RELAX, MISS SIMMONS—IT'LL TURN OUT TO BE **NOTHING**. I **GUARANTEE** IT.

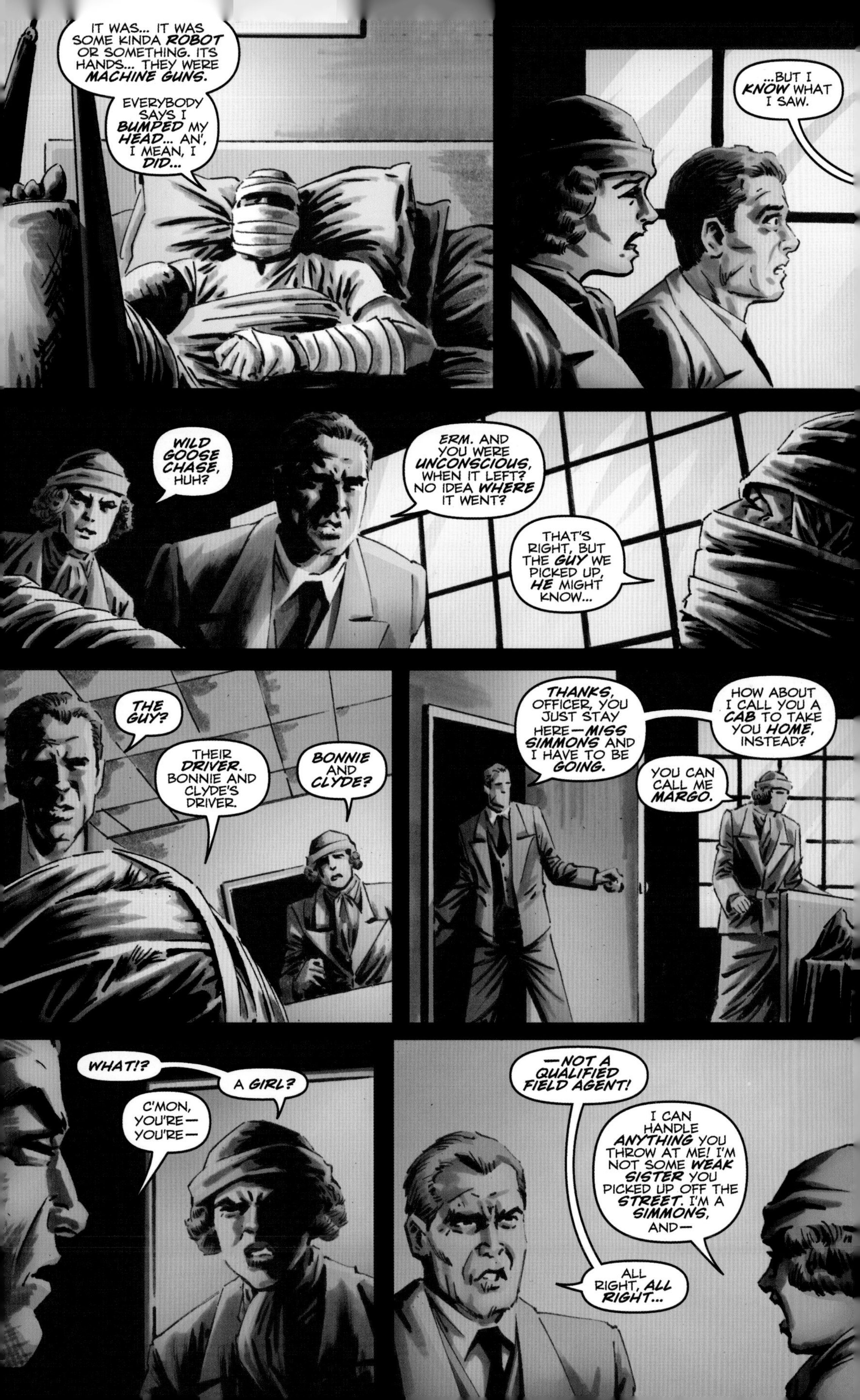
IT WAS... IT WAS SOME KINDA ROBOT OR SOMETHING. ITS HANDS... THEY WERE MACHINE GUNS.
EVERYBODY SAYS I BUMPED MY HEAD... AN', I MEAN, I DID...
...BUT I KNOW WHAT I SAW.
WILD GOOSE CHASE, HUH?
ERM. AND YOU WERE UNCONSCIOUS, WHEN IT LEFT? NO IDEA WHERE IT WENT?
THAT'S RIGHT, BUT THE GUY WE PICKED UP, HE MIGHT KNOW...
THE GUY?
THEIR DRIVER. BONNIE AND CLYDE'S DRIVER.
BONNIE AND CLYDE?
THANKS, OFFICER, YOU JUST STAY HERE—MISS SIMMONS AND I HAVE TO BE GOING.
HOW ABOUT I CALL YOU A CAB TO TAKE YOU HOME, INSTEAD?
YOU CAN CALL ME MARGO.
WHAT!?
A GIRL?
C'MON, YOU'RE— YOU'RE—
—NOT A QUALIFIED FIELD AGENT!
I CAN HANDLE ANYTHING YOU THROW AT ME! I'M NOT SOME WEAK SISTER YOU PICKED UP OFF THE STREET. I'M A SIMMONS, AND—
ALL RIGHT, ALL RIGHT...

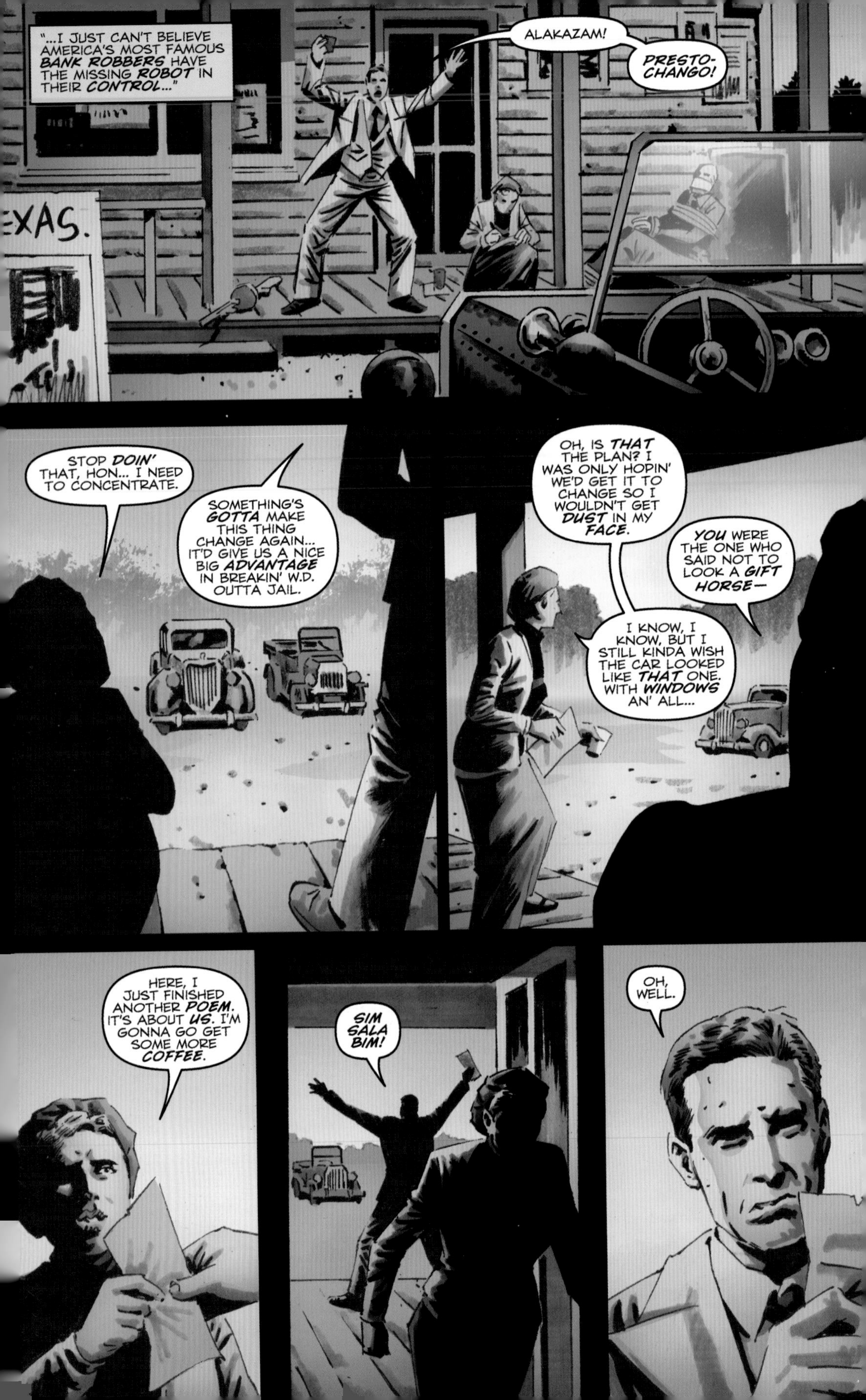
"...I JUST CAN'T BELIEVE AMERICA'S MOST FAMOUS BANK ROBBERS HAVE THE MISSING ROBOT IN THEIR CONTROL..."
ALAKAZAM!
PRESTO-CHANGO!
EXAS.
STOP DOIN' THAT, HON... I NEED TO CONCENTRATE.
SOMETHING'S GOTTA MAKE THIS THING CHANGE AGAIN... IT'D GIVE US A NICE BIG ADVANTAGE IN BREAKIN' W.D. OUTTA JAIL.
OH, IS THAT THE PLAN? I WAS ONLY HOPIN' WE'D GET IT TO CHANGE SO I WOULDN'T GET DUST IN MY FACE.
YOU WERE THE ONE WHO SAID NOT TO LOOK A GIFT HORSE—
I KNOW, I KNOW, BUT I STILL KINDA WISH THE CAR LOOKED LIKE THAT ONE. WITH WINDOWS AN' ALL...
HERE, I JUST FINISHED ANOTHER POEM. IT'S ABOUT US. I'M GONNA GO GET SOME MORE COFFEE.
SIM SALA BIM!
OH, WELL.

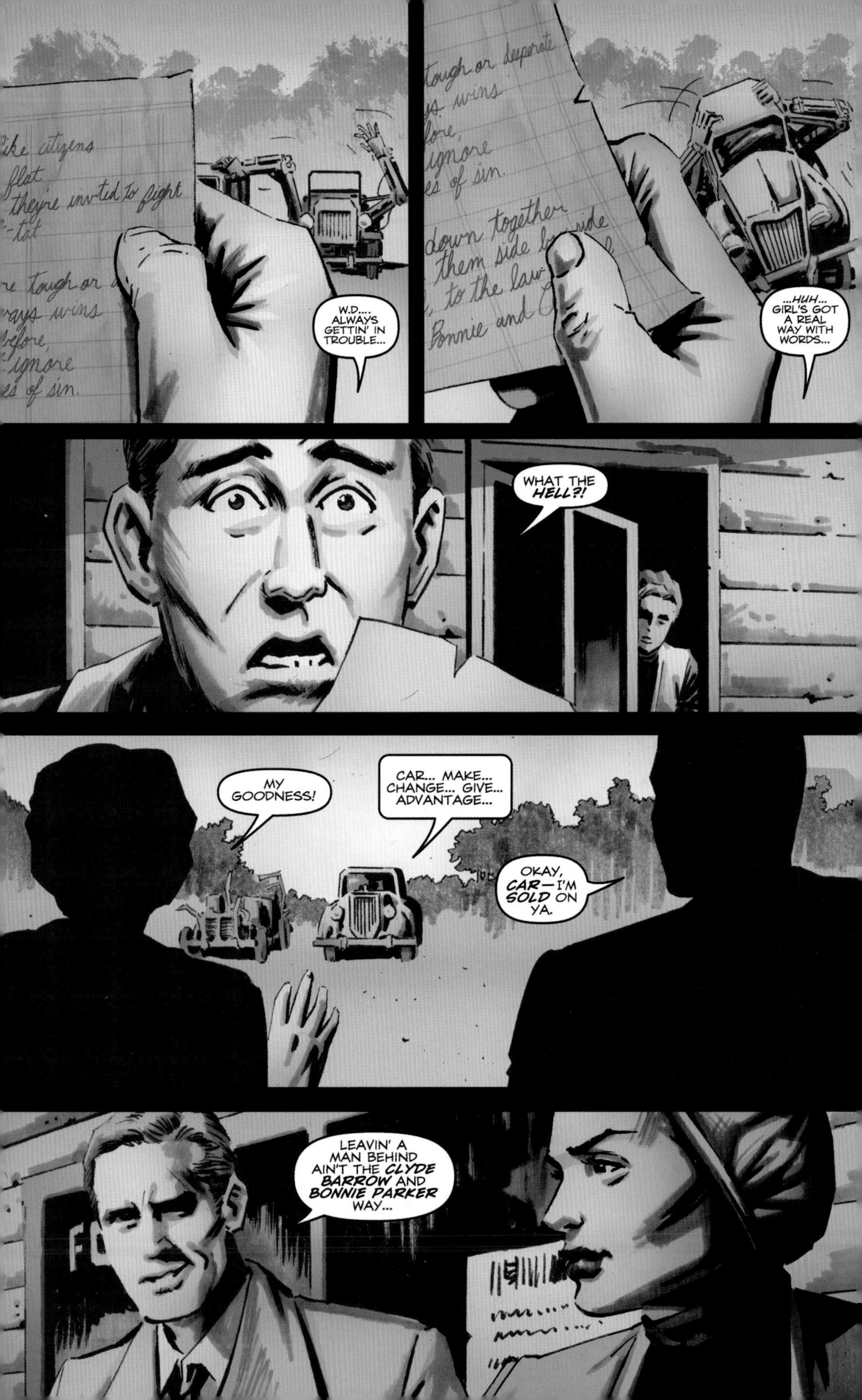
W.D.... ALWAYS GETTIN' IN TROUBLE...
...HUH... GIRL'S GOT A REAL WAY WITH WORDS...
WHAT THE HELL?!
MY GOODNESS!
CAR... MAKE... CHANGE... GIVE... ADVANTAGE...
OKAY, CAR—I'M SOLD ON YA.
LEAVIN' A MAN BEHIND AIN'T THE CLYDE BARROW AND BONNIE PARKER WAY...

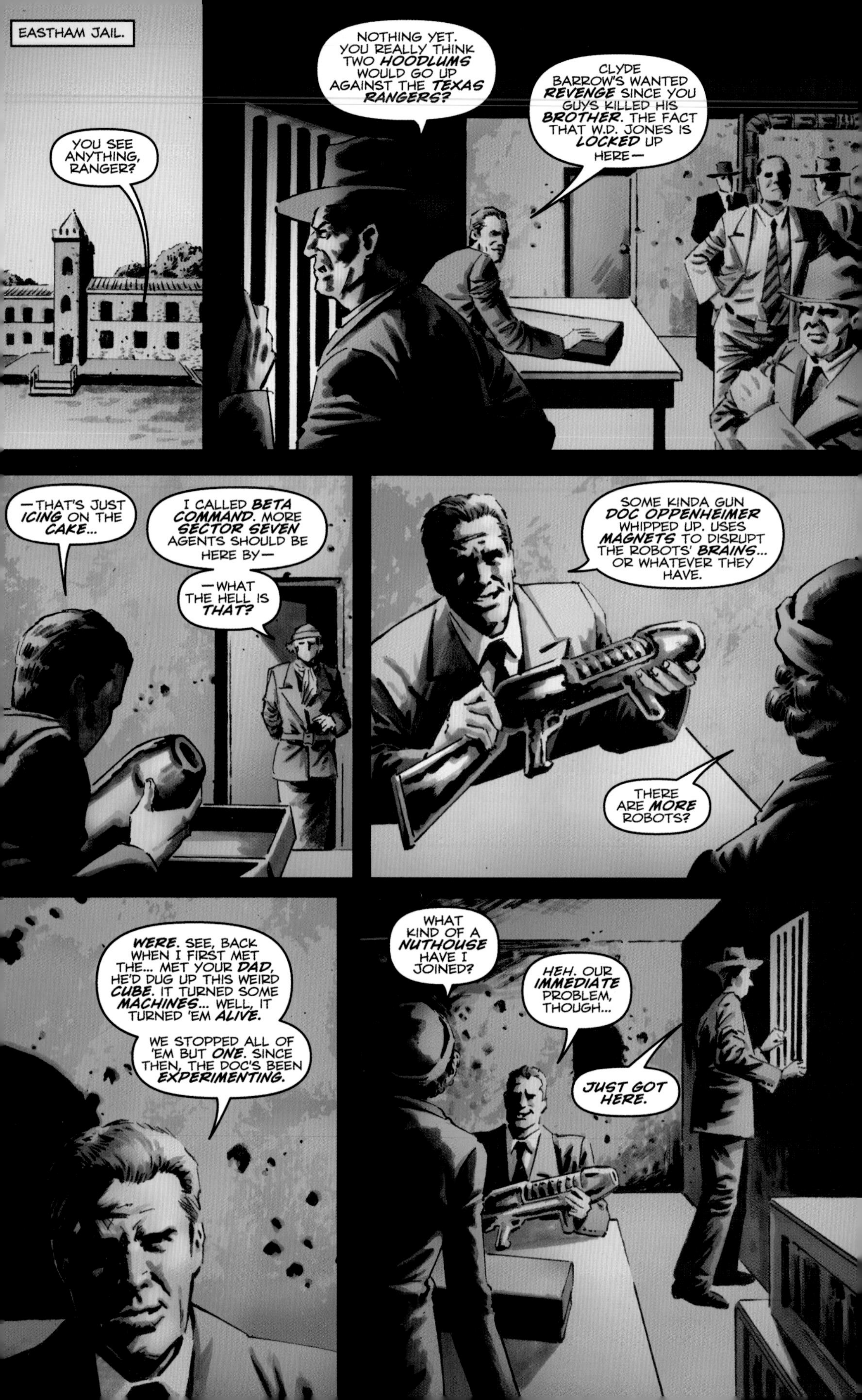
EASTHAM JAIL.
YOU SEE ANYTHING, RANGER?
NOTHING YET. YOU REALLY THINK TWO HOODLUMS WOULD GO UP AGAINST THE TEXAS RANGERS?
CLYDE BARROW'S WANTED REVENGE SINCE YOU GUYS KILLED HIS BROTHER. THE FACT THAT W.D. JONES IS LOCKED UP HERE—
—THAT'S JUST ICING ON THE CAKE...
I CALLED BETA COMMAND. MORE SECTOR SEVEN AGENTS SHOULD BE HERE BY—
—WHAT THE HELL IS THAT?
SOME KINDA GUN DOC OPPENHEIMER WHIPPED UP. USES MAGNETS TO DISRUPT THE ROBOTS' BRAINS... OR WHATEVER THEY HAVE.
THERE ARE MORE ROBOTS?
WERE. SEE, BACK WHEN I FIRST MET THE... MET YOUR DAD, HE'D DUG UP THIS WEIRD CUBE. IT TURNED SOME MACHINES... WELL, IT TURNED 'EM ALIVE.
WE STOPPED ALL OF 'EM BUT ONE. SINCE THEN, THE DOC'S BEEN EXPERIMENTING.
WHAT KIND OF A NUTHOUSE HAVE I JOINED?
HEH. OUR IMMEDIATE PROBLEM, THOUGH...
JUST GOT HERE.

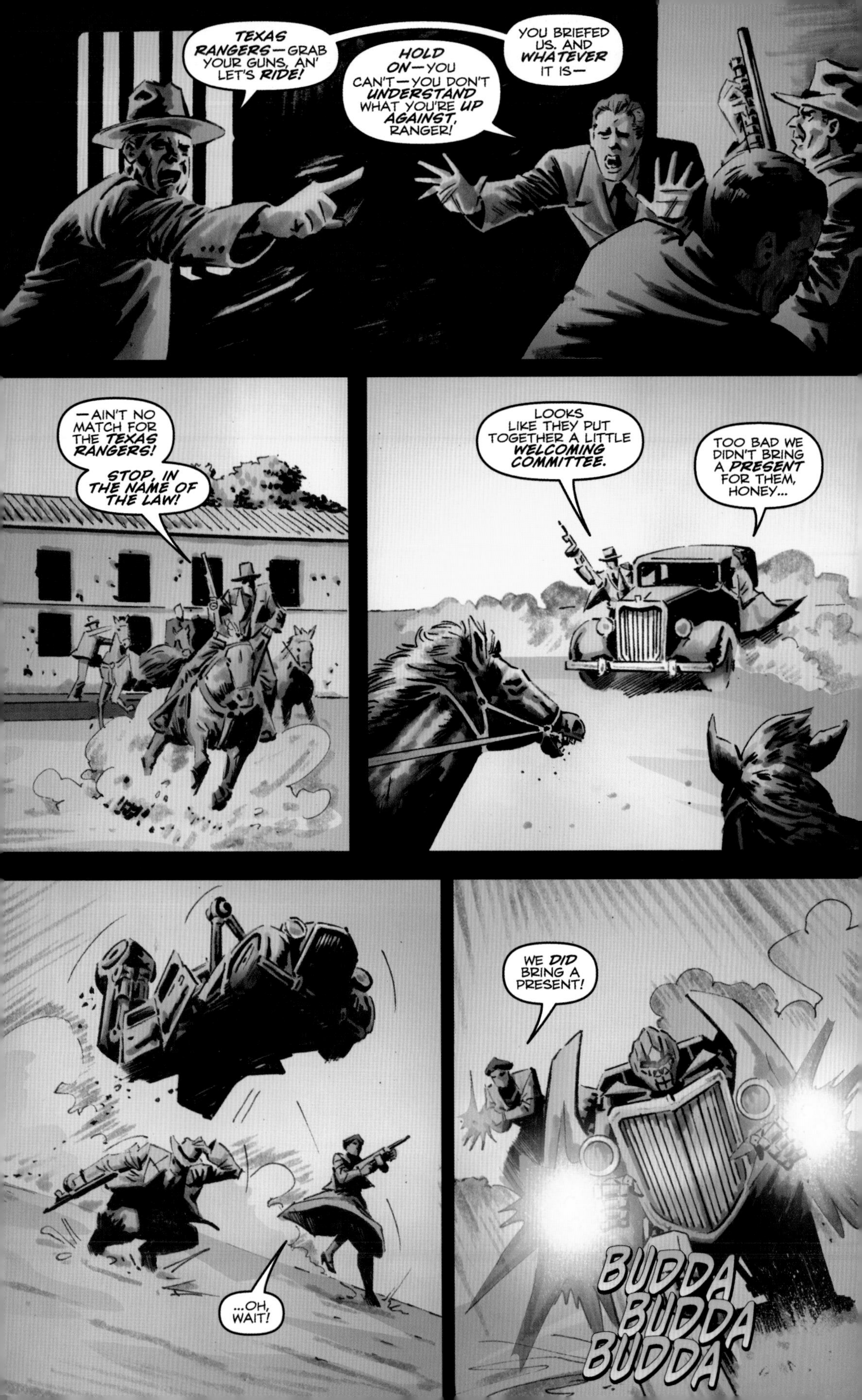
TEXAS RANGERS—GRAB YOUR GUNS, AN' LET'S RIDE!
HOLD ON—YOU CAN'T—YOU DON'T UNDERSTAND WHAT YOU'RE UP AGAINST, RANGER!
YOU BRIEFED US. AND WHATEVER IT IS—
—AIN'T NO MATCH FOR THE TEXAS RANGERS!
STOP, IN THE NAME OF THE LAW!
LOOKS LIKE THEY PUT TOGETHER A LITTLE WELCOMING COMMITTEE.
TOO BAD WE DIDN'T BRING A PRESENT FOR THEM, HONEY...
...OH, WAIT!
WE DID BRING A PRESENT!
BUDDA BUDDA BUDDA

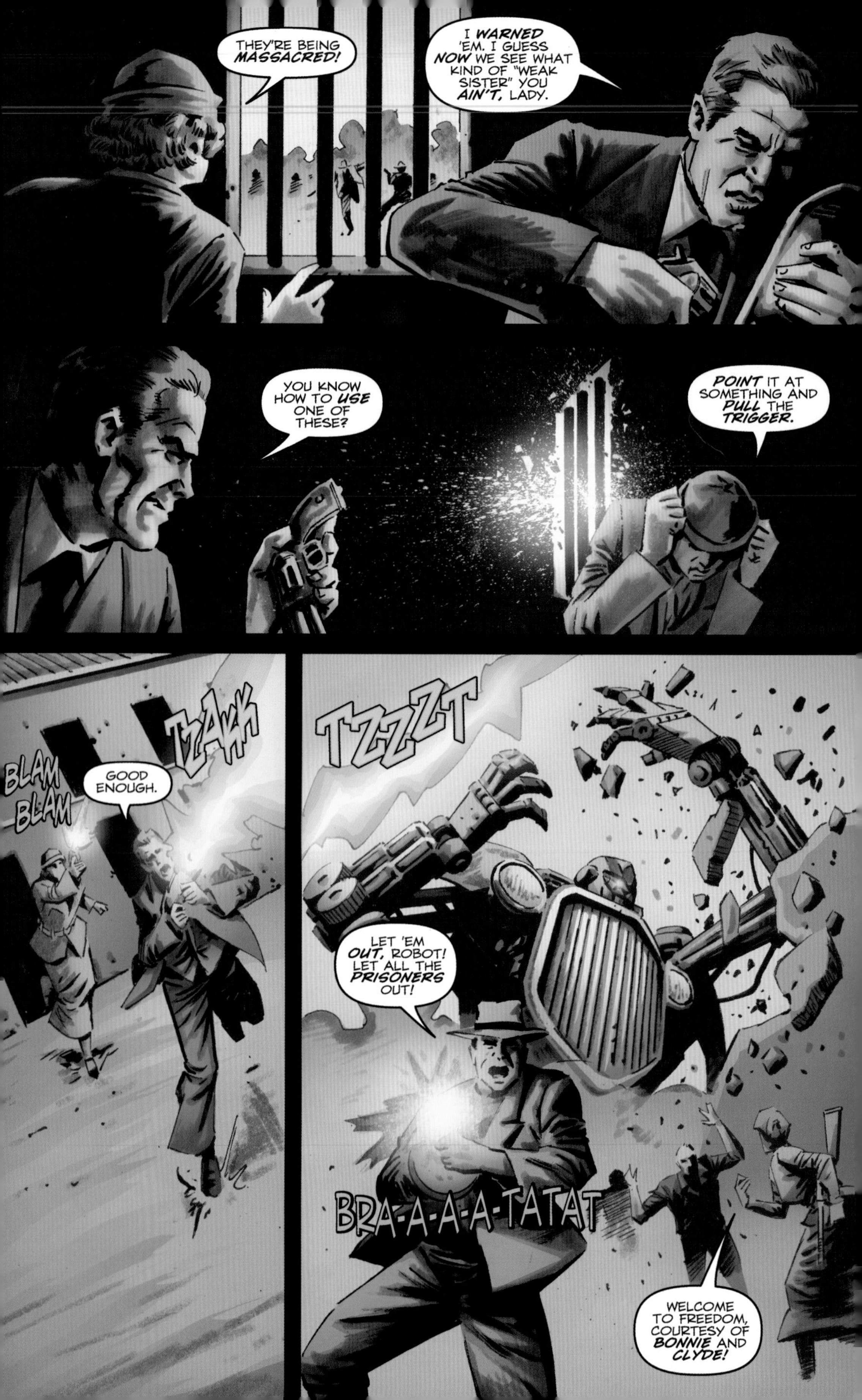
THEY'RE BEING MASSACRED!
I WARNED 'EM. I GUESS NOW WE SEE WHAT KIND OF "WEAK SISTER" YOU AIN'T, LADY.
YOU KNOW HOW TO USE ONE OF THESE?
POINT IT AT SOMETHING AND PULL THE TRIGGER.
BLAM BLAM
TZAKK
GOOD ENOUGH.
TZZZT
LET 'EM OUT, ROBOT! LET ALL THE PRISONERS OUT!
BRA-A-A-A-TATAT
WELCOME TO FREEDOM, COURTESY OF BONNIE AND CLYDE!

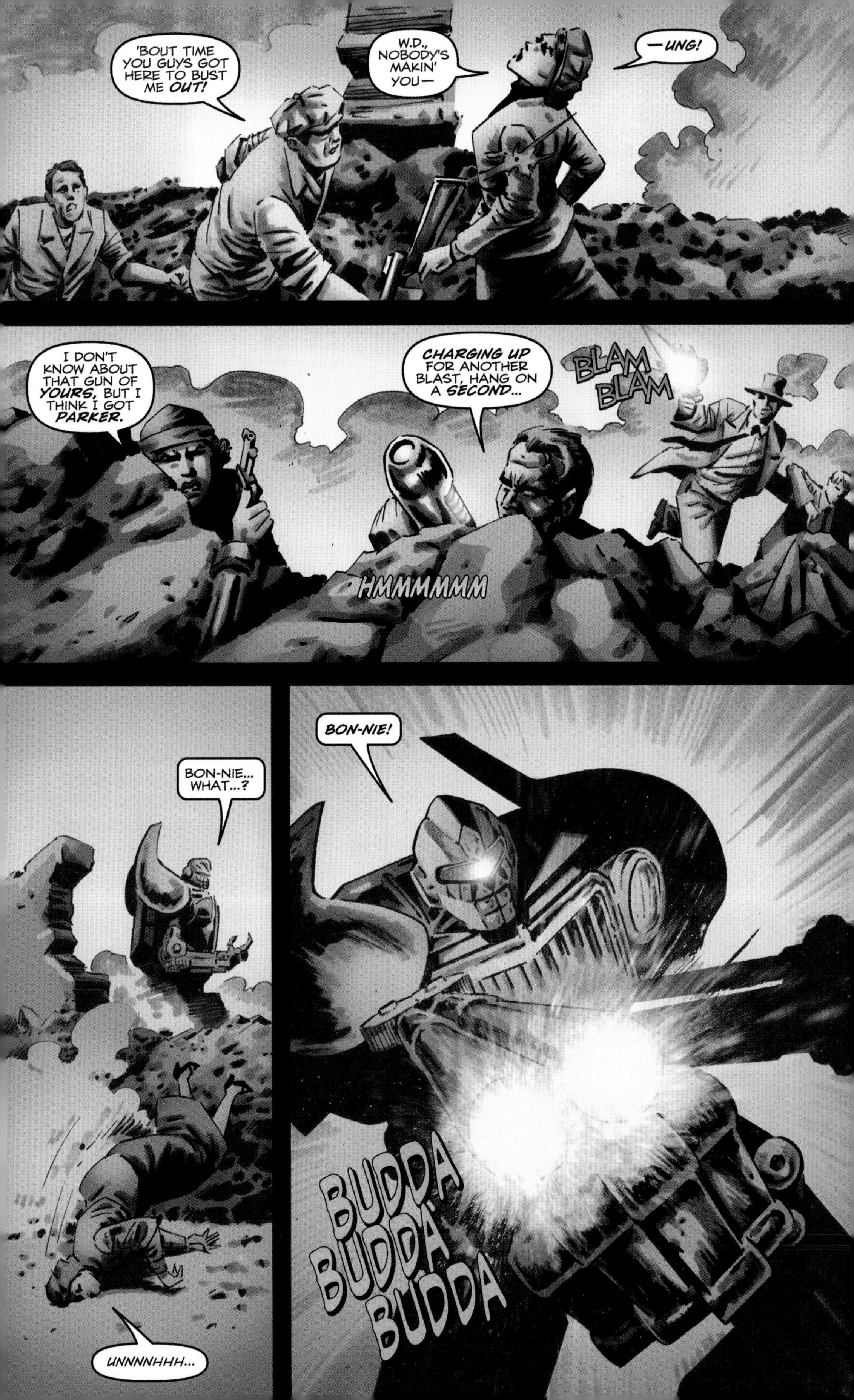
'BOUT TIME YOU GUYS GOT HERE TO BUST ME OUT!
W.D., NOBODY'S MAKIN' YOU—
—UNG!
I DON'T KNOW ABOUT THAT GUN OF YOURS, BUT I THINK I GOT PARKER.
CHARGING UP FOR ANOTHER BLAST, HANG ON A SECOND...
BLAM BLAM
HMMMMMM
BON-NIE... WHAT...?
UNNNNHHH...
BON-NIE!
BUDDA BUDDA BUDDA

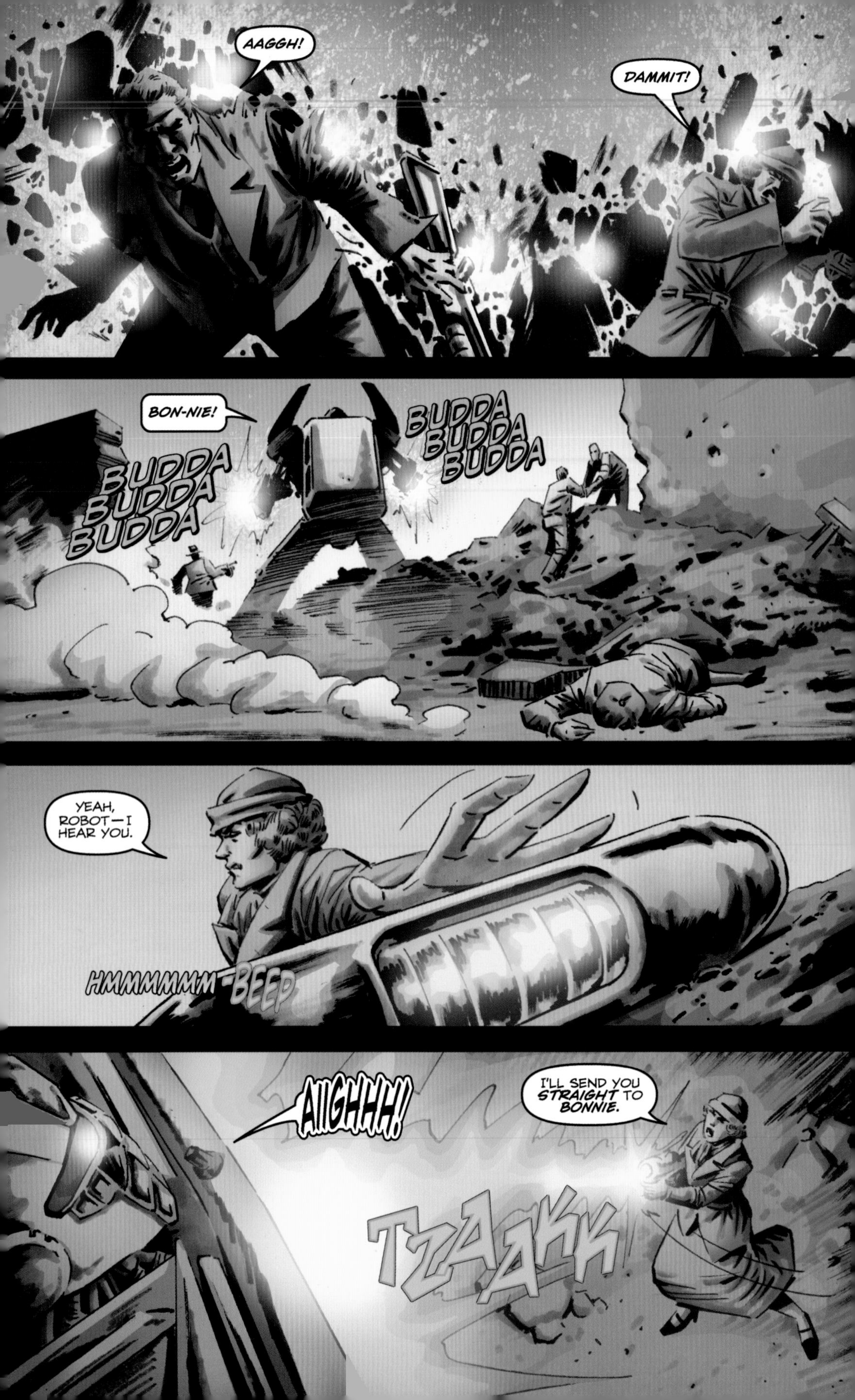
AAGGH!
DAMMIT!
BON-NIE!
BUDDA BUDDA BUDDA
BUDDA BUDDA BUDDA
YEAH, ROBOT—I HEAR YOU.
HMMMMMM-BEEP
AIIGHHH!
I'LL SEND YOU STRAIGHT TO BONNIE.
TZAAKK

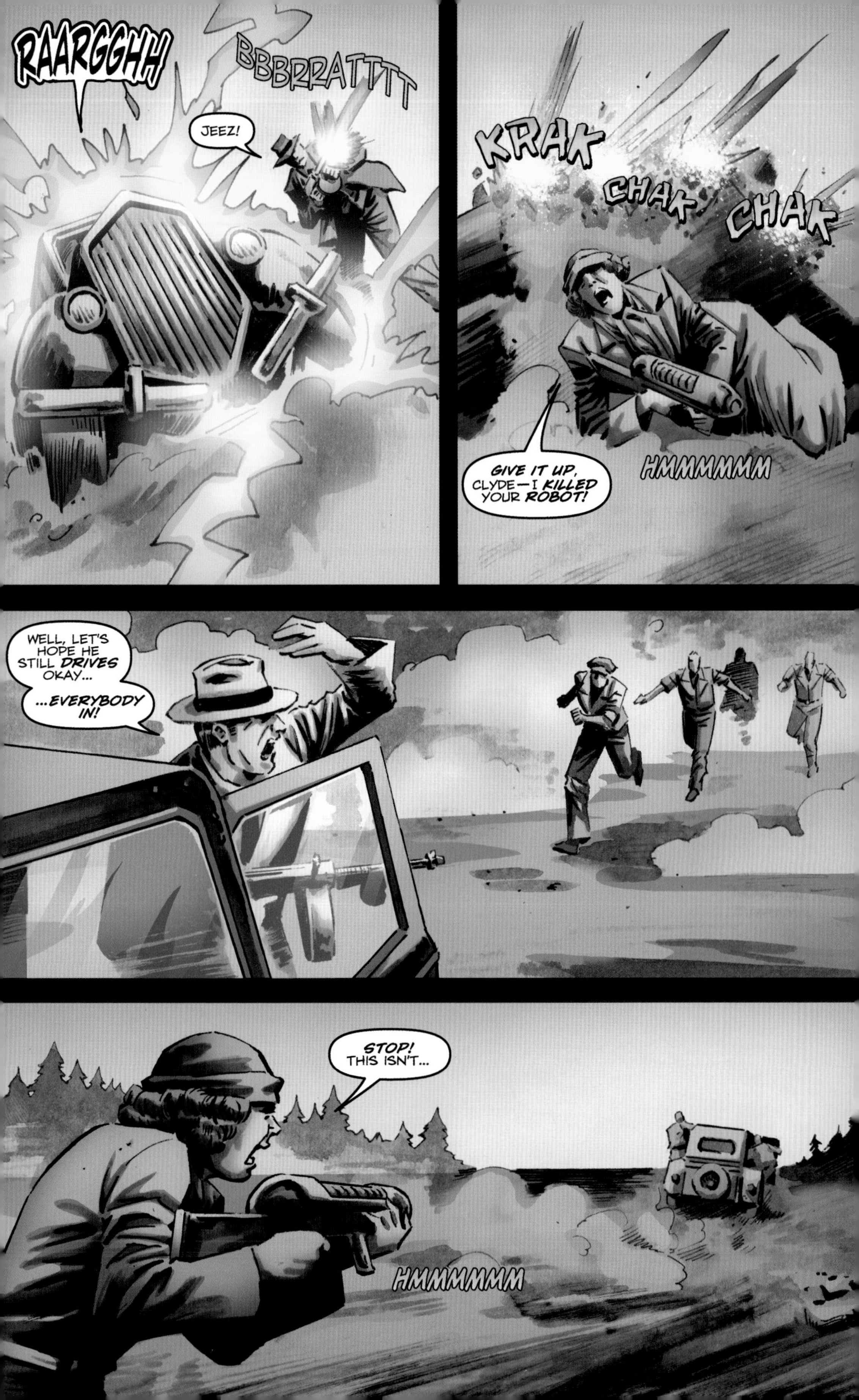
RAARGGHH
BBBRRATTTTT
JEEZ!
KRAK
CHAK
CHAK
GIVE IT UP, CLYDE—I KILLED YOUR ROBOT!
HMMMMMM
WELL, LET'S HOPE HE STILL DRIVES OKAY...
...EVERYBODY IN!
STOP! THIS ISN'T...
HMMMMMM

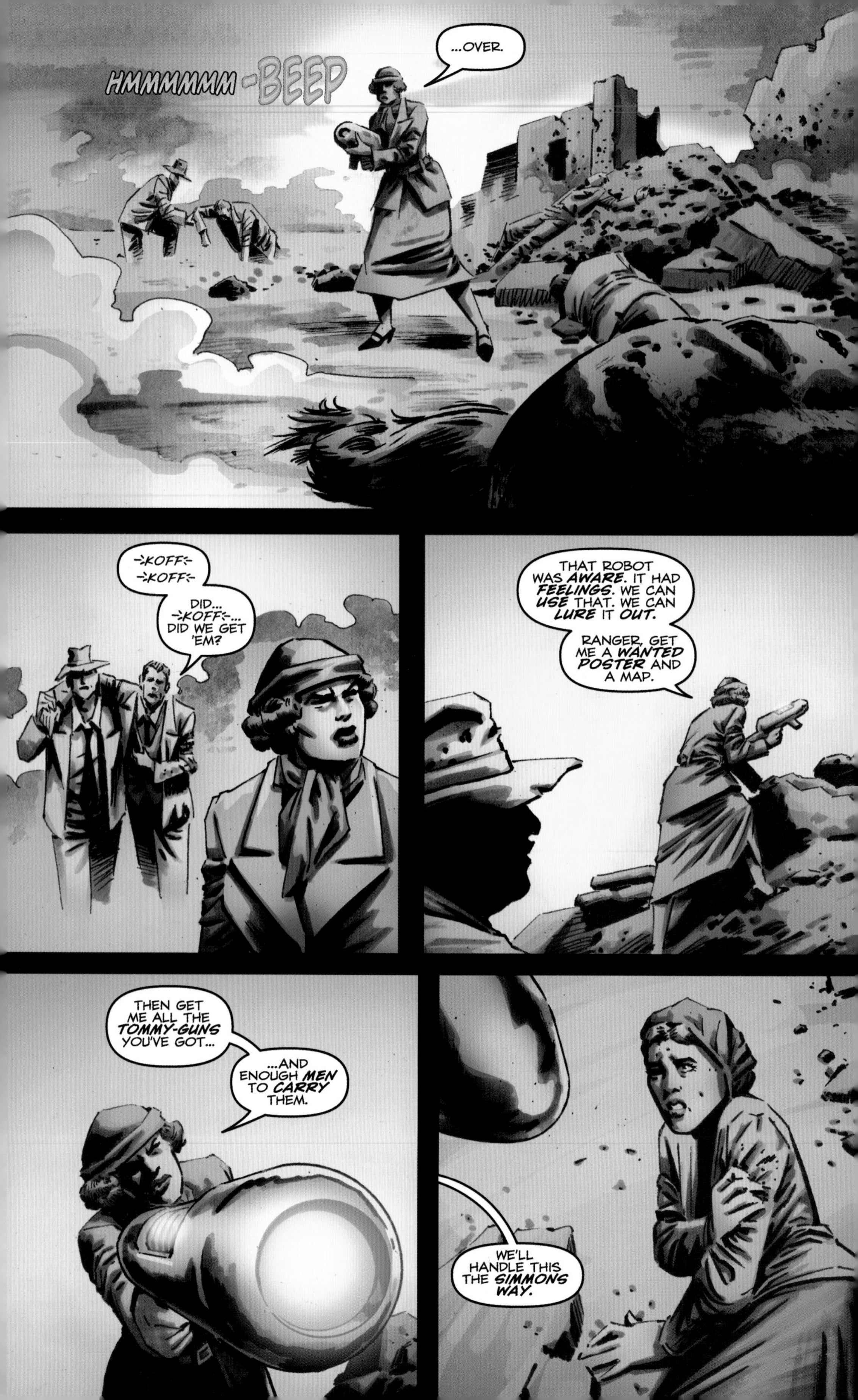

HMMMMMM -BEEP
...OVER.
-KOFF-
-KOFF-
DID... -KOFF-... DID WE GET 'EM?
THAT ROBOT WAS AWARE. IT HAD FEELINGS. WE CAN USE THAT. WE CAN LURE IT OUT.
RANGER, GET ME A WANTED POSTER AND A MAP.
THEN GET ME ALL THE TOMMY-GUNS YOU'VE GOT...
...AND ENOUGH MEN TO CARRY THEM.
WE'LL HANDLE THIS THE SIMMONS WAY.

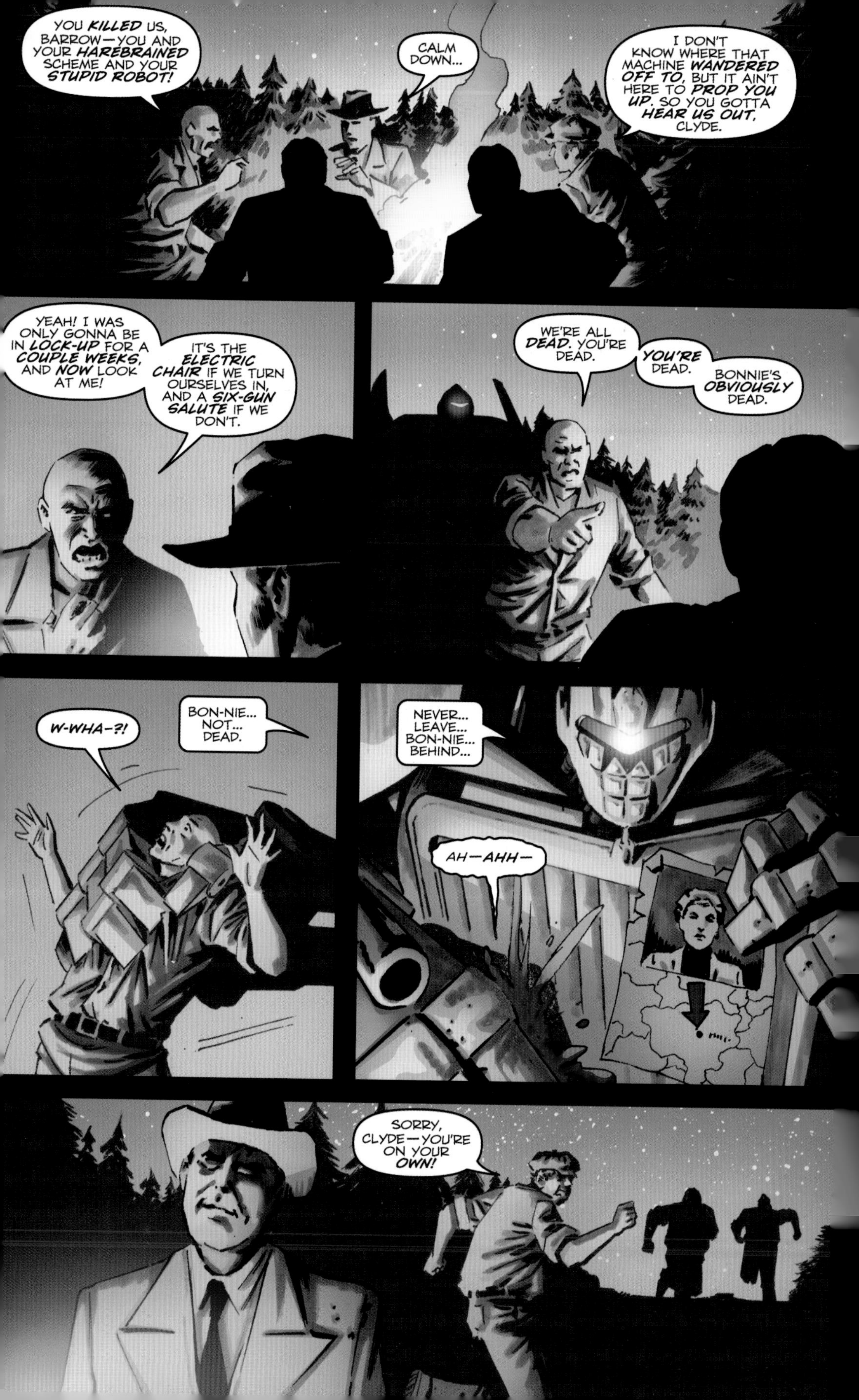
YOU KILLED US, BARROW—YOU AND YOUR HAREBRAINED SCHEME AND YOUR STUPID ROBOT!
CALM DOWN...
I DON'T KNOW WHERE THAT MACHINE WANDERED OFF TO, BUT IT AIN'T HERE TO PROP YOU UP. SO YOU GOTTA HEAR US OUT, CLYDE.
YEAH! I WAS ONLY GONNA BE IN LOCK-UP FOR A COUPLE WEEKS, AND NOW LOOK AT ME!
IT'S THE ELECTRIC CHAIR IF WE TURN OURSELVES IN, AND A SIX-GUN SALUTE IF WE DON'T.
WE'RE ALL DEAD. YOU'RE DEAD.
YOU'RE DEAD.
BONNIE'S OBVIOUSLY DEAD.
W-WHA-?!
BON-NIE... NOT... DEAD.
NEVER... LEAVE... BON-NIE... BEHIND...
AH—AHH—
SORRY, CLYDE—YOU'RE ON YOUR OWN!

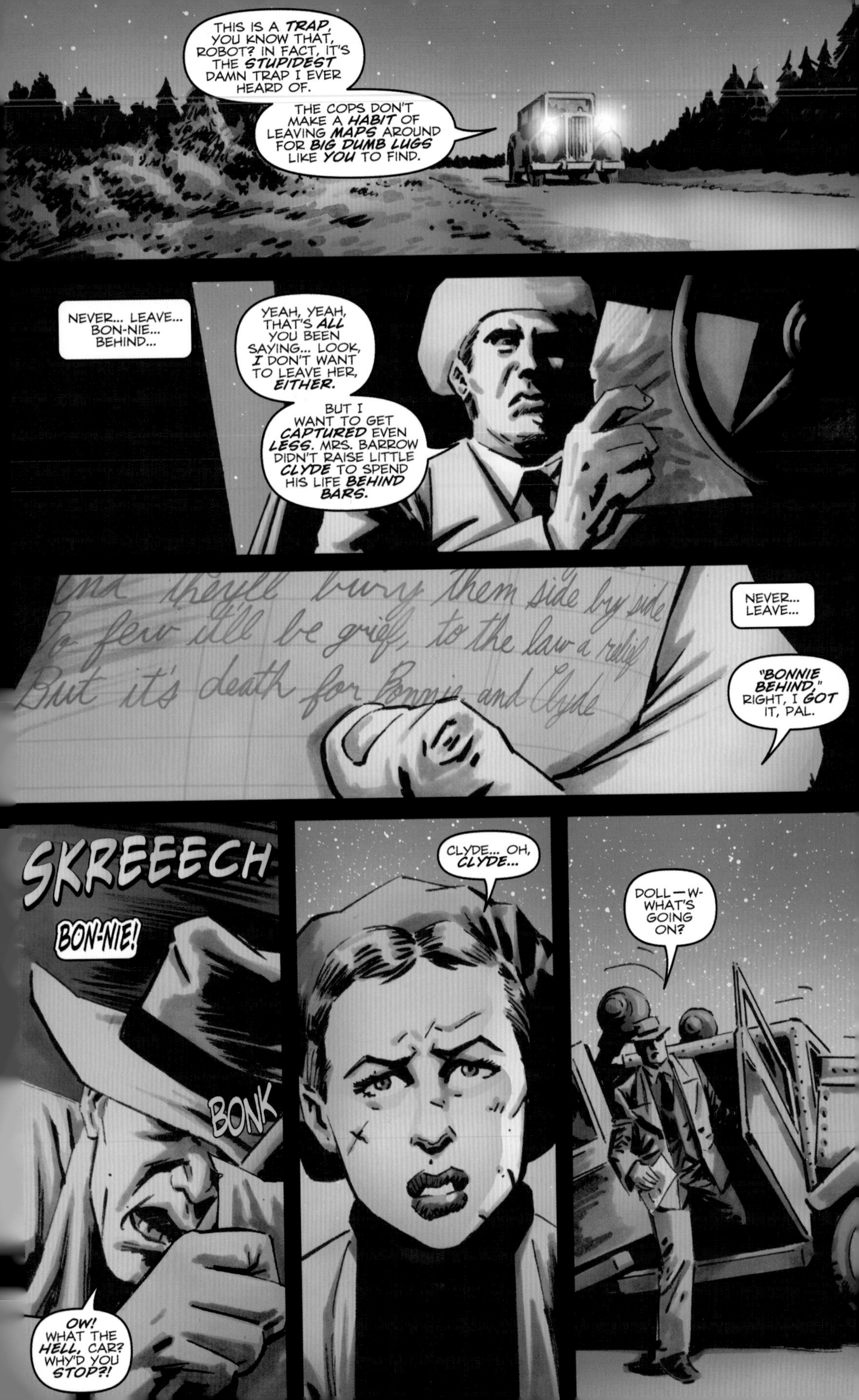

THIS IS A TRAP, YOU KNOW THAT, ROBOT? IN FACT, IT'S THE STUPIDEST DAMN TRAP I EVER HEARD OF.
THE COPS DON'T MAKE A HABIT OF LEAVING MAPS AROUND FOR BIG DUMB LUGS LIKE YOU TO FIND.
NEVER... LEAVE... BON-NIE... BEHIND...
YEAH, YEAH, THAT'S ALL YOU BEEN SAYING... LOOK, I DON'T WANT TO LEAVE HER, EITHER.
BUT I WANT TO GET CAPTURED EVEN LESS. MRS. BARROW DIDN'T RAISE LITTLE CLYDE TO SPEND HIS LIFE BEHIND BARS.
And they'll bury them side by side
To few it'll be grief, to the law a relief
But it's death for Bonnie and Clyde
NEVER... LEAVE...
"BONNIE BEHIND," RIGHT, I GOT IT, PAL.
SKREEECH
BON-NIE!
BONK
OW! WHAT THE HELL, CAR? WHY'D YOU STOP?!
CLYDE... OH, CLYDE...
DOLL—W-WHAT'S GOING ON?

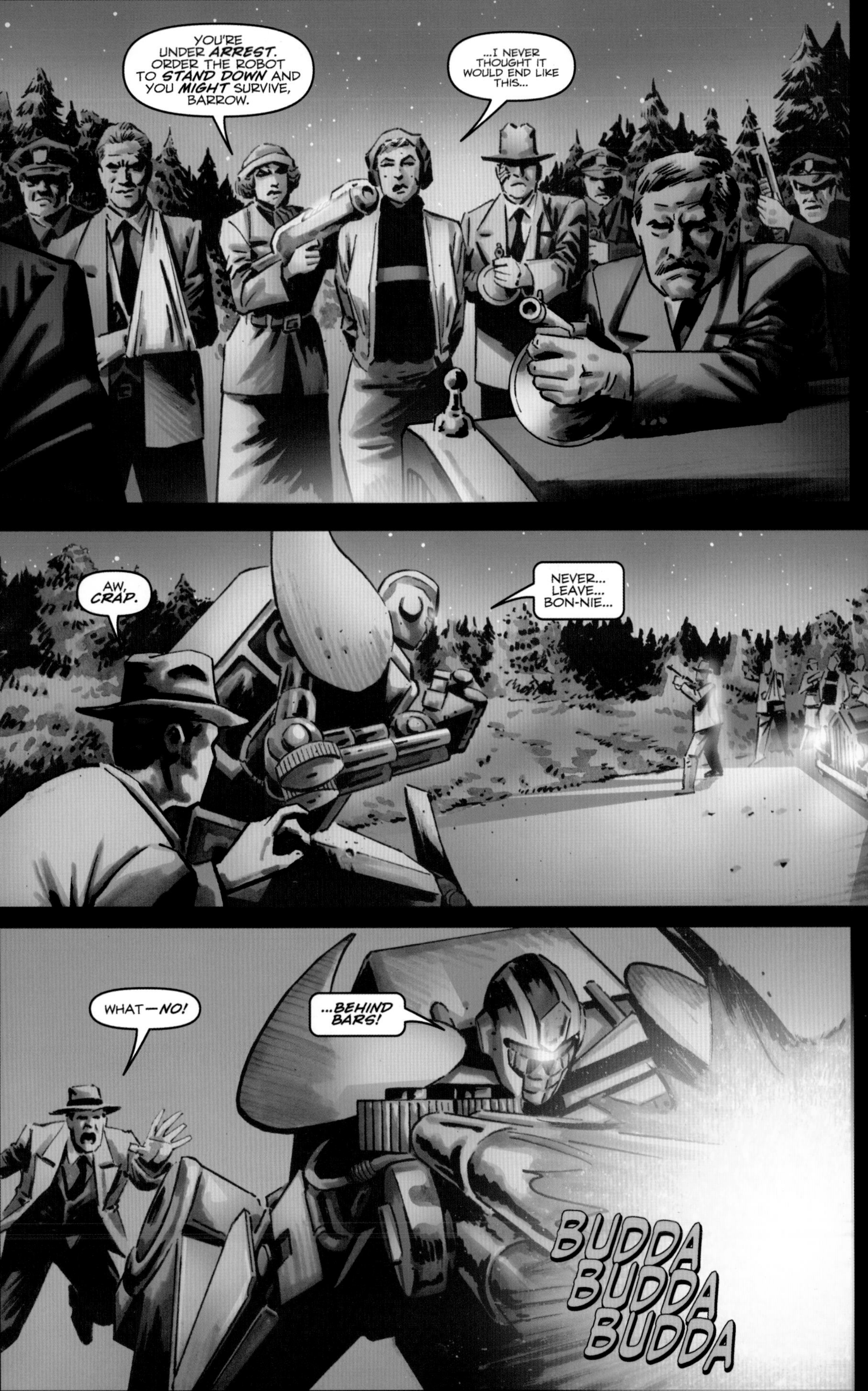
YOU'RE UNDER ARREST. ORDER THE ROBOT TO STAND DOWN AND YOU MIGHT SURVIVE, BARROW.
...I NEVER THOUGHT IT WOULD END LIKE THIS...
AW, CRAP.
NEVER... LEAVE... BON-NIE...
WHAT—NO!
...BEHIND BARS!
BUDDA BUDDA BUDDA

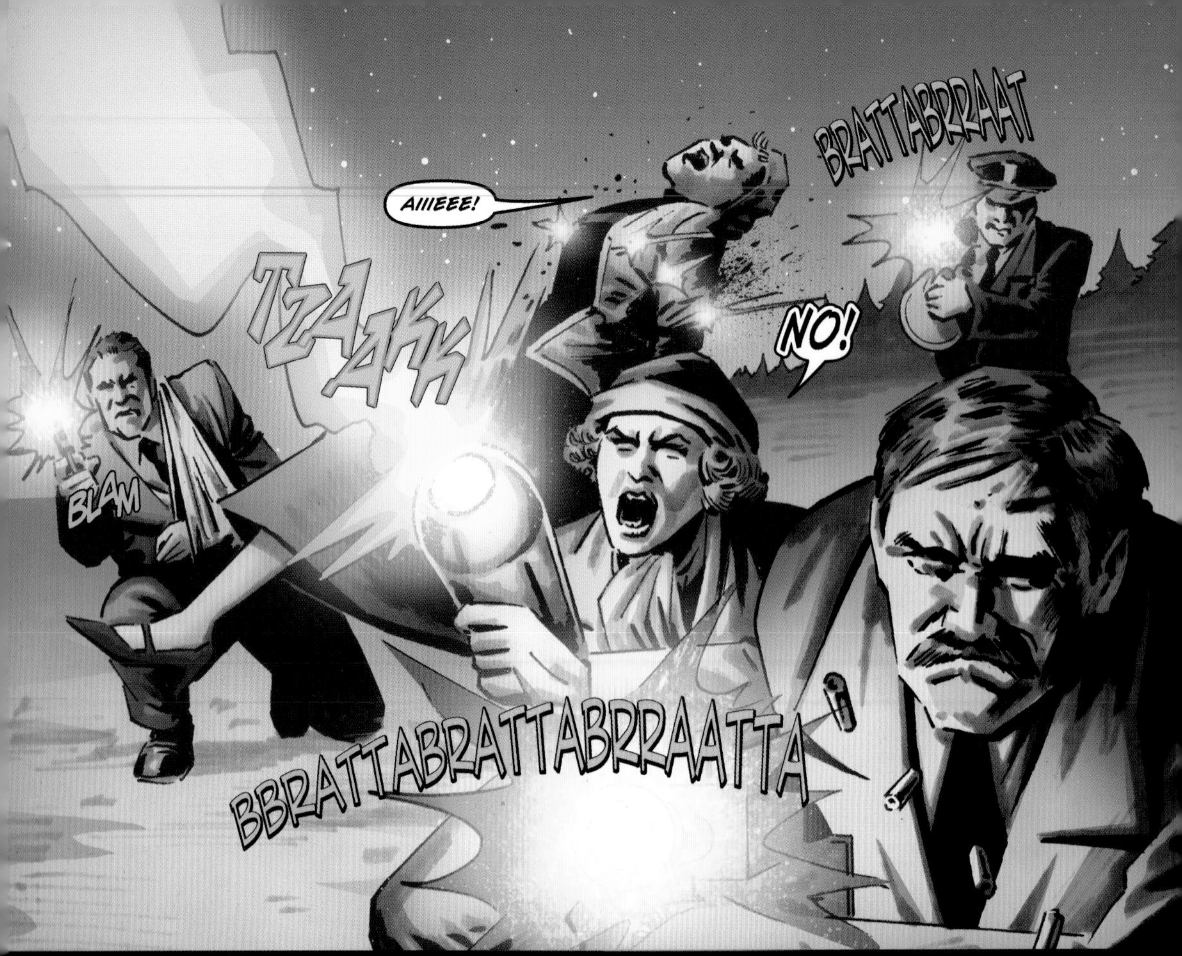
AIIIEEE!
BRATTABRRAAT
TZAAKK
NO!
BLAM
BBRATTABRATTABRRAATTA

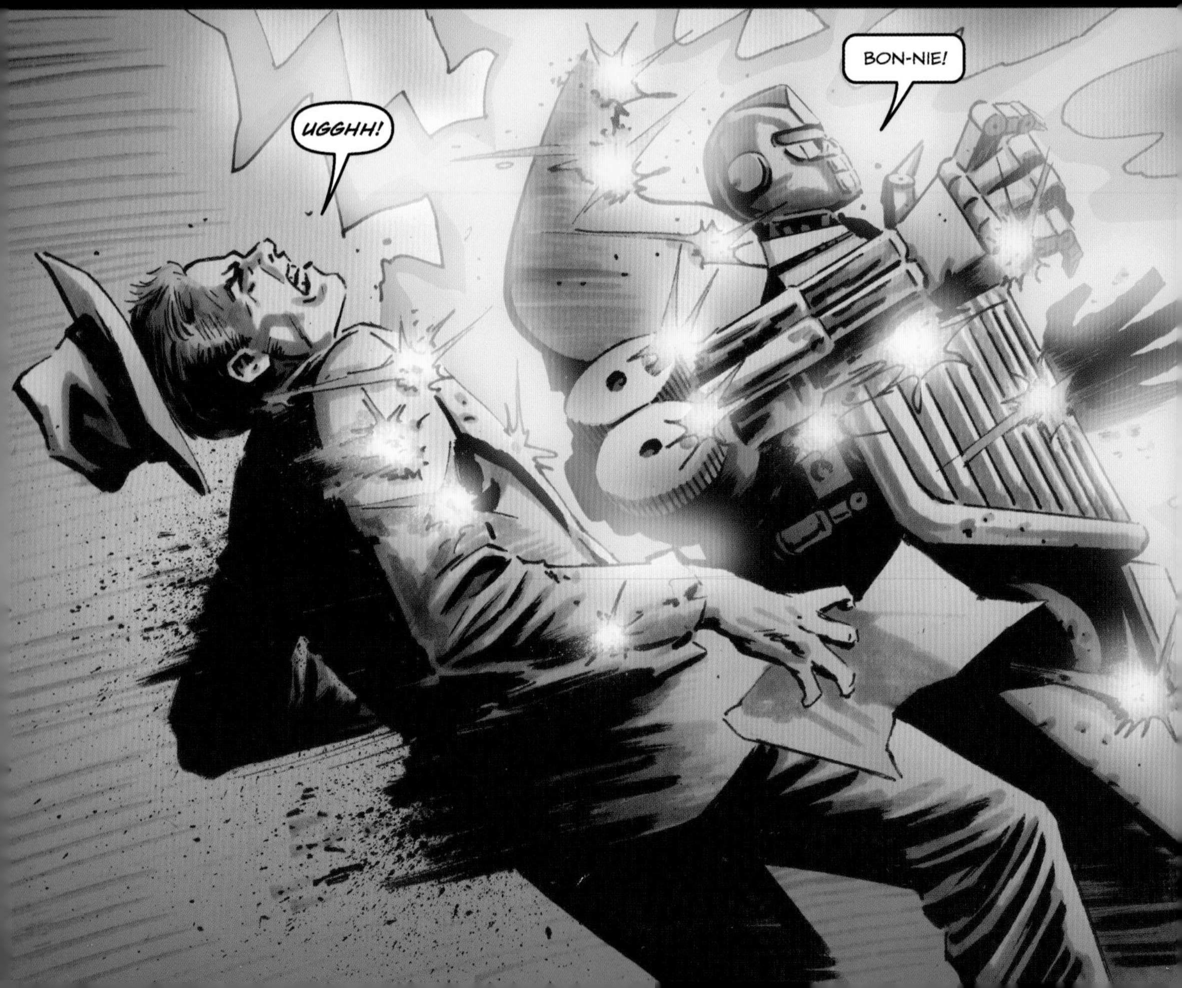
BON-NIE!
UGGHH!

BRATTABRRAAT

HMMMMMMMMMMMMMM

BLAM

BBRATTABRATTA

...PLEASE...

...ONLY... WAY... NO... JAIL...

BBRATTA BRATTA BRRAA

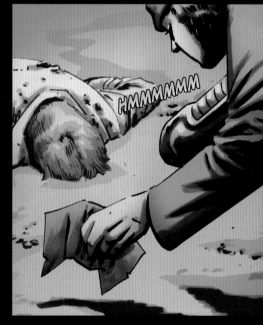

HMMMMM

...I'M... SORRY...

HMMMMMM-BEEP

...BON... NIE...

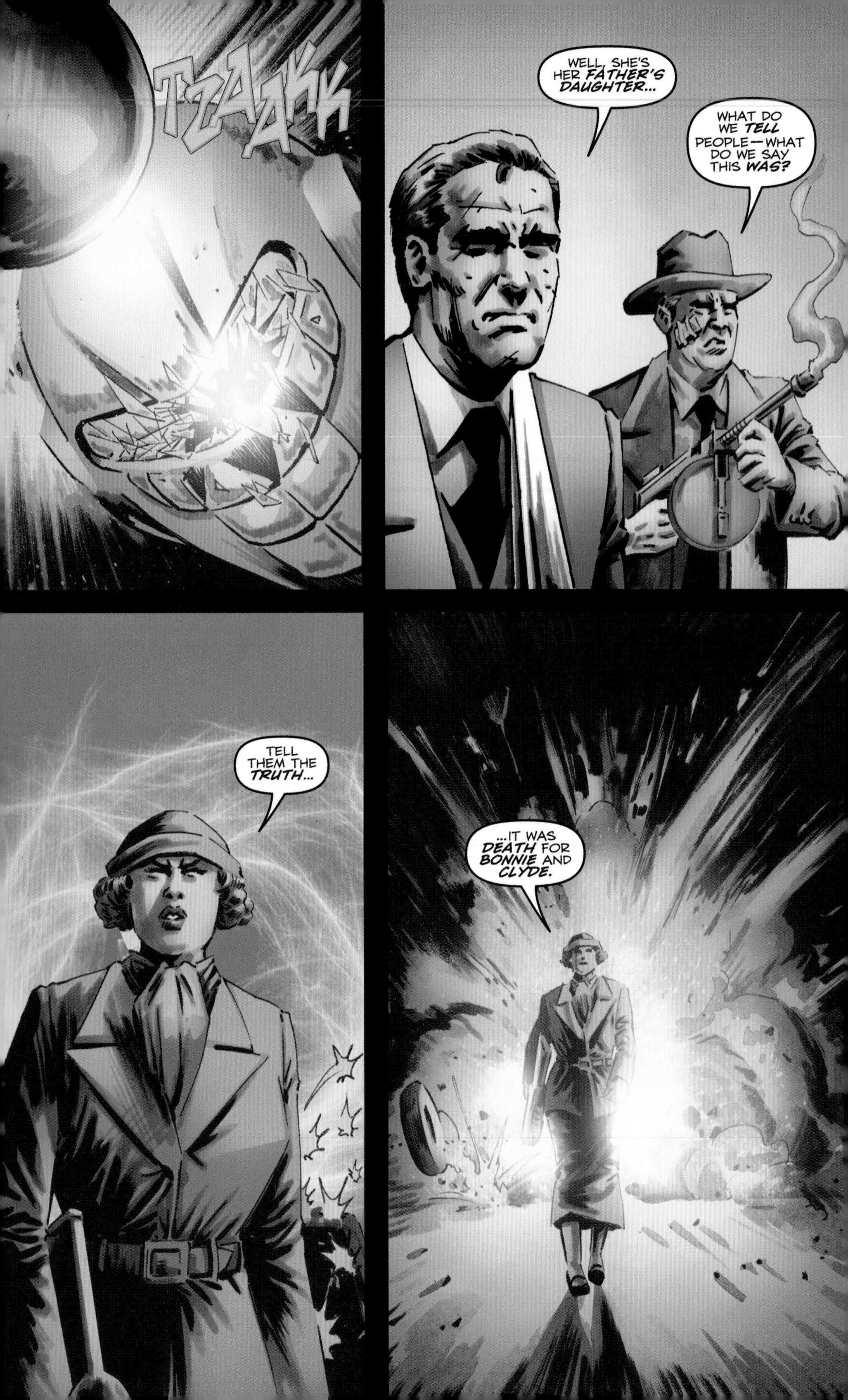
TZAAKK
WELL, SHE'S HER FATHER'S DAUGHTER...
WHAT DO WE TELL PEOPLE—WHAT DO WE SAY THIS WAS?
TELL THEM THE TRUTH...
...IT WAS DEATH FOR BONNIE AND CLYDE.

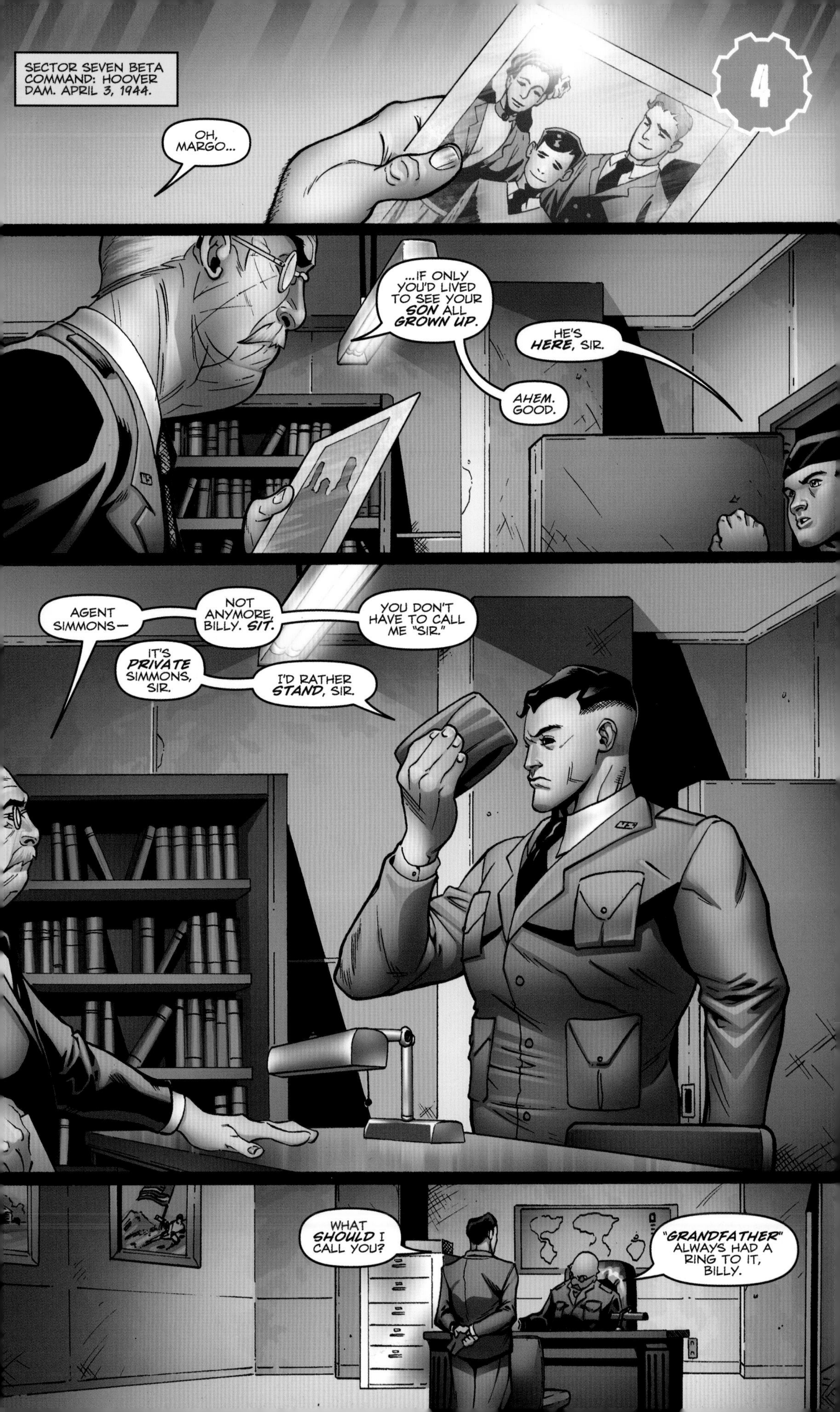

SECTOR SEVEN BETA COMMAND: HOOVER DAM. APRIL 3, 1944.
4
OH, MARGO...
...IF ONLY YOU'D LIVED TO SEE YOUR SON ALL GROWN UP.
HE'S HERE, SIR.
AHEM. GOOD.
AGENT SIMMONS—
NOT ANYMORE, BILLY. SIT.
YOU DON'T HAVE TO CALL ME "SIR."
IT'S PRIVATE SIMMONS, SIR.
I'D RATHER STAND, SIR.
WHAT SHOULD I CALL YOU?
"GRANDFATHER" ALWAYS HAD A RING TO IT, BILLY.

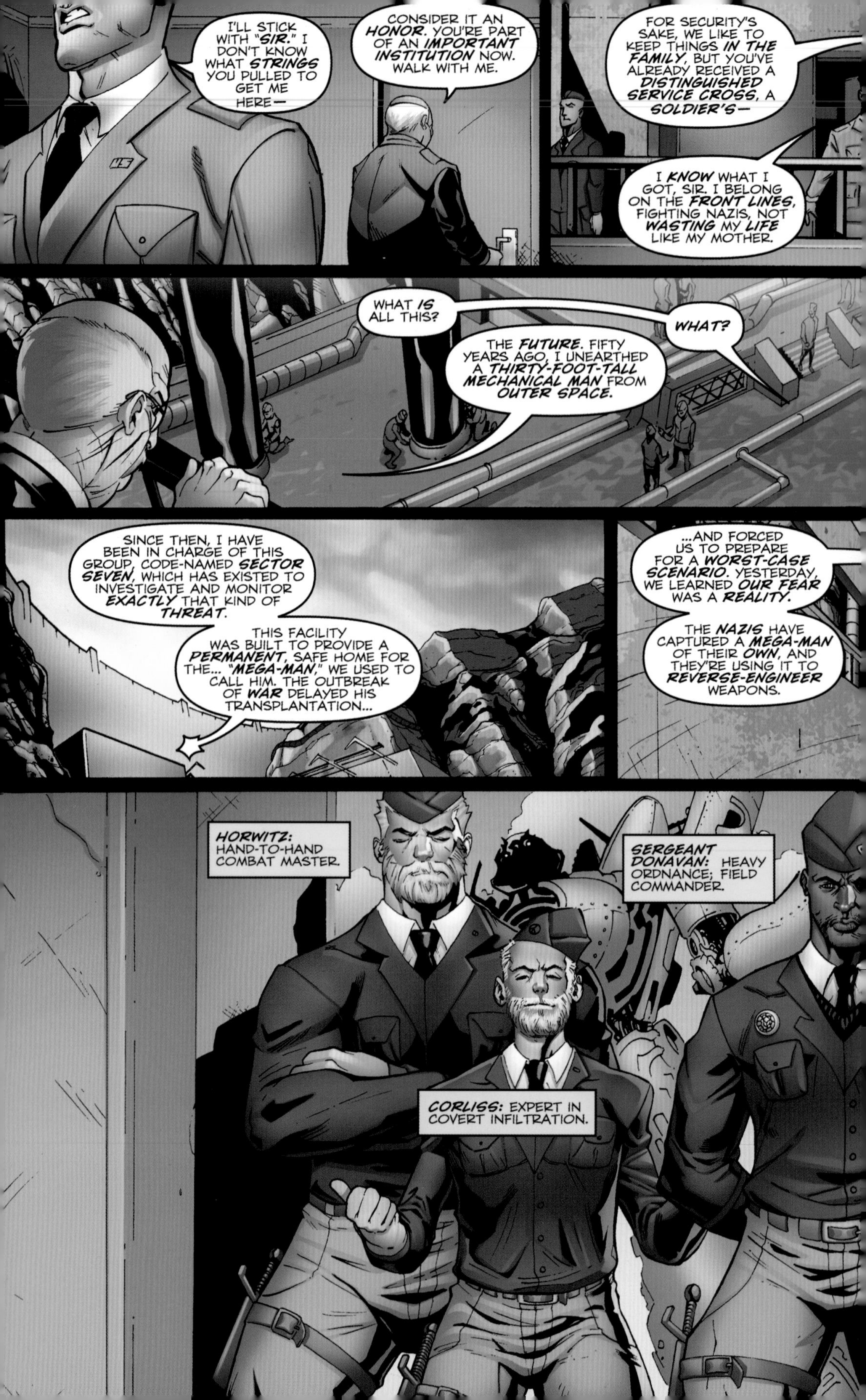
I'LL STICK WITH "SIR." I DON'T KNOW WHAT STRINGS YOU PULLED TO GET ME HERE—
CONSIDER IT AN HONOR. YOU'RE PART OF AN IMPORTANT INSTITUTION NOW. WALK WITH ME.
FOR SECURITY'S SAKE, WE LIKE TO KEEP THINGS IN THE FAMILY, BUT YOU'VE ALREADY RECEIVED A DISTINGUISHED SERVICE CROSS, A SOLDIER'S—
I KNOW WHAT I GOT, SIR. I BELONG ON THE FRONT LINES, FIGHTING NAZIS, NOT WASTING MY LIFE LIKE MY MOTHER.
WHAT IS ALL THIS?
WHAT?
THE FUTURE. FIFTY YEARS AGO, I UNEARTHED A THIRTY-FOOT-TALL MECHANICAL MAN FROM OUTER SPACE.
SINCE THEN, I HAVE BEEN IN CHARGE OF THIS GROUP, CODE-NAMED SECTOR SEVEN, WHICH HAS EXISTED TO INVESTIGATE AND MONITOR EXACTLY THAT KIND OF THREAT.
THIS FACILITY WAS BUILT TO PROVIDE A PERMANENT, SAFE HOME FOR THE... "MEGA-MAN," WE USED TO CALL HIM. THE OUTBREAK OF WAR DELAYED HIS TRANSPLANTATION...
...AND FORCED US TO PREPARE FOR A WORST-CASE SCENARIO. YESTERDAY, WE LEARNED OUR FEAR WAS A REALITY.
THE NAZIS HAVE CAPTURED A MEGA-MAN OF THEIR OWN, AND THEY'RE USING IT TO REVERSE-ENGINEER WEAPONS.
HORWITZ: HAND-TO-HAND COMBAT MASTER.
SERGEANT DONAVAN: HEAVY ORDNANCE; FIELD COMMANDER.
CORLISS: EXPERT IN COVERT INFILTRATION.

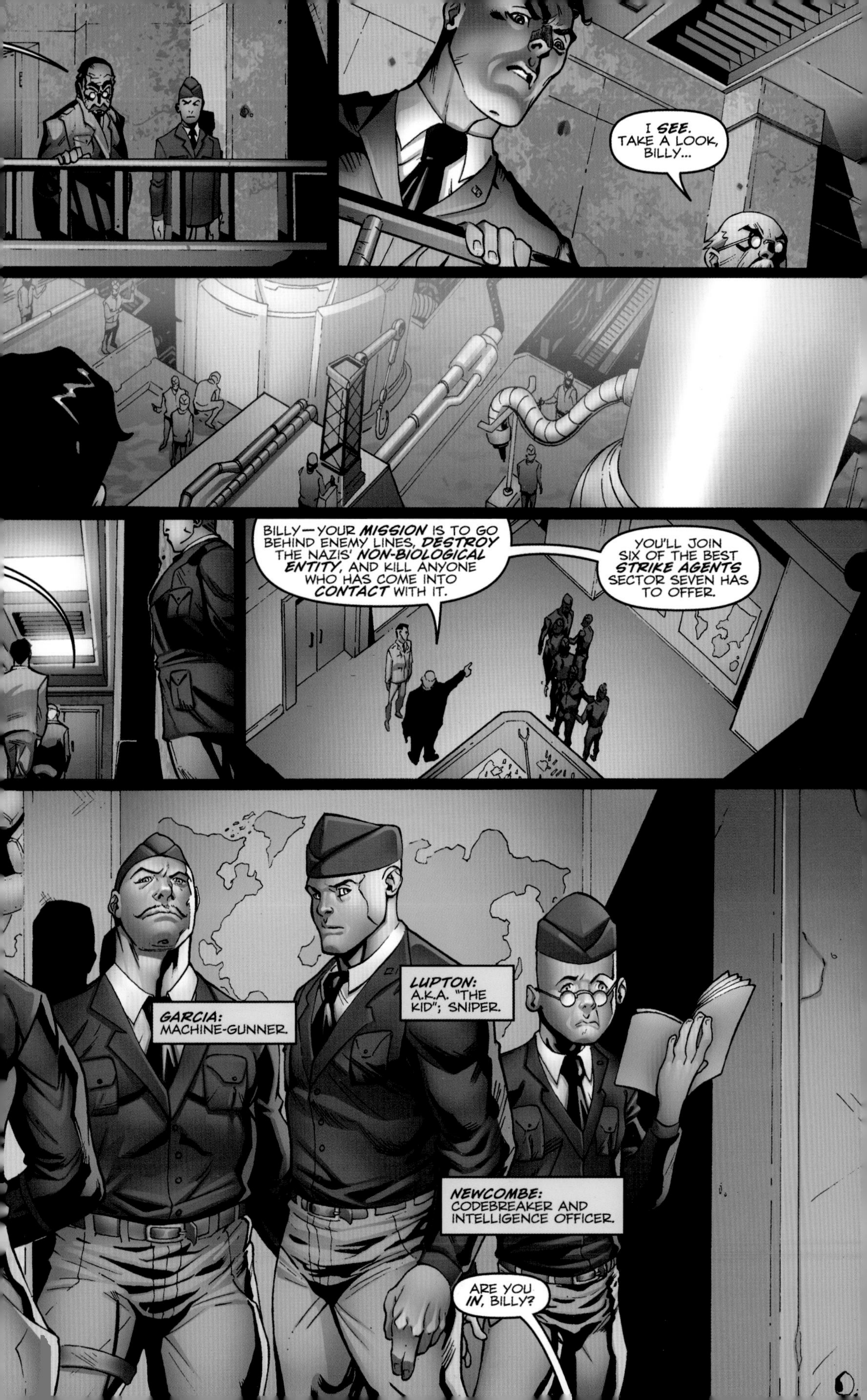
I SEE. TAKE A LOOK, BILLY...
BILLY—YOUR MISSION IS TO GO BEHIND ENEMY LINES, DESTROY THE NAZIS' NON-BIOLOGICAL ENTITY, AND KILL ANYONE WHO HAS COME INTO CONTACT WITH IT.
YOU'LL JOIN SIX OF THE BEST STRIKE AGENTS SECTOR SEVEN HAS TO OFFER.
GARCIA: MACHINE-GUNNER.
LUPTON: A.K.A. "THE KID"; SNIPER.
NEWCOMBE: CODEBREAKER AND INTELLIGENCE OFFICER.
ARE YOU IN, BILLY?

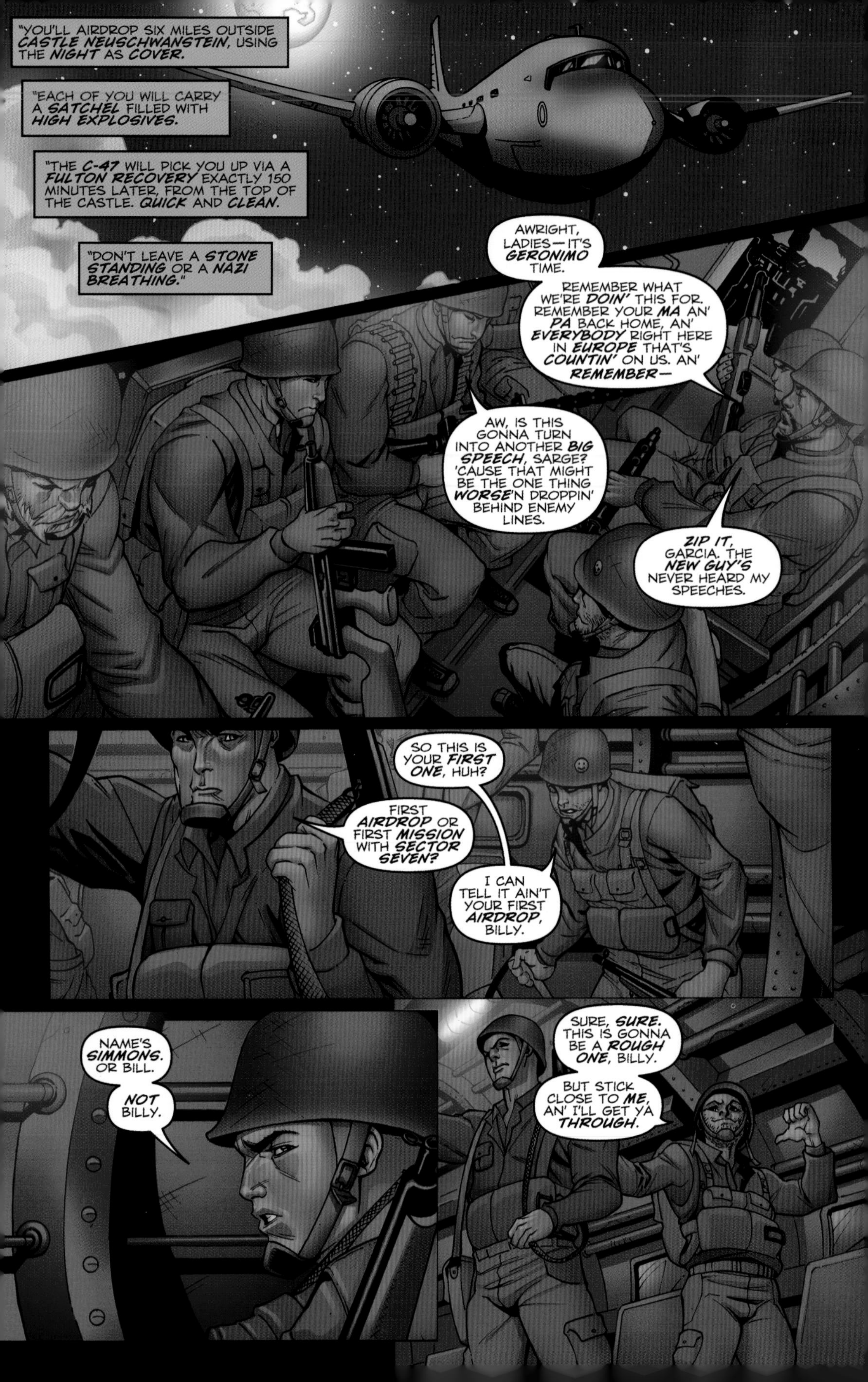
"YOU'LL AIRDROP SIX MILES OUTSIDE CASTLE NEUSCHWANSTEIN, USING THE NIGHT AS COVER.
"EACH OF YOU WILL CARRY A SATCHEL FILLED WITH HIGH EXPLOSIVES.
"THE C-47 WILL PICK YOU UP VIA A FULTON RECOVERY EXACTLY 150 MINUTES LATER, FROM THE TOP OF THE CASTLE. QUICK AND CLEAN.
"DON'T LEAVE A STONE STANDING OR A NAZI BREATHING."
AWRIGHT, LADIES—IT'S GERONIMO TIME.
REMEMBER WHAT WE'RE DOIN' THIS FOR. REMEMBER YOUR MA AN' PA BACK HOME, AN' EVERYBODY RIGHT HERE IN EUROPE THAT'S COUNTIN' ON US. AN' REMEMBER—
AW, IS THIS GONNA TURN INTO ANOTHER BIG SPEECH, SARGE? 'CAUSE THAT MIGHT BE THE ONE THING WORSE'N DROPPIN' BEHIND ENEMY LINES.
ZIP IT, GARCIA. THE NEW GUY'S NEVER HEARD MY SPEECHES.
SO THIS IS YOUR FIRST ONE, HUH?
FIRST AIRDROP OR FIRST MISSION WITH SECTOR SEVEN?
I CAN TELL IT AIN'T YOUR FIRST AIRDROP, BILLY.
NAME'S SIMMONS. OR BILL.
NOT BILLY.
SURE, SURE. THIS IS GONNA BE A ROUGH ONE, BILLY.
BUT STICK CLOSE TO ME, AN' I'LL GET YA THROUGH.

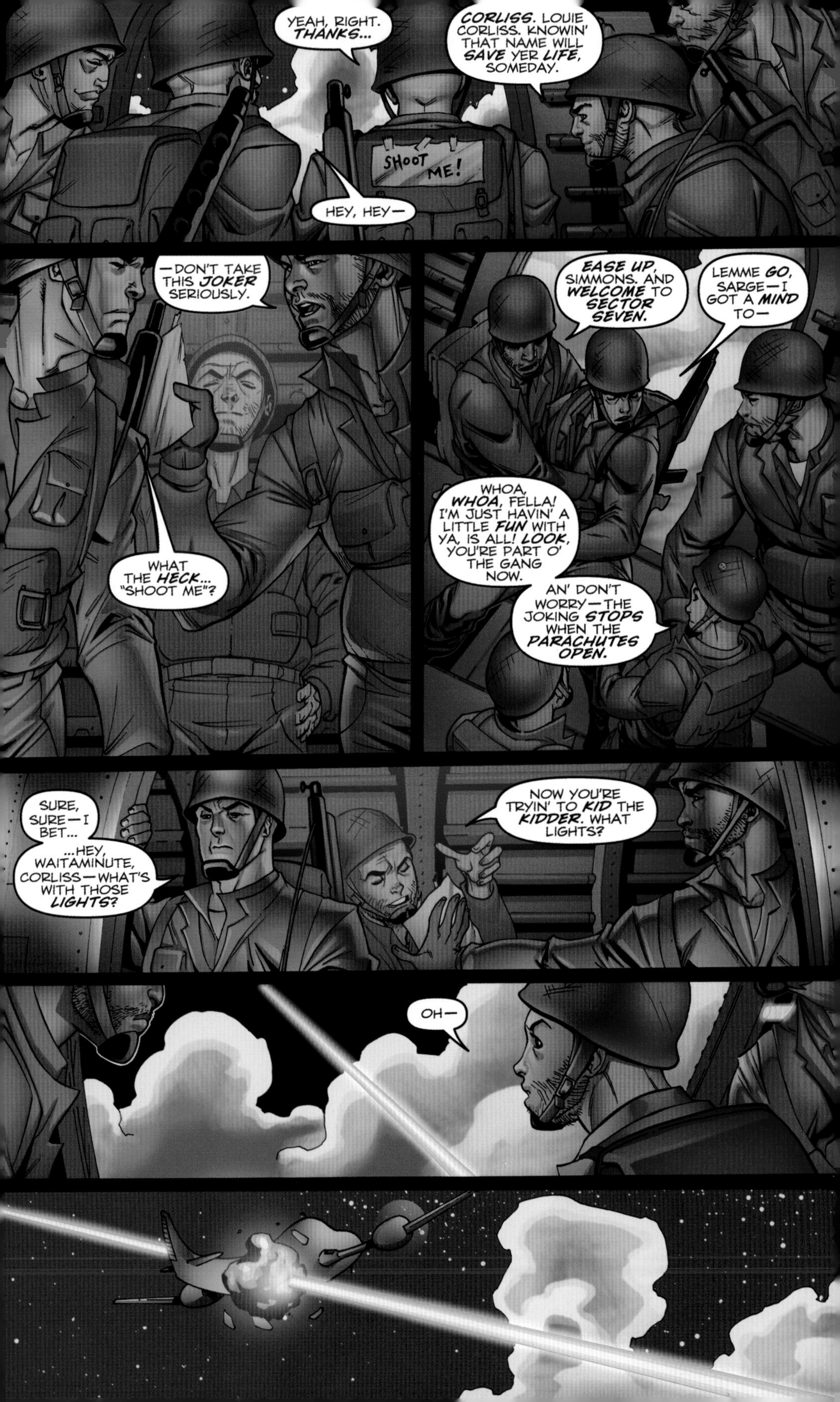
YEAH, RIGHT. THANKS...
CORLISS. LOUIE CORLISS. KNOWIN' THAT NAME WILL SAVE YER LIFE, SOMEDAY.
SHOOT ME!
HEY, HEY—
—DON'T TAKE THIS JOKER SERIOUSLY.
WHAT THE HECK... "SHOOT ME"?
EASE UP, SIMMONS. AND WELCOME TO SECTOR SEVEN.
LEMME GO, SARGE—I GOT A MIND TO—
WHOA, WHOA, FELLA! I'M JUST HAVIN' A LITTLE FUN WITH YA, IS ALL! LOOK, YOU'RE PART O' THE GANG NOW.
AN' DON'T WORRY—THE JOKING STOPS WHEN THE PARACHUTES OPEN.
SURE, SURE—I BET...
...HEY, WAITAMINUTE, CORLISS—WHAT'S WITH THOSE LIGHTS?
NOW YOU'RE TRYIN' TO KID THE KIDDER. WHAT LIGHTS?
OH—

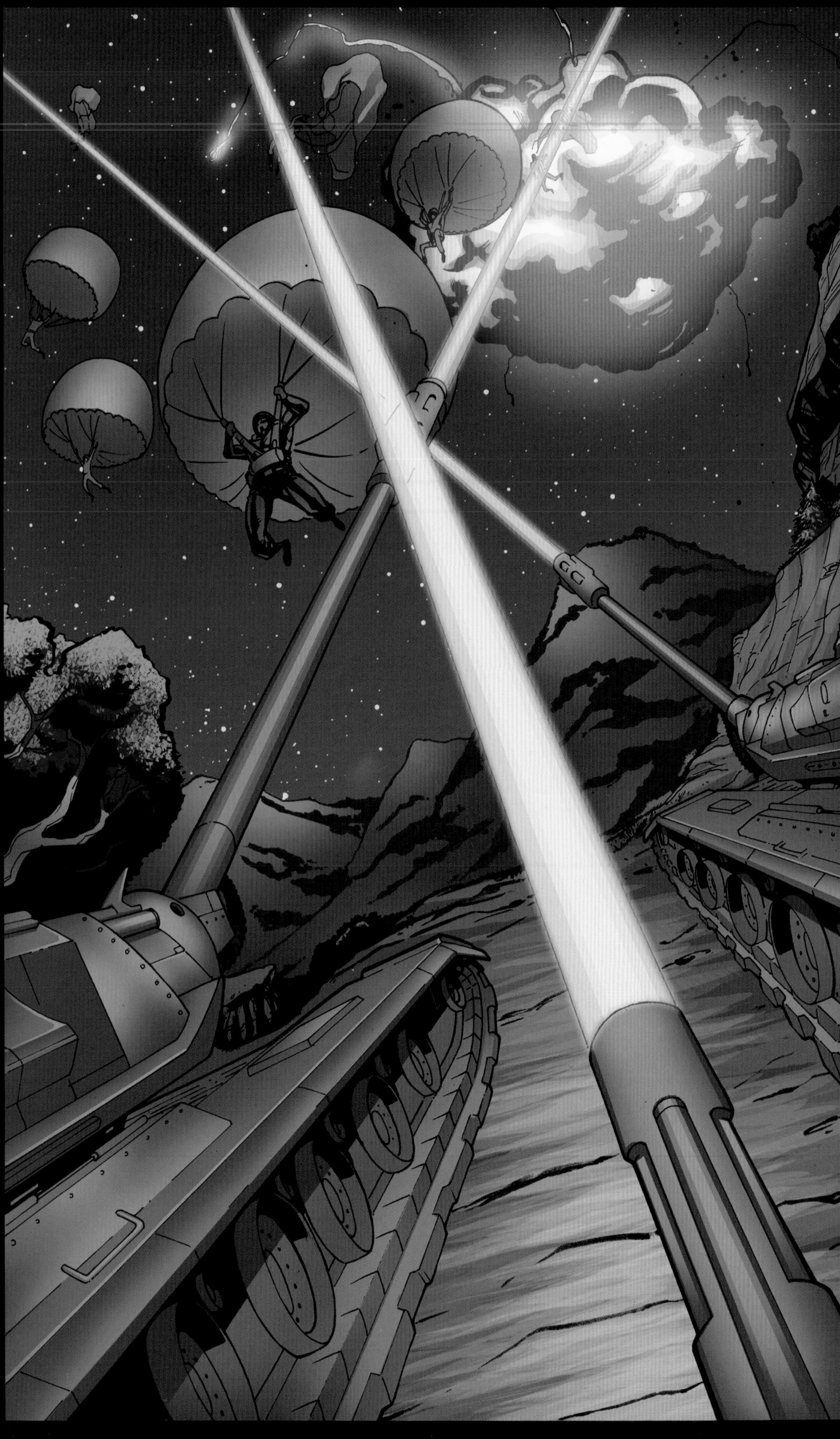

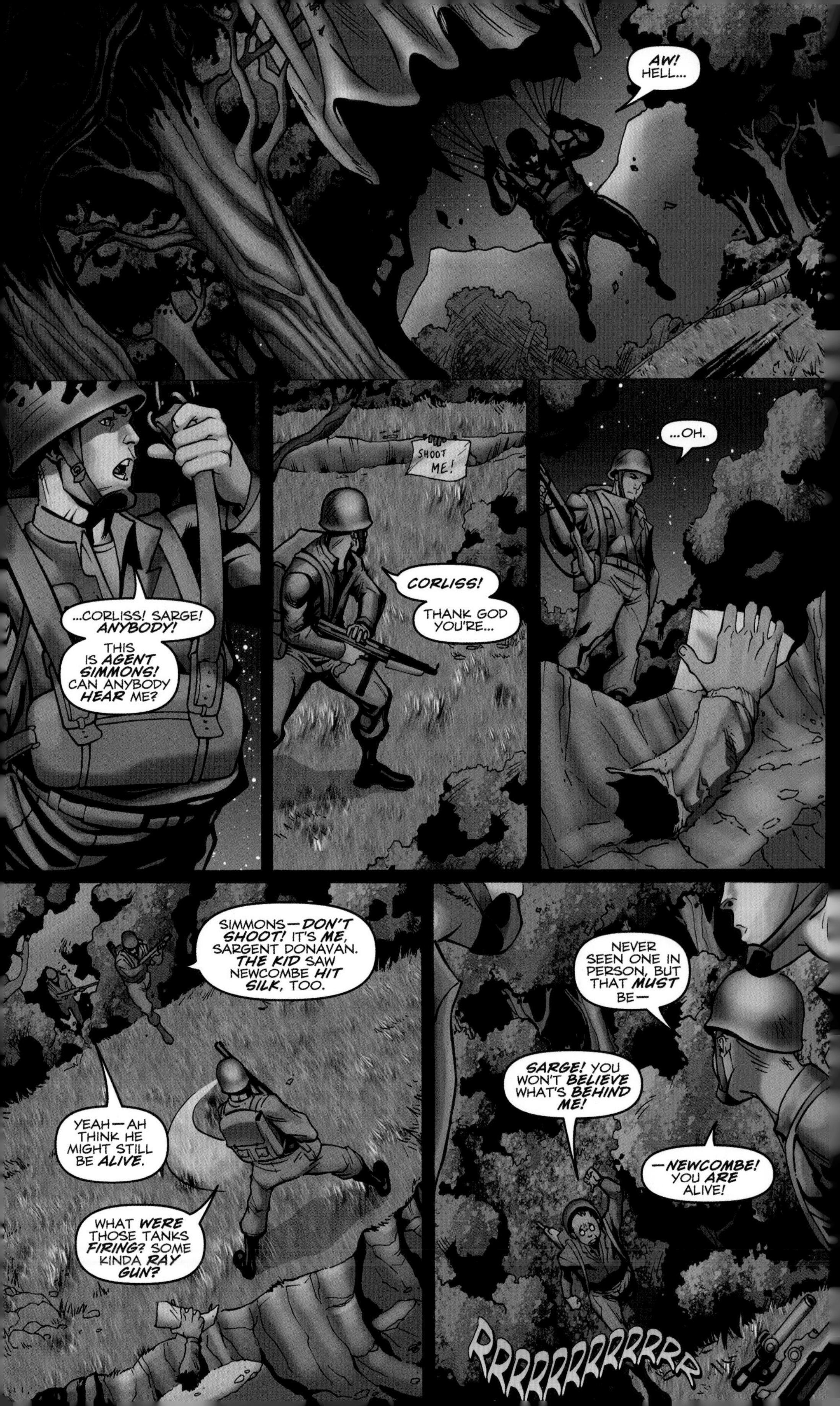
AW! HELL...
...CORLISS! SARGE! ANYBODY!
THIS IS AGENT SIMMONS! CAN ANYBODY HEAR ME?
SHOOT ME!
CORLISS!
THANK GOD YOU'RE...
...OH.
SIMMONS—DON'T SHOOT! IT'S ME, SARGENT DONAVAN. THE KID SAW NEWCOMBE HIT SILK, TOO.
YEAH—AH THINK HE MIGHT STILL BE ALIVE.
WHAT WERE THOSE TANKS FIRING? SOME KINDA RAY GUN?
NEVER SEEN ONE IN PERSON, BUT THAT MUST BE—
SARGE! YOU WON'T BELIEVE WHAT'S BEHIND ME!
—NEWCOMBE! YOU ARE ALIVE!
RRRRRRRRRRRR

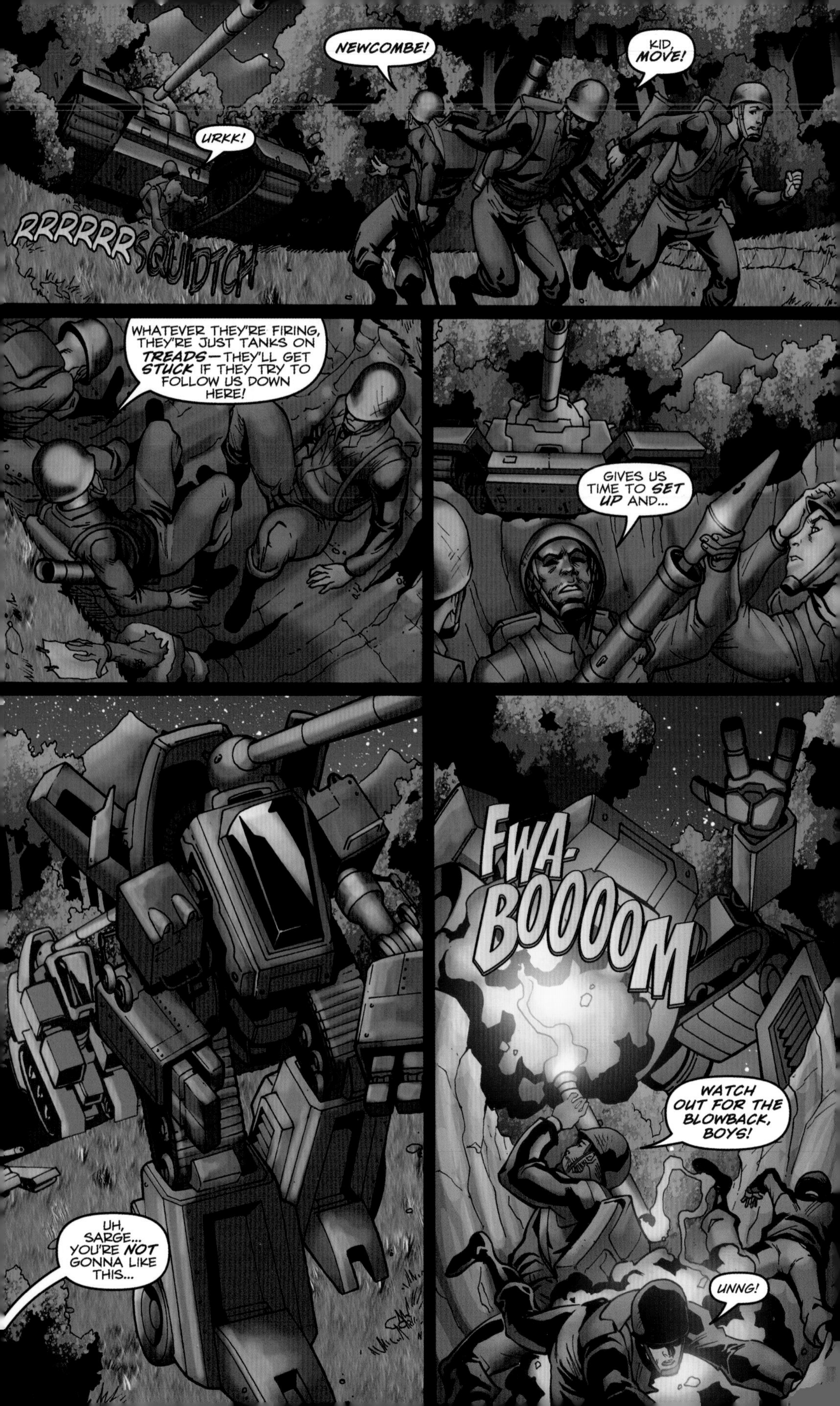
NEWCOMBE!
KID, MOVE!
URKK!
RRRRRRSQUIDTCH
WHATEVER THEY'RE FIRING, THEY'RE JUST TANKS ON TREADS—THEY'LL GET STUCK IF THEY TRY TO FOLLOW US DOWN HERE!
GIVES US TIME TO SET UP AND...
UH, SARGE... YOU'RE NOT GONNA LIKE THIS...
FWA-BOOOOM
WATCH OUT FOR THE BLOWBACK, BOYS!
UNNG!

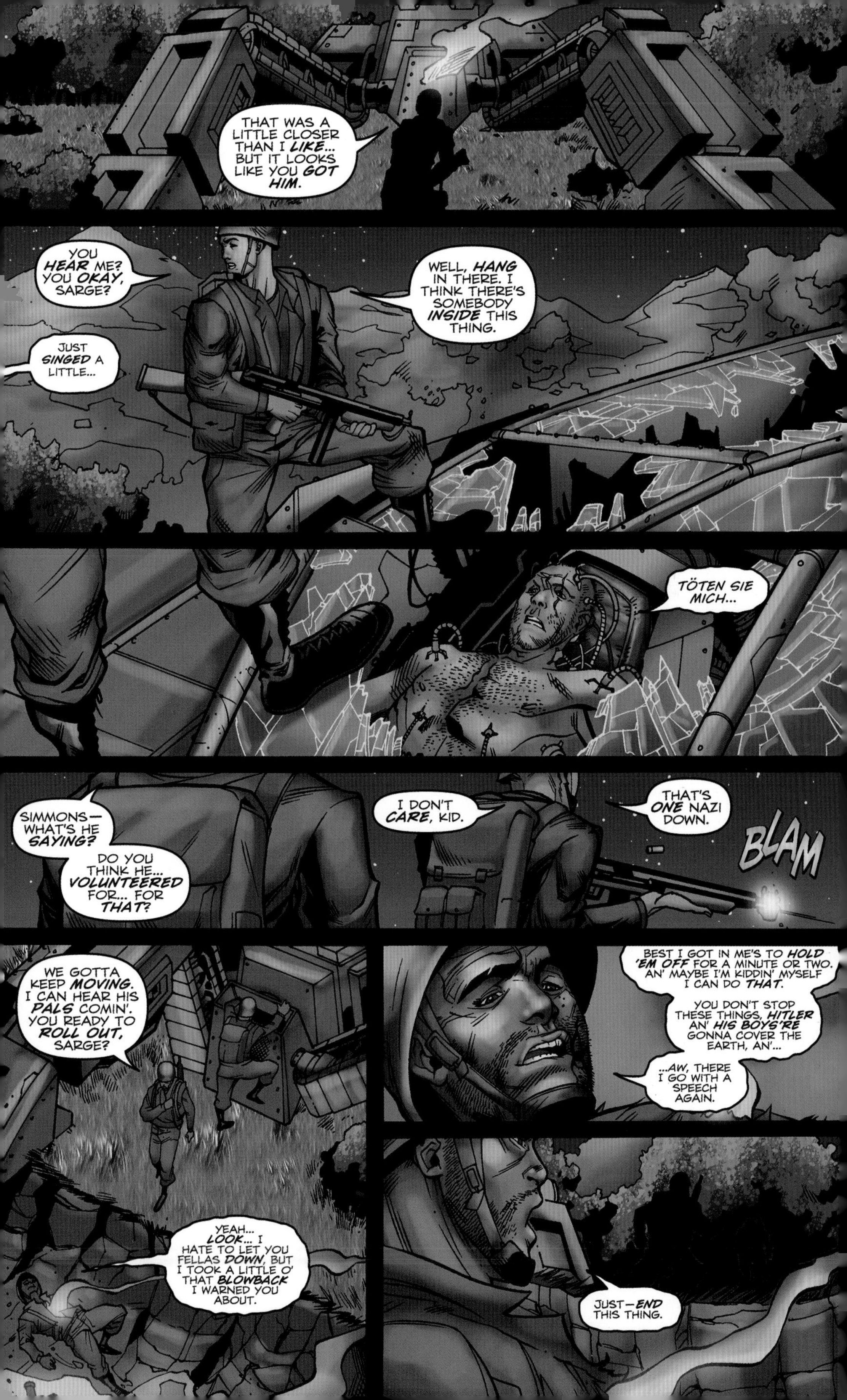
THAT WAS A LITTLE CLOSER THAN I LIKE... BUT IT LOOKS LIKE YOU GOT HIM.
YOU HEAR ME? YOU OKAY, SARGE?
JUST SINGED A LITTLE...
WELL, HANG IN THERE. I THINK THERE'S SOMEBODY INSIDE THIS THING.
TÖTEN SIE MICH...
SIMMONS—WHAT'S HE SAYING?
DO YOU THINK HE... VOLUNTEERED FOR... FOR THAT?
I DON'T CARE, KID.
THAT'S ONE NAZI DOWN.
BLAM
WE GOTTA KEEP MOVING. I CAN HEAR HIS PALS COMIN'. YOU READY TO ROLL OUT, SARGE?
YEAH... LOOK... I HATE TO LET YOU FELLAS DOWN, BUT I TOOK A LITTLE O' THAT BLOWBACK I WARNED YOU ABOUT.
BEST I GOT IN ME'S TO HOLD 'EM OFF FOR A MINUTE OR TWO. AN' MAYBE I'M KIDDIN' MYSELF I CAN DO THAT.
YOU DON'T STOP THESE THINGS, HITLER AN' HIS BOYS'RE GONNA COVER THE EARTH, AN'...
...AW, THERE I GO WITH A SPEECH AGAIN.
JUST—END THIS THING.

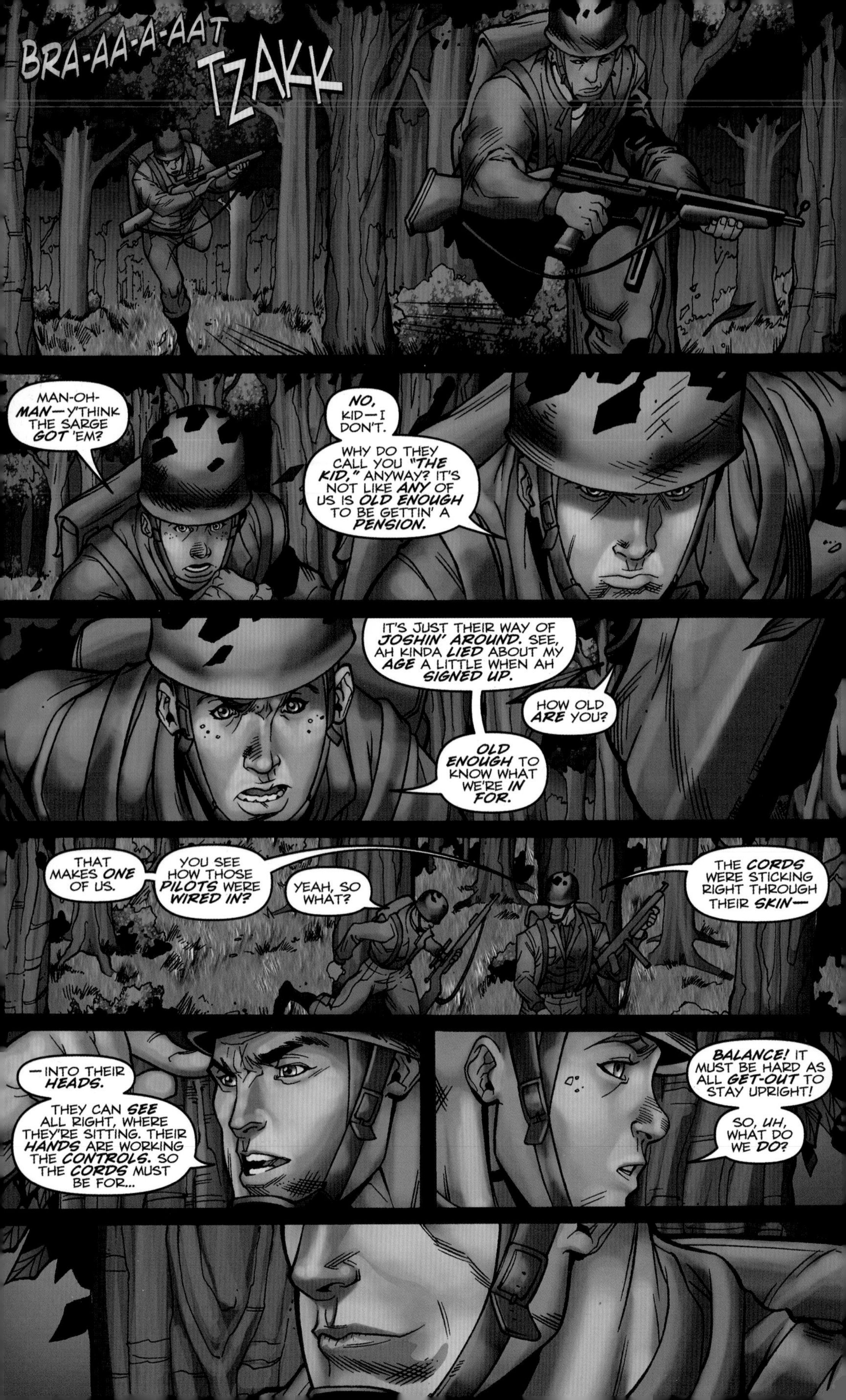
BRA-AA-A-AAT
TZAKK
MAN-OH-MAN—Y'THINK THE SARGE GOT 'EM?
NO, KID—I DON'T.
WHY DO THEY CALL YOU "THE KID," ANYWAY? IT'S NOT LIKE ANY OF US IS OLD ENOUGH TO BE GETTIN' A PENSION.
IT'S JUST THEIR WAY OF JOSHIN' AROUND. SEE, AH KINDA LIED ABOUT MY AGE A LITTLE WHEN AH SIGNED UP.
HOW OLD ARE YOU?
OLD ENOUGH TO KNOW WHAT WE'RE IN FOR.
THAT MAKES ONE OF US.
YOU SEE HOW THOSE PILOTS WERE WIRED IN?
YEAH, SO WHAT?
THE CORDS WERE STICKING RIGHT THROUGH THEIR SKIN—
—INTO THEIR HEADS.
THEY CAN SEE ALL RIGHT, WHERE THEY'RE SITTING. THEIR HANDS ARE WORKING THE CONTROLS. SO THE CORDS MUST BE FOR...
BALANCE! IT MUST BE HARD AS ALL GET-OUT TO STAY UPRIGHT!
SO, UH, WHAT DO WE DO?

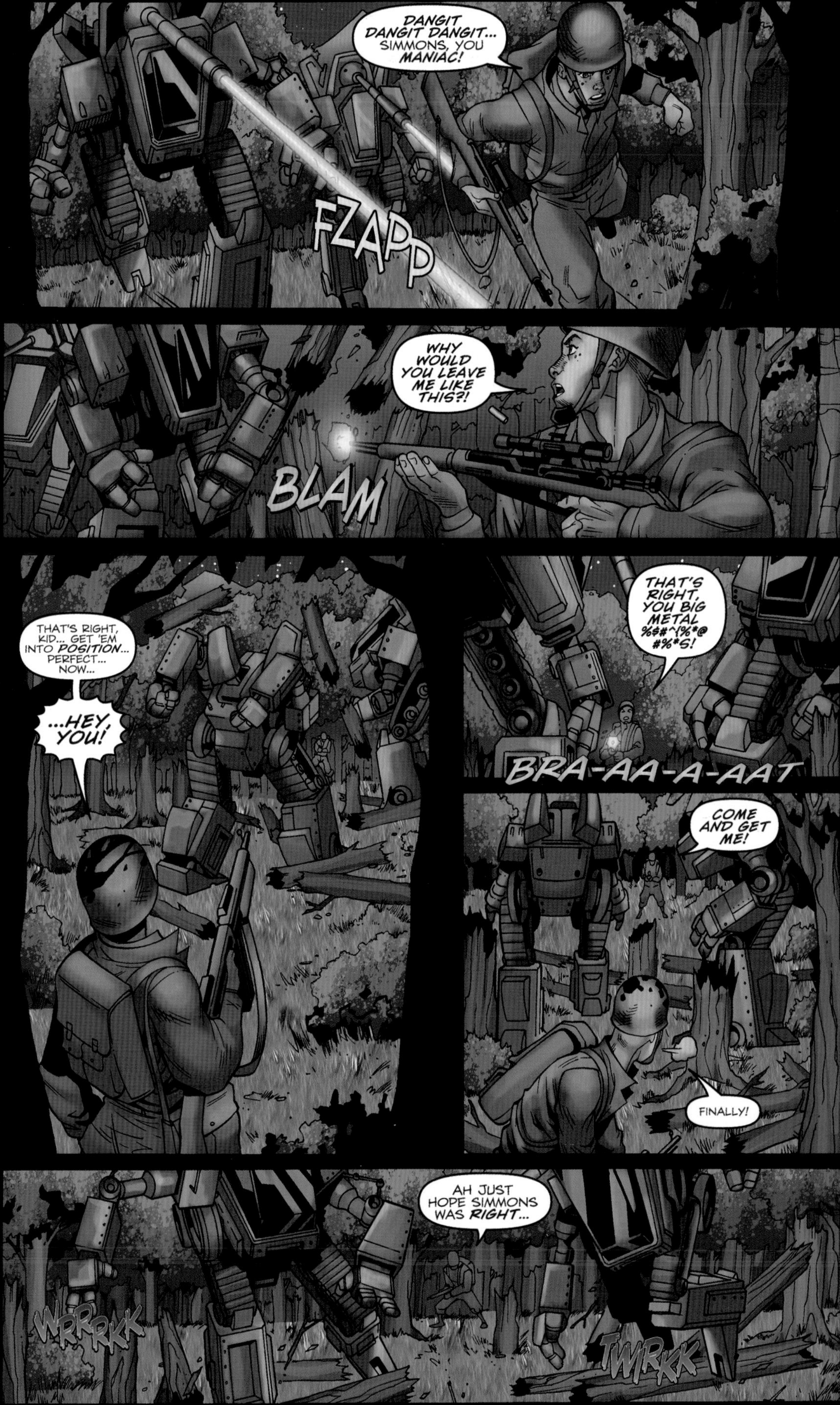
DANGIT DANGIT DANGIT... SIMMONS, YOU MANIAC!
FZAPP
WHY WOULD YOU LEAVE ME LIKE THIS?!
BLAM
THAT'S RIGHT, KID... GET 'EM INTO POSITION... PERFECT... NOW...
...HEY, YOU!
THAT'S RIGHT, YOU BIG METAL %$#^{%*@ #%*S!
BRA-AA-A-AAT
COME AND GET ME!
FINALLY!
AH JUST HOPE SIMMONS WAS RIGHT...
WRRRKK
TWRKK

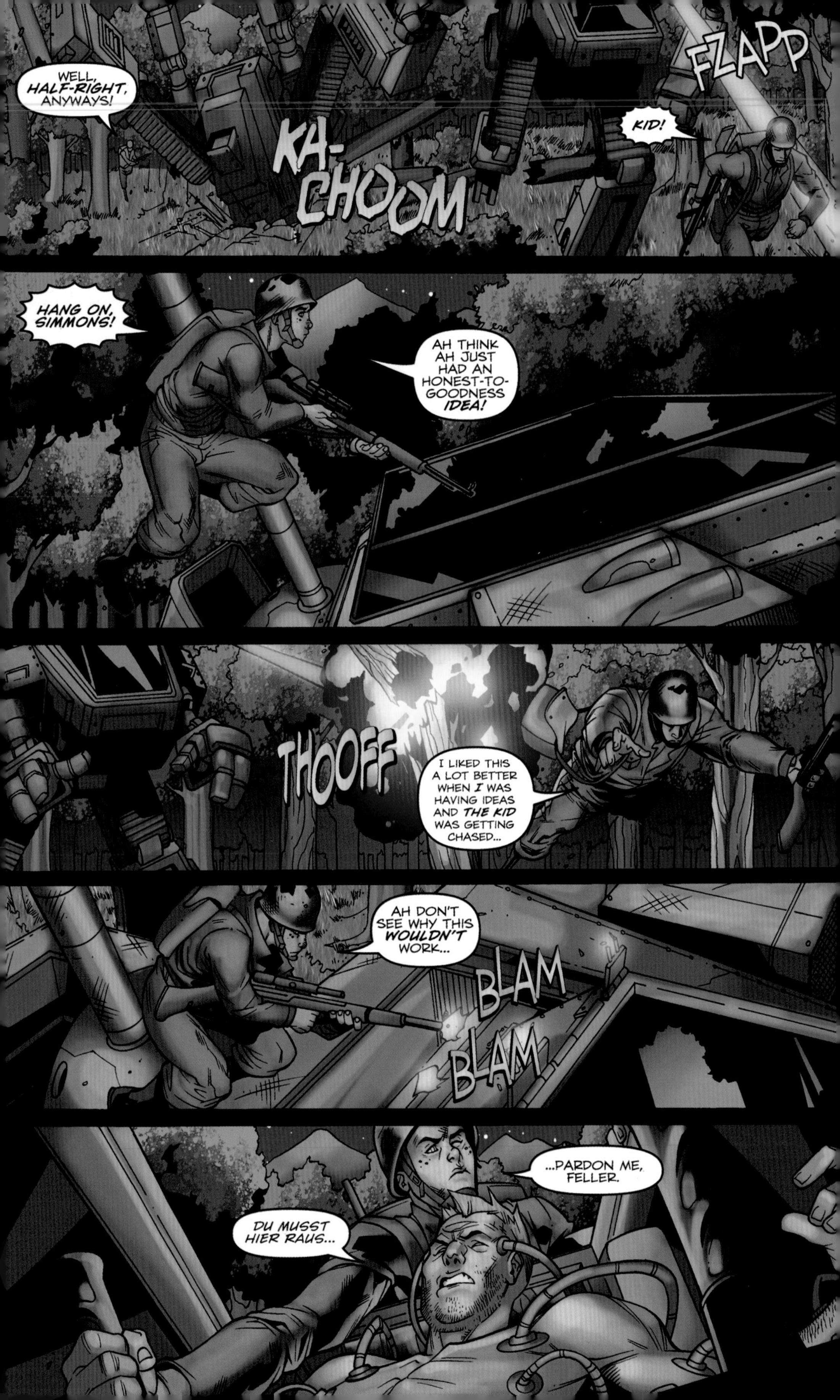

WELL, HALF-RIGHT, ANYWAYS!
KA-CHOOM
FZAPP
KID!
HANG ON, SIMMONS!
AH THINK AH JUST HAD AN HONEST-TO-GOODNESS IDEA!
THOOFF
I LIKED THIS A LOT BETTER WHEN I WAS HAVING IDEAS AND THE KID WAS GETTING CHASED...
AH DON'T SEE WHY THIS WOULDN'T WORK...
BLAM
BLAM
...PARDON ME, FELLER.
DU MUSST HIER RAUS...

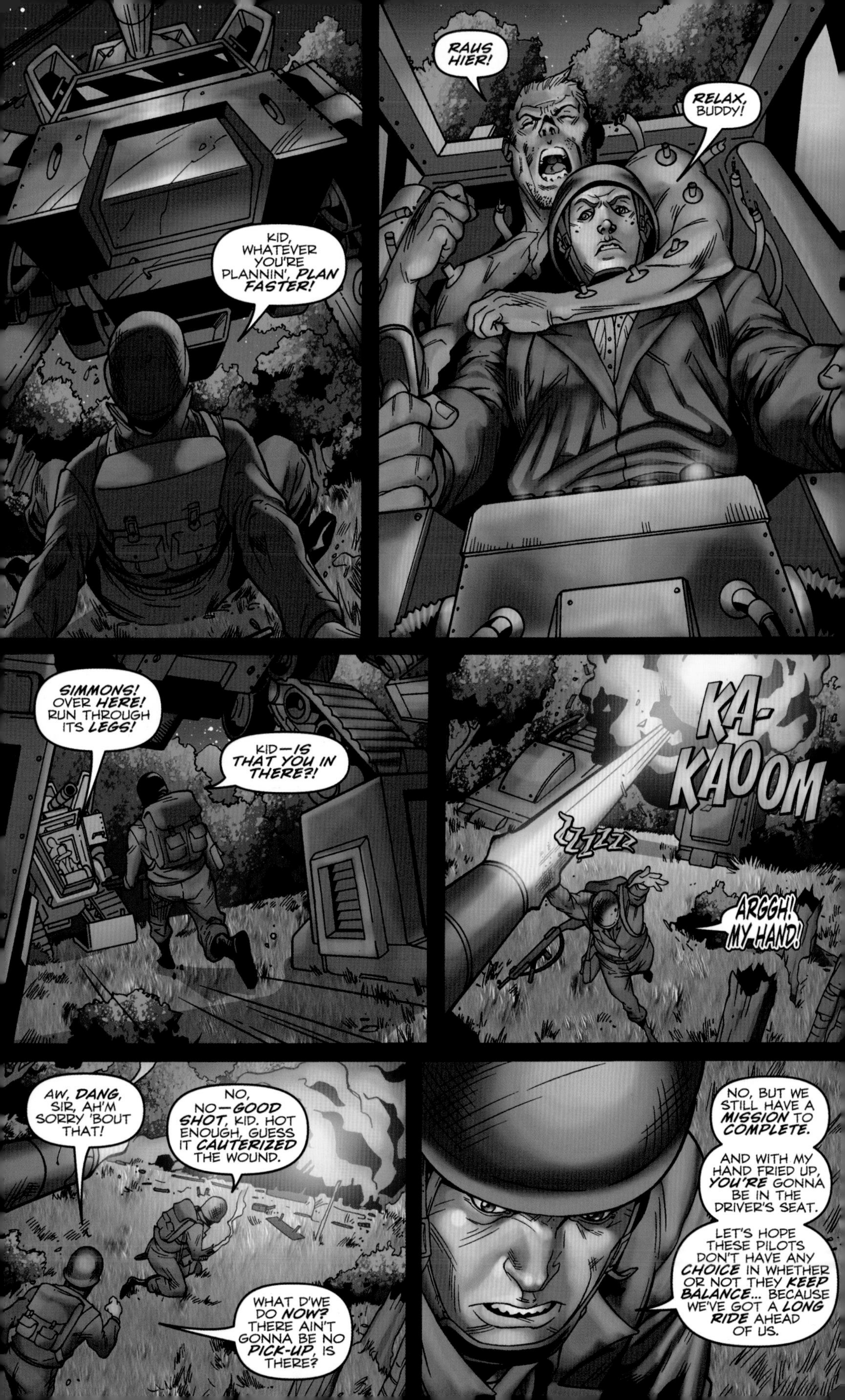
KID, WHATEVER YOU'RE PLANNIN', PLAN FASTER!
RAUS HIER!
RELAX, BUDDY!
SIMMONS! OVER HERE! RUN THROUGH ITS LEGS!
KID—IS THAT YOU IN THERE?!
KA-KAOOM
ZZZZZZ
ARGGH! MY HAND!
AW, DANG, SIR, AH'M SORRY 'BOUT THAT!
NO, NO—GOOD SHOT, KID. HOT ENOUGH, GUESS IT CAUTERIZED THE WOUND.
WHAT D'WE DO NOW? THERE AIN'T GONNA BE NO PICK-UP, IS THERE?
NO, BUT WE STILL HAVE A MISSION TO COMPLETE.
AND WITH MY HAND FRIED UP, YOU'RE GONNA BE IN THE DRIVER'S SEAT.
LET'S HOPE THESE PILOTS DON'T HAVE ANY CHOICE IN WHETHER OR NOT THEY KEEP BALANCE... BECAUSE WE'VE GOT A LONG RIDE AHEAD OF US.

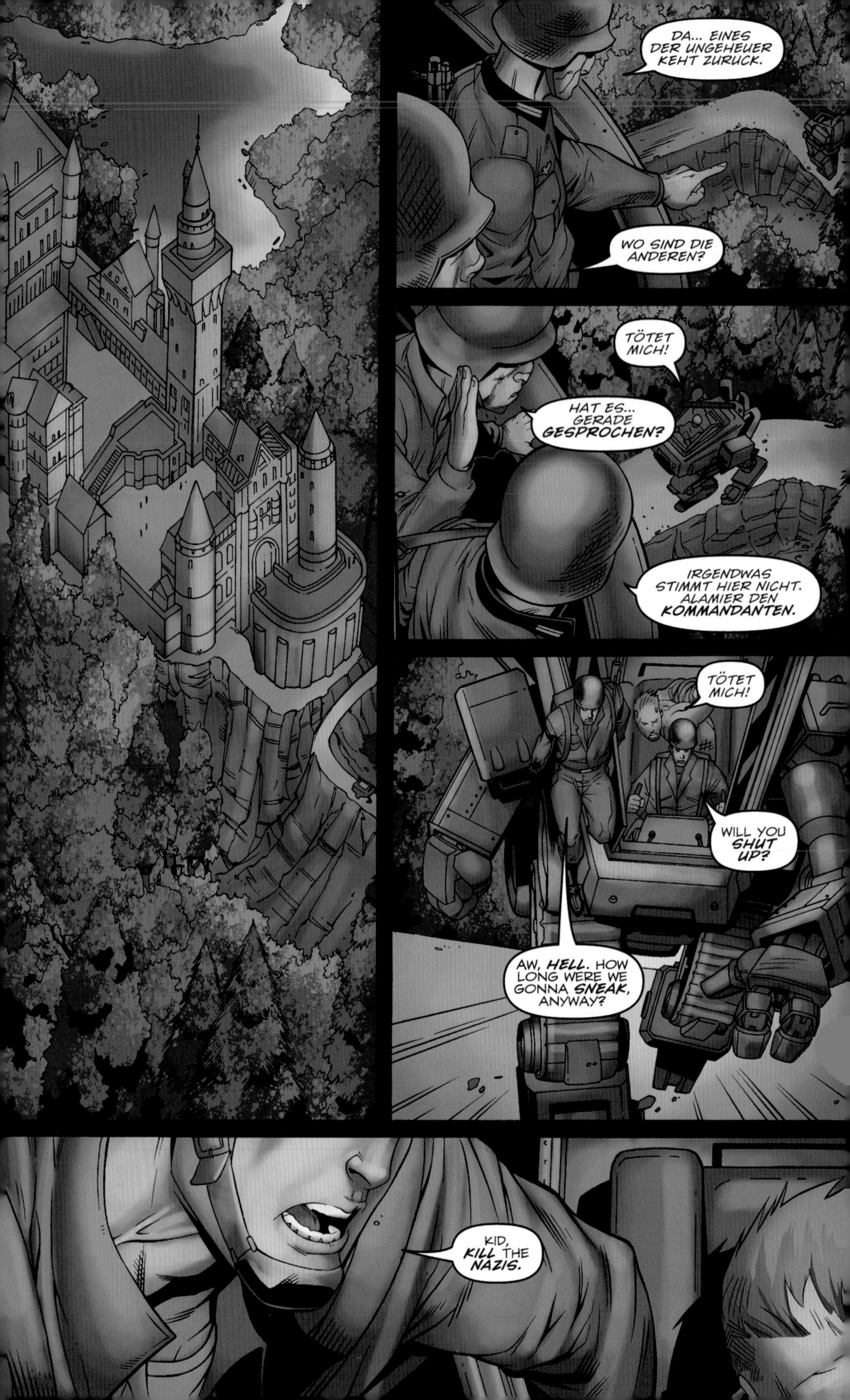
DA... EINES DER UNGEHEUER KEHT ZURUCK.
WO SIND DIE ANDEREN?
TÖTET MICH!
HAT ES... GERADE GESPROCHEN?
IRGENDWAS STIMMT HIER NICHT. ALAMIER DEN KOMMANDANTEN.
TÖTET MICH!
WILL YOU SHUT UP?
AW, HELL. HOW LONG WERE WE GONNA SNEAK, ANYWAY?
KID, KILL THE NAZIS.

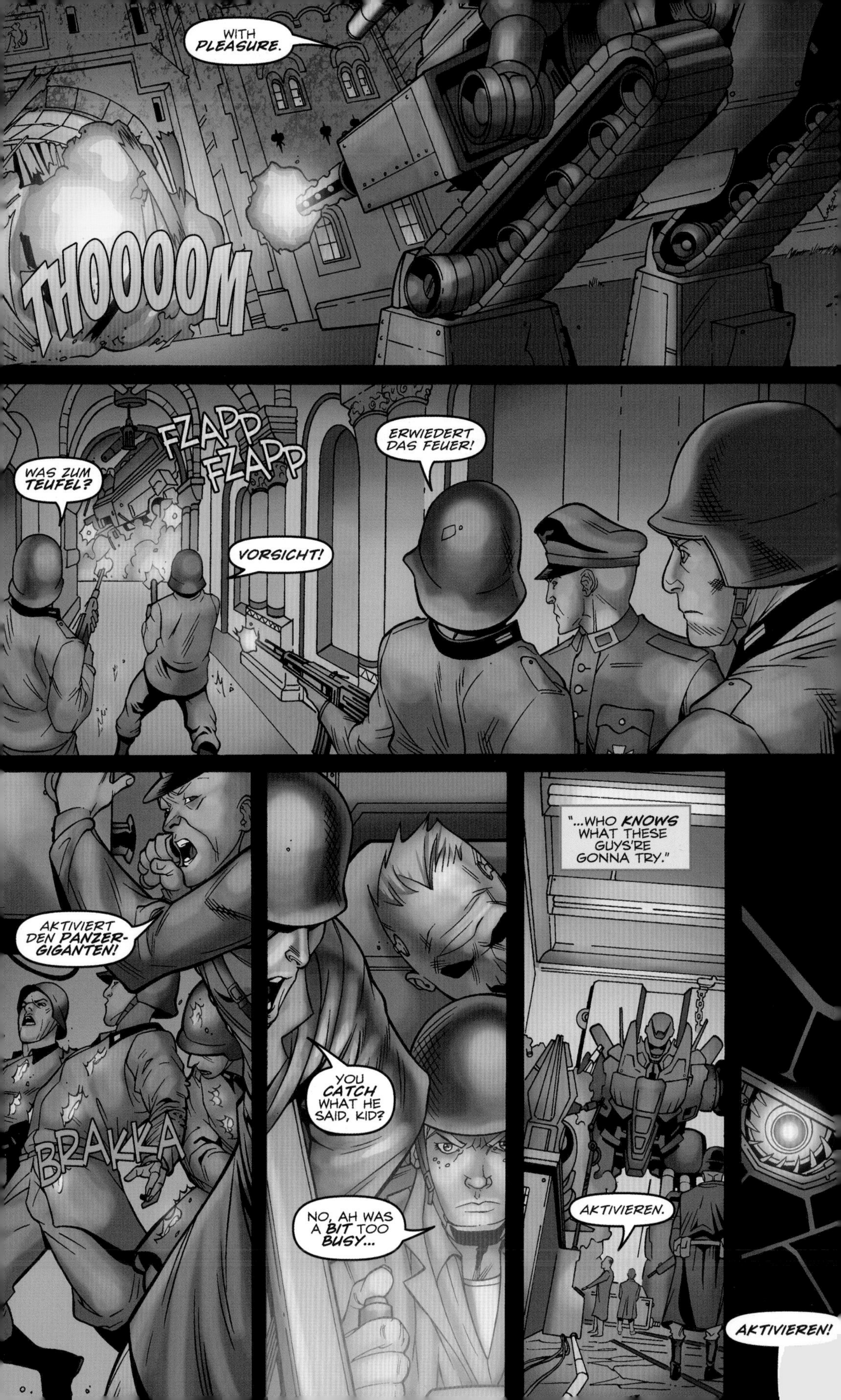
WITH PLEASURE.
THOOOOM
FZAPP FZAPP
WAS ZUM TEUFEL?
VORSICHT!
ERWIEDERT DAS FEUER!
AKTIVIERT DEN PANZER-GIGANTEN!
BRAKKA
YOU CATCH WHAT HE SAID, KID?
NO, AH WAS A BIT TOO BUSY...
"...WHO KNOWS WHAT THESE GUYS'RE GONNA TRY."
AKTIVIEREN.
AKTIVIEREN!

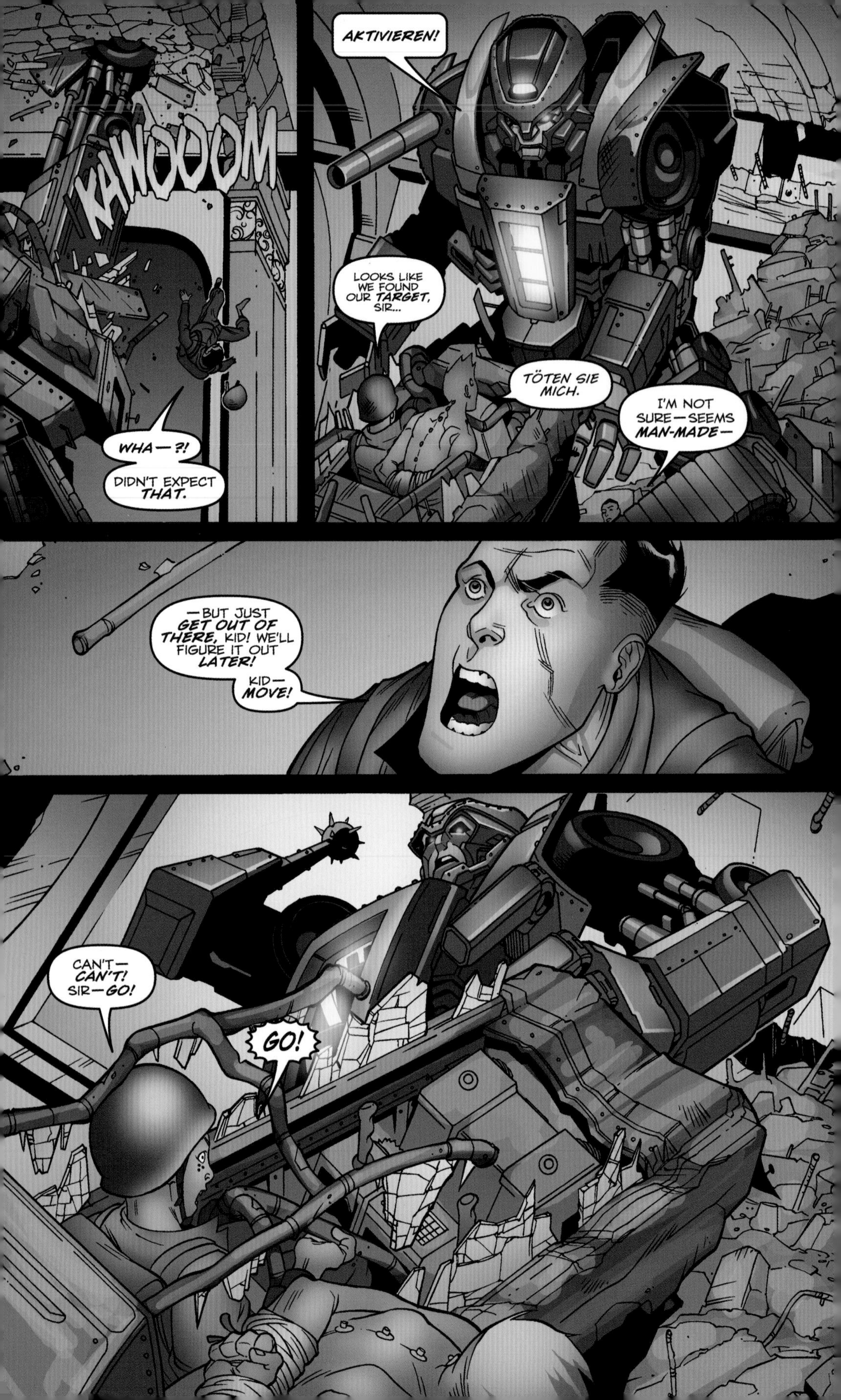
KAWOOOM
WHA—?!
DIDN'T EXPECT THAT.
AKTIVIEREN!
LOOKS LIKE WE FOUND OUR TARGET, SIR...
TÖTEN SIE MICH.
I'M NOT SURE—SEEMS MAN-MADE—
—BUT JUST GET OUT OF THERE, KID! WE'LL FIGURE IT OUT LATER!
KID—MOVE!
CAN'T—CAN'T! SIR—GO!
GO!

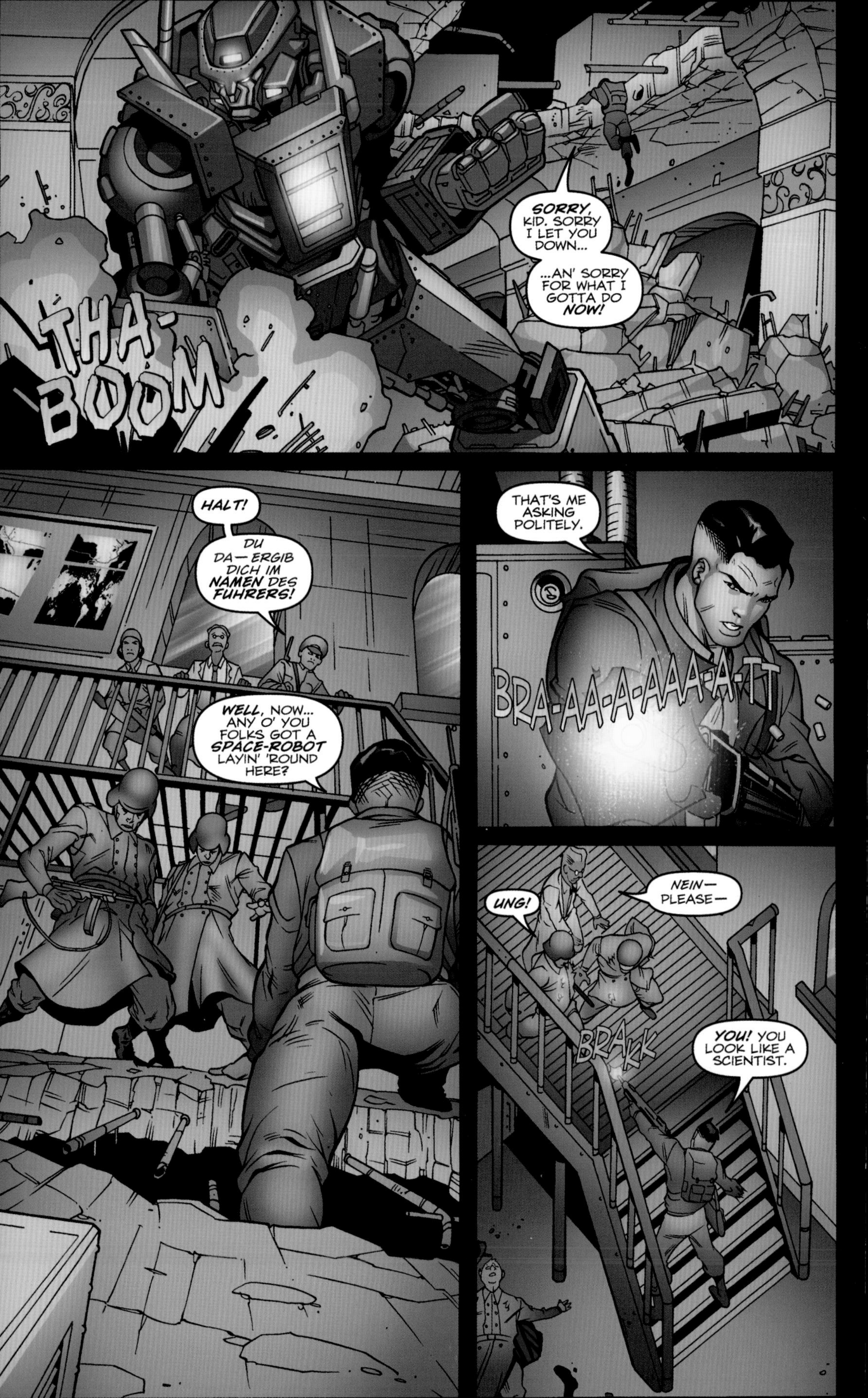
SORRY, KID. SORRY I LET YOU DOWN...
...AN' SORRY FOR WHAT I GOTTA DO NOW!
THA-BOOM
HALT!
DU DA—ERGIB DICH IM NAMEN DES FUHRERS!
WELL, NOW... ANY O' YOU FOLKS GOT A SPACE-ROBOT LAYIN' 'ROUND HERE?
THAT'S ME ASKING POLITELY.
BRA-AA-A-AAA-A-TT
UNG!
NEIN—PLEASE—
BRAKK
YOU! YOU LOOK LIKE A SCIENTIST.

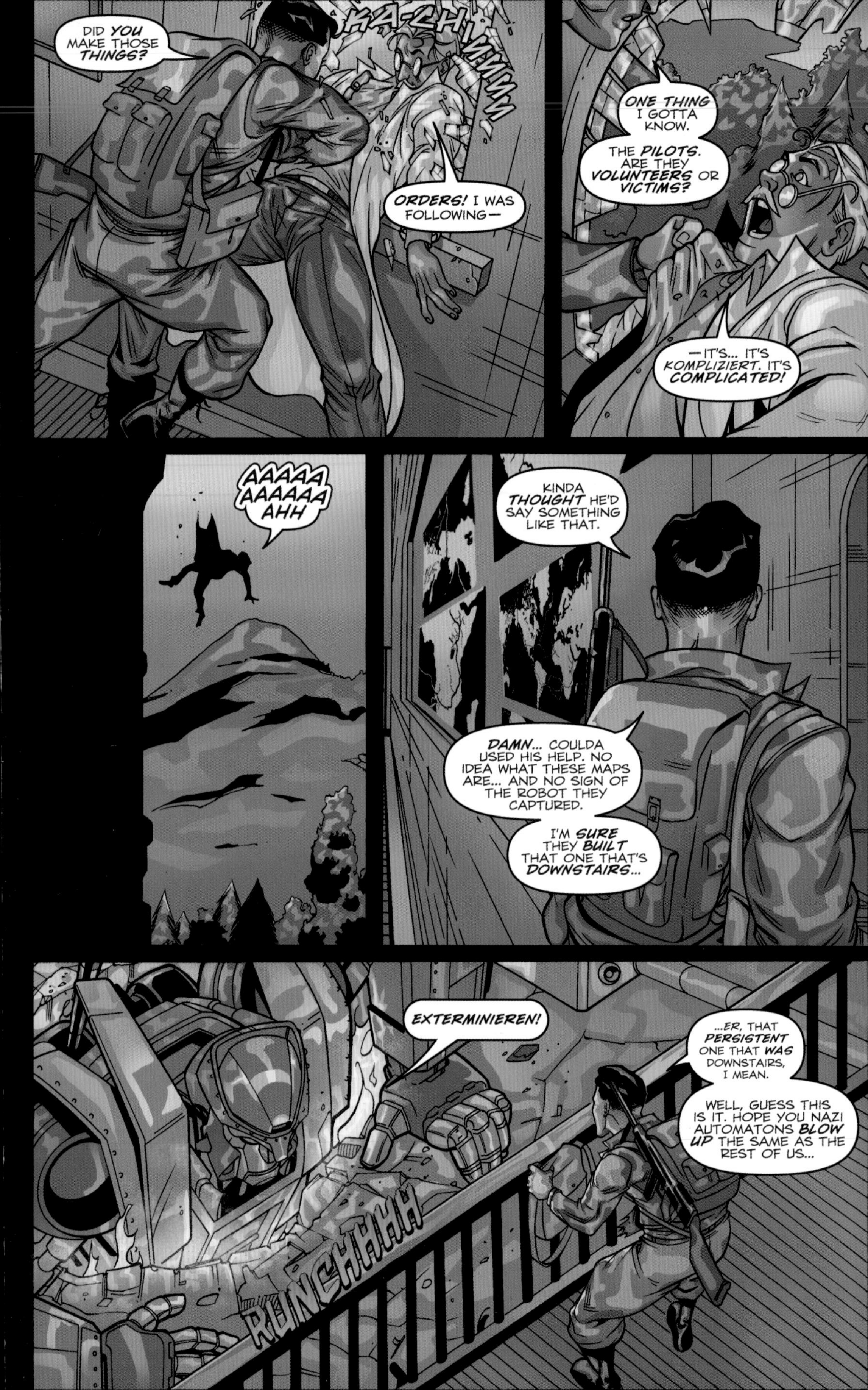
DID YOU MAKE THOSE THINGS?
KA-CHINNNN
ORDERS! I WAS FOLLOWING—
ONE THING I GOTTA KNOW.
THE PILOTS. ARE THEY VOLUNTEERS OR VICTIMS?
—IT'S... IT'S KOMPLIZIERT. IT'S COMPLICATED!
AAAAA AAAAAA AHH
KINDA THOUGHT HE'D SAY SOMETHING LIKE THAT.
DAMN... COULDA USED HIS HELP. NO IDEA WHAT THESE MAPS ARE... AND NO SIGN OF THE ROBOT THEY CAPTURED.
I'M SURE THEY BUILT THAT ONE THAT'S DOWNSTAIRS...
EXTERMINIEREN!
...ER, THAT PERSISTENT ONE THAT WAS DOWNSTAIRS, I MEAN.
WELL, GUESS THIS IS IT. HOPE YOU NAZI AUTOMATONS BLOW UP THE SAME AS THE REST OF US...
RUNCHHHH

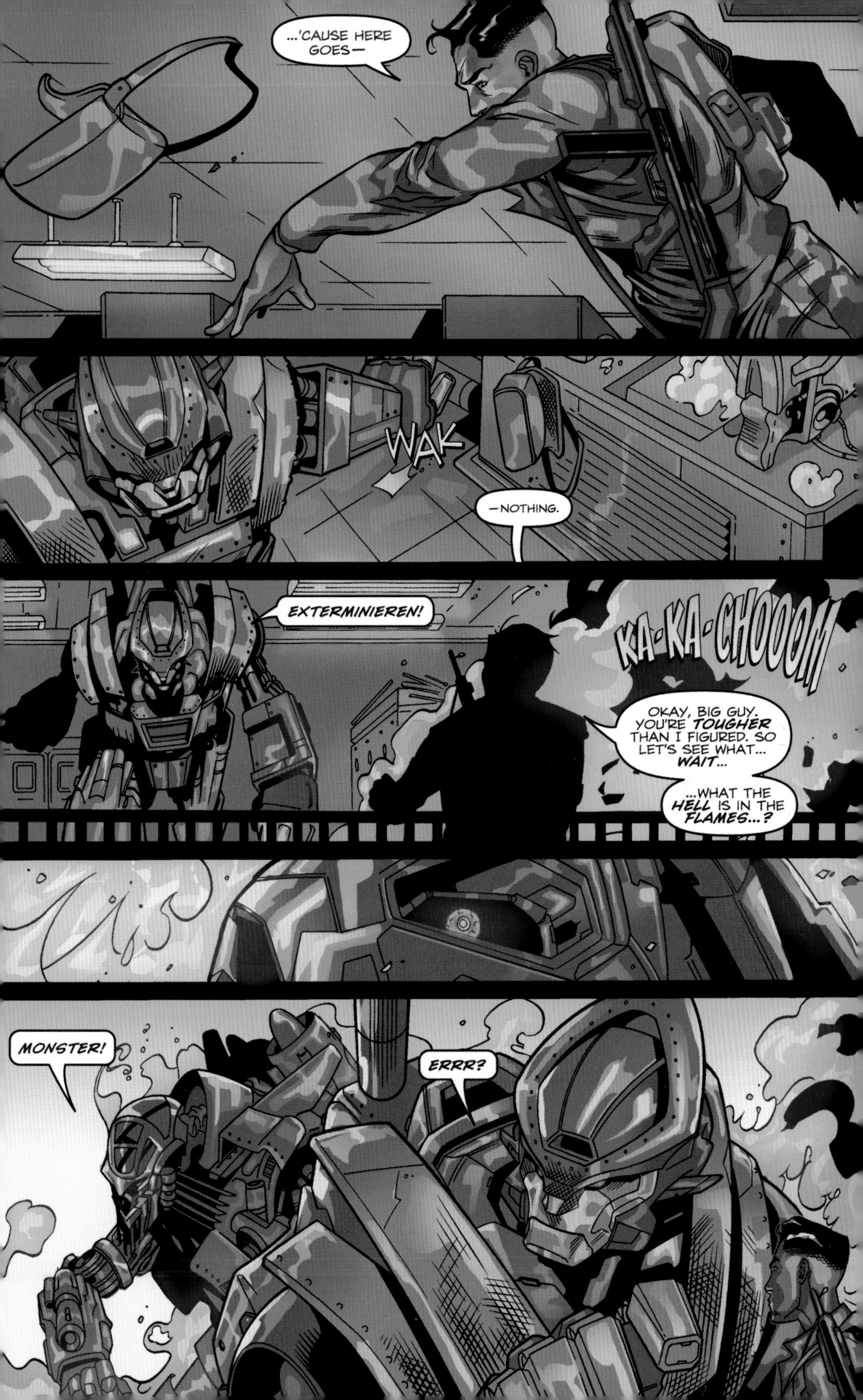
...'CAUSE HERE GOES—
WAK
—NOTHING.
EXTERMINIEREN!
KA-KA-CHOOOM
OKAY, BIG GUY. YOU'RE TOUGHER THAN I FIGURED. SO LET'S SEE WHAT... WAIT...
...WHAT THE HELL IS IN THE FLAMES...?
MONSTER!
ERRR?

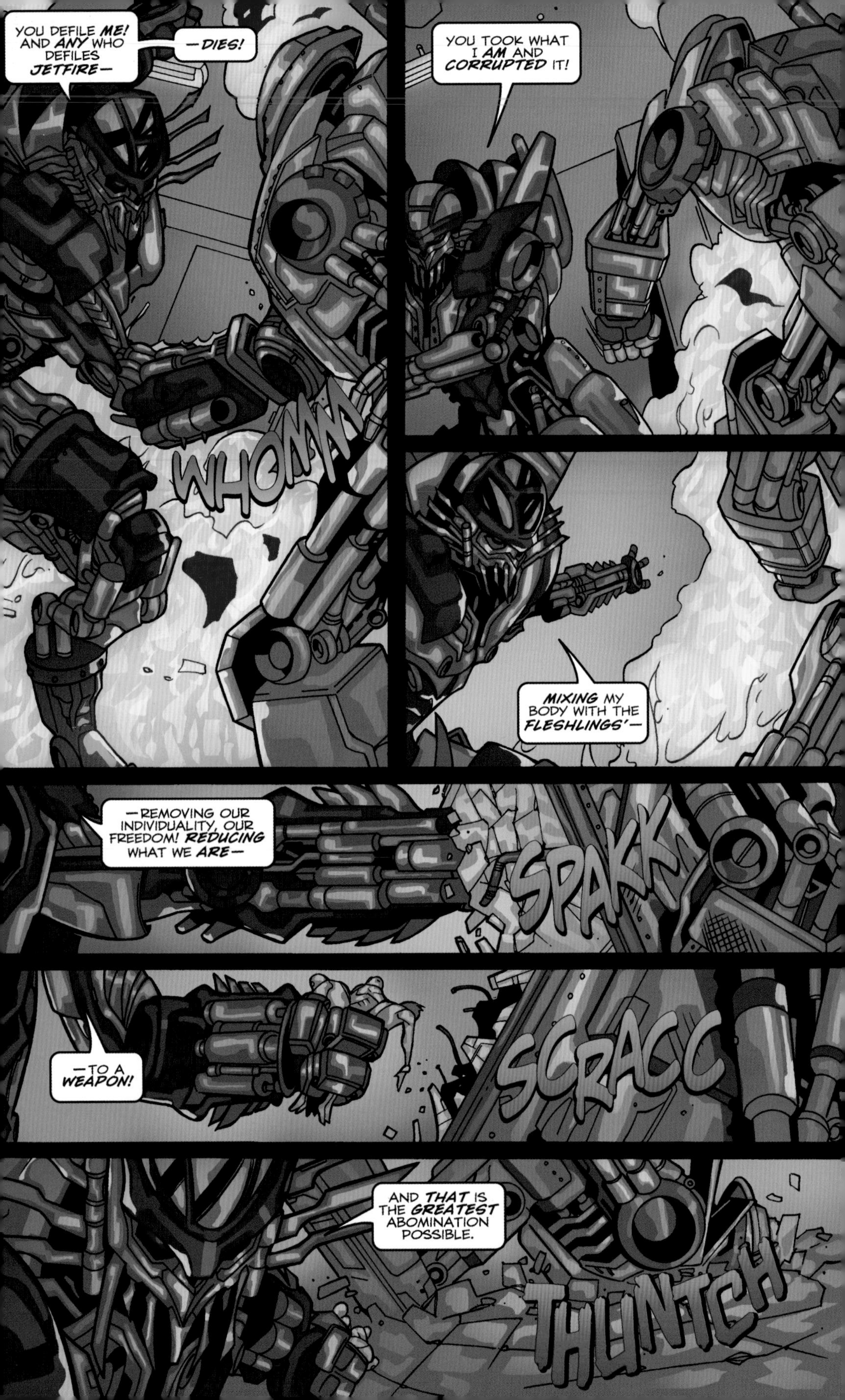

YOU DEFILE *ME!* AND *ANY* WHO DEFILES *JETFIRE*—
—*DIES!*
WHOMM
YOU TOOK WHAT I *AM* AND *CORRUPTED* IT!
MIXING MY BODY WITH THE *FLESHLINGS'*—
—REMOVING OUR INDIVIDUALITY, OUR FREEDOM! *REDUCING* WHAT WE *ARE*—
SPAKK
—TO A *WEAPON!*
SCRACC
AND *THAT* IS THE *GREATEST* ABOMINATION POSSIBLE.
THUNTCH

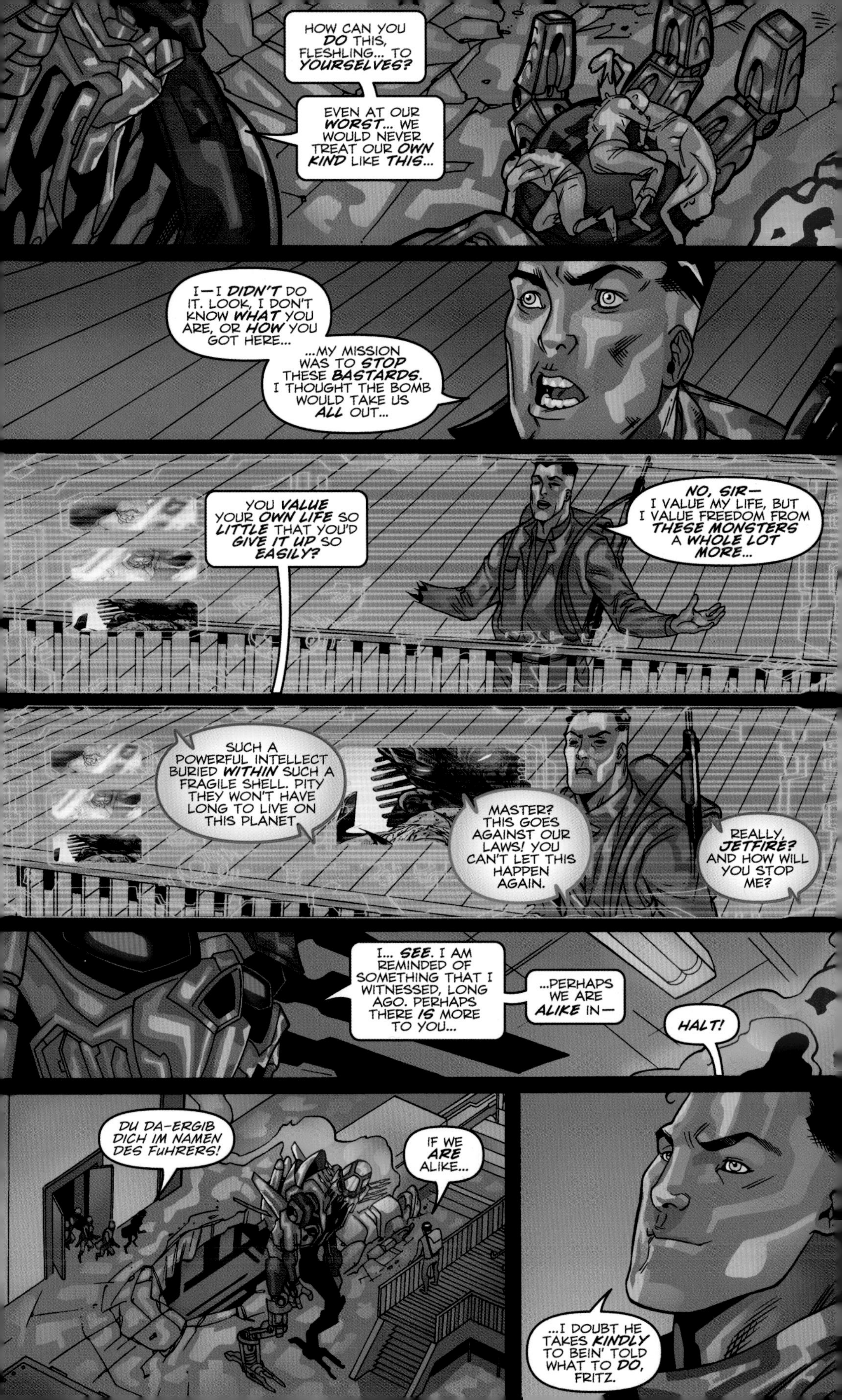
HOW CAN YOU DO THIS, FLESHLING... TO YOURSELVES?
EVEN AT OUR WORST... WE WOULD NEVER TREAT OUR OWN KIND LIKE THIS...
I—I DIDN'T DO IT. LOOK, I DON'T KNOW WHAT YOU ARE, OR HOW YOU GOT HERE...
...MY MISSION WAS TO STOP THESE BASTARDS. I THOUGHT THE BOMB WOULD TAKE US ALL OUT...
YOU VALUE YOUR OWN LIFE SO LITTLE THAT YOU'D GIVE IT UP SO EASILY?
NO, SIR— I VALUE MY LIFE, BUT I VALUE FREEDOM FROM THESE MONSTERS A WHOLE LOT MORE...
SUCH A POWERFUL INTELLECT BURIED WITHIN SUCH A FRAGILE SHELL. PITY THEY WON'T HAVE LONG TO LIVE ON THIS PLANET.
MASTER? THIS GOES AGAINST OUR LAWS! YOU CAN'T LET THIS HAPPEN AGAIN.
REALLY, JETFIRE? AND HOW WILL YOU STOP ME?
I... SEE. I AM REMINDED OF SOMETHING THAT I WITNESSED, LONG AGO. PERHAPS THERE IS MORE TO YOU...
...PERHAPS WE ARE ALIKE IN—
HALT!
DU DA-ERGIB DICH IM NAMEN DES FUHRERS!
IF WE ARE ALIKE...
...I DOUBT HE TAKES KINDLY TO BEIN' TOLD WHAT TO DO, FRITZ.

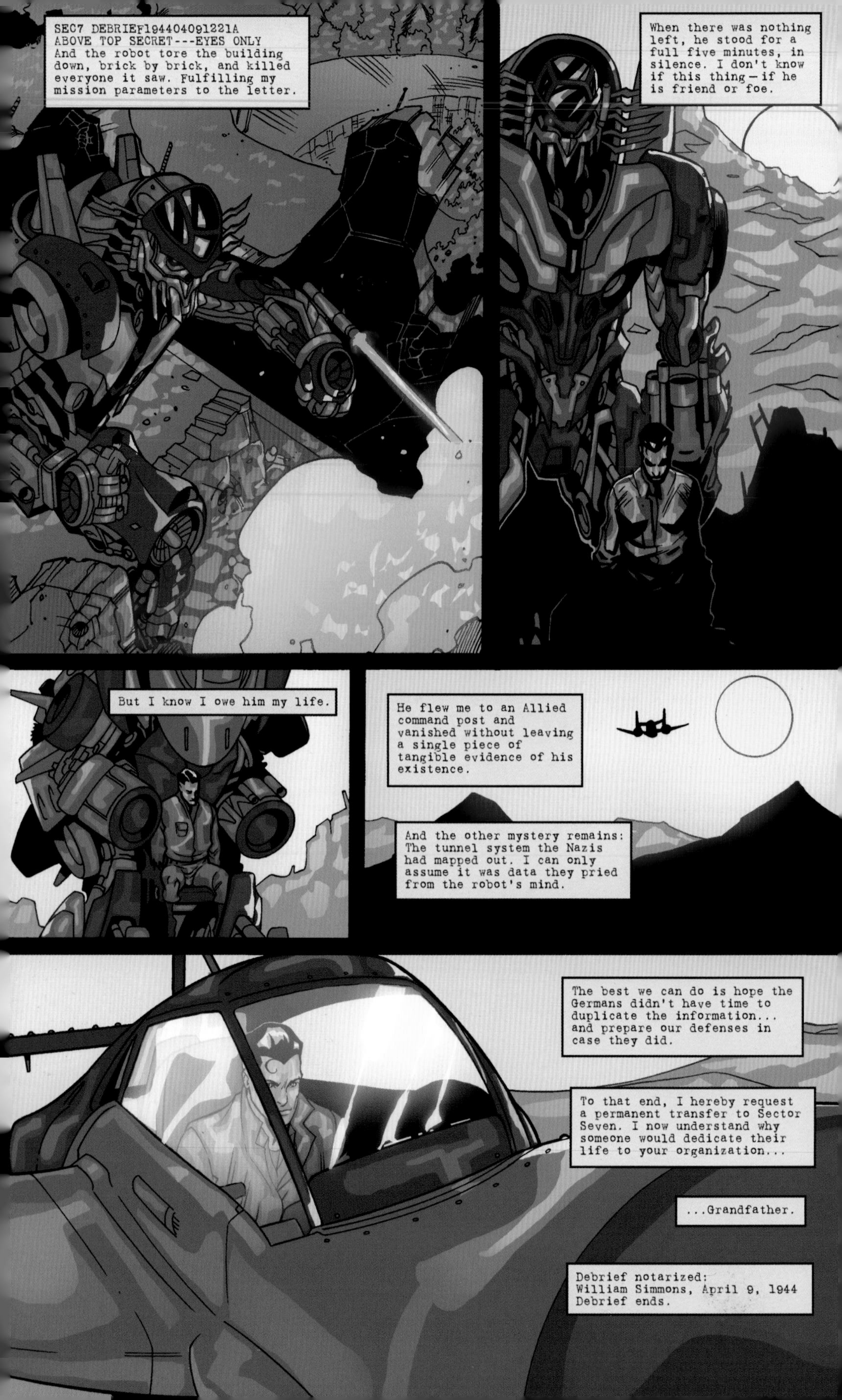
SEC7 DEBRIEF194404091221A
ABOVE TOP SECRET---EYES ONLY
And the robot tore the building down, brick by brick, and killed everyone it saw. Fulfilling my mission parameters to the letter.
When there was nothing left, he stood for a full five minutes, in silence. I don't know if this thing—if he is friend or foe.
But I know I owe him my life.
He flew me to an Allied command post and vanished without leaving a single piece of tangible evidence of his existence.
And the other mystery remains: The tunnel system the Nazis had mapped out. I can only assume it was data they pried from the robot's mind.
The best we can do is hope the Germans didn't have time to duplicate the information... and prepare our defenses in case they did.
To that end, I hereby request a permanent transfer to Sector Seven. I now understand why someone would dedicate their life to your organization...
...Grandfather.
Debrief notarized:
William Simmons, April 9, 1944
Debrief ends.

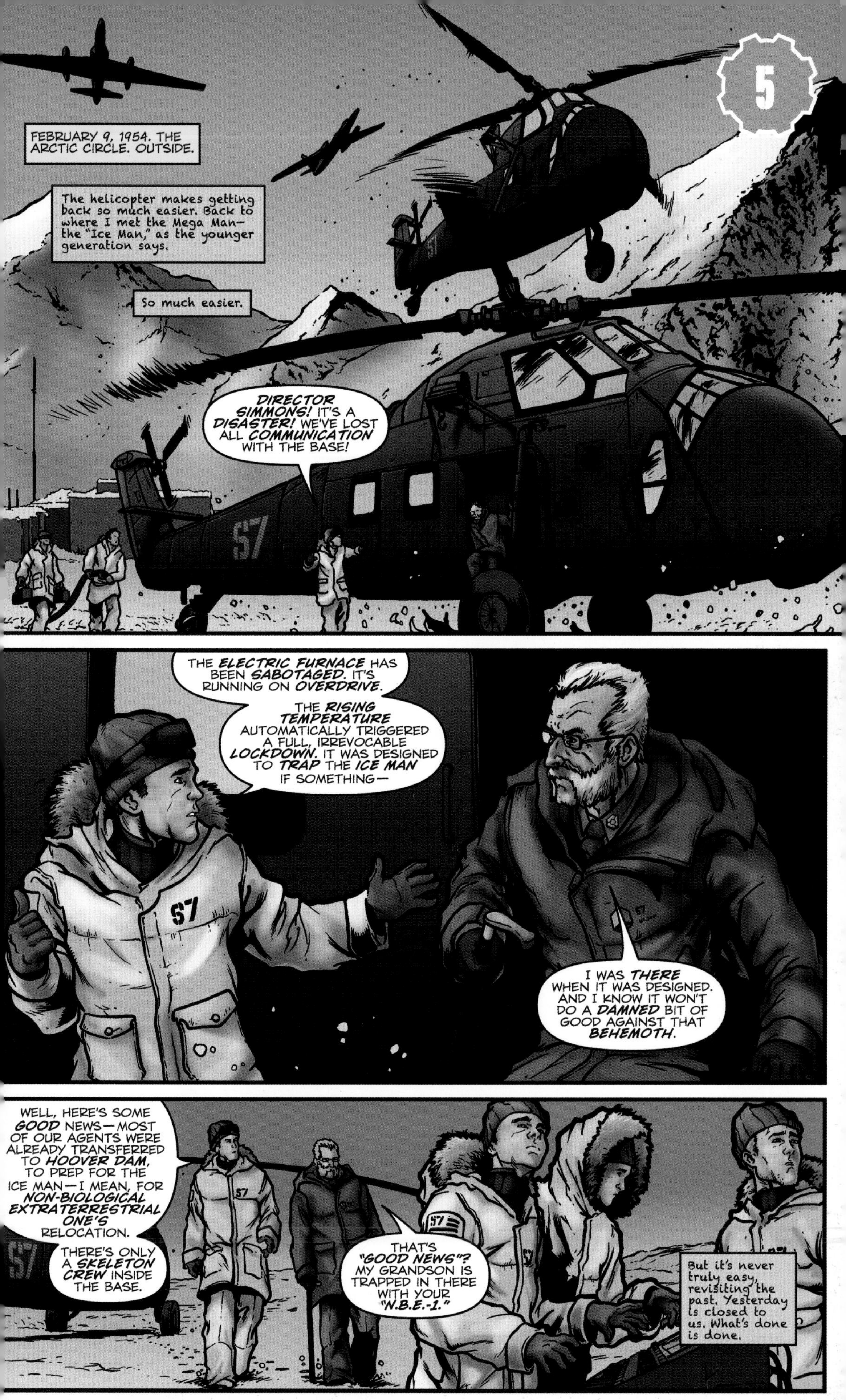
5
FEBRUARY 9, 1954. THE ARCTIC CIRCLE. OUTSIDE.
The helicopter makes getting back so much easier. Back to where I met the Mega Man—the "Ice Man," as the younger generation says.
So much easier.
DIRECTOR SIMMONS! IT'S A DISASTER! WE'VE LOST ALL COMMUNICATION WITH THE BASE!
THE ELECTRIC FURNACE HAS BEEN SABOTAGED. IT'S RUNNING ON OVERDRIVE.
THE RISING TEMPERATURE AUTOMATICALLY TRIGGERED A FULL, IRREVOCABLE LOCKDOWN. IT WAS DESIGNED TO TRAP THE ICE MAN IF SOMETHING—
I WAS THERE WHEN IT WAS DESIGNED. AND I KNOW IT WON'T DO A DAMNED BIT OF GOOD AGAINST THAT BEHEMOTH.
WELL, HERE'S SOME GOOD NEWS—MOST OF OUR AGENTS WERE ALREADY TRANSFERRED TO HOOVER DAM, TO PREP FOR THE ICE MAN—I MEAN, FOR NON-BIOLOGICAL EXTRATERRESTRIAL ONE'S RELOCATION.
THERE'S ONLY A SKELETON CREW INSIDE THE BASE.
THAT'S "GOOD NEWS"? MY GRANDSON IS TRAPPED IN THERE WITH YOUR "N.B.E.-1."
But it's never truly easy, revisiting the past. Yesterday is closed to us. What's done is done.

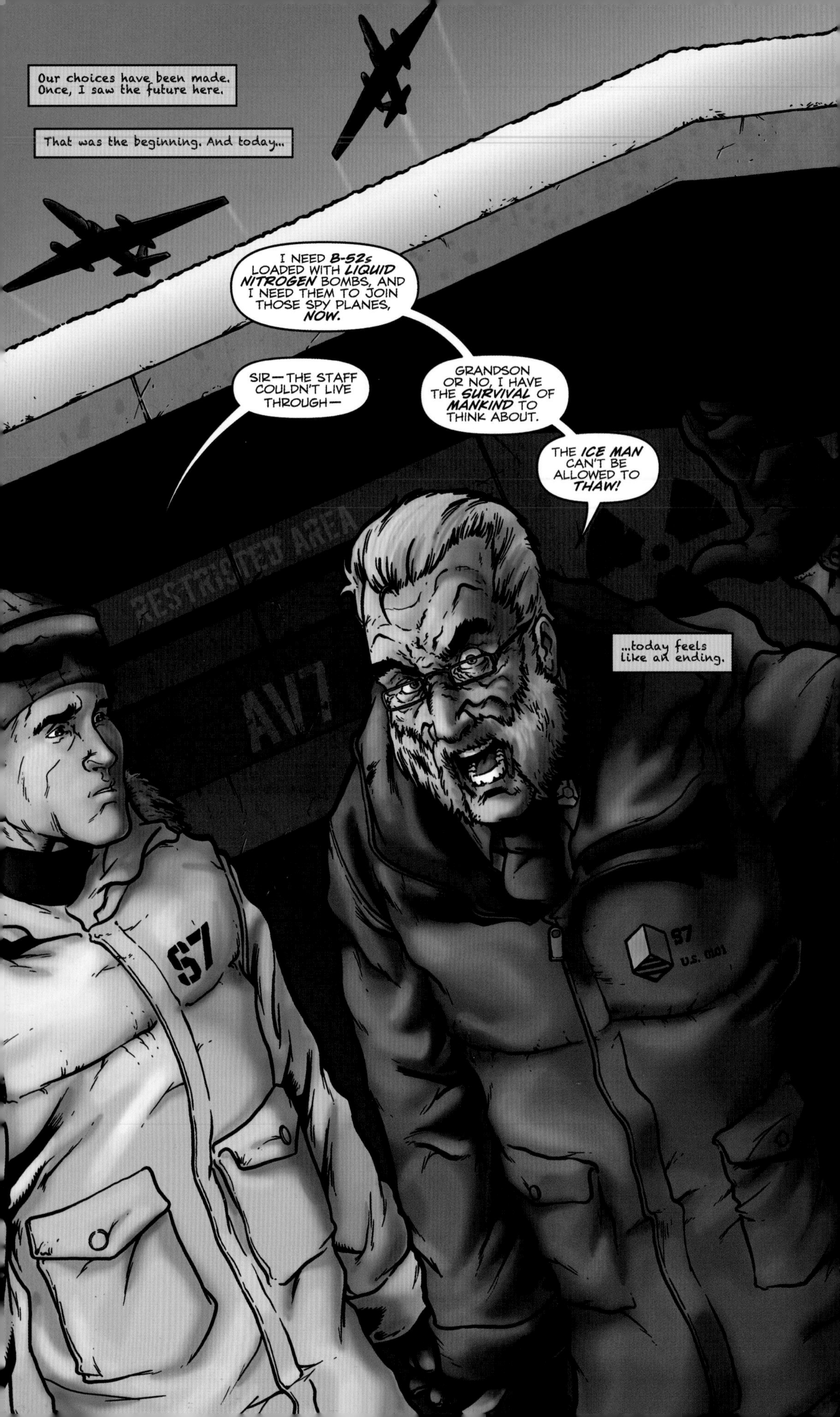
Our choices have been made. Once, I saw the future here.
That was the beginning. And today...
I NEED B-52s LOADED WITH LIQUID NITROGEN BOMBS, AND I NEED THEM TO JOIN THOSE SPY PLANES, NOW.
SIR—THE STAFF COULDN'T LIVE THROUGH—
GRANDSON OR NO, I HAVE THE SURVIVAL OF MANKIND TO THINK ABOUT.
THE ICE MAN CAN'T BE ALLOWED TO THAW!
RESTRICTED AREA
...today feels like an ending.

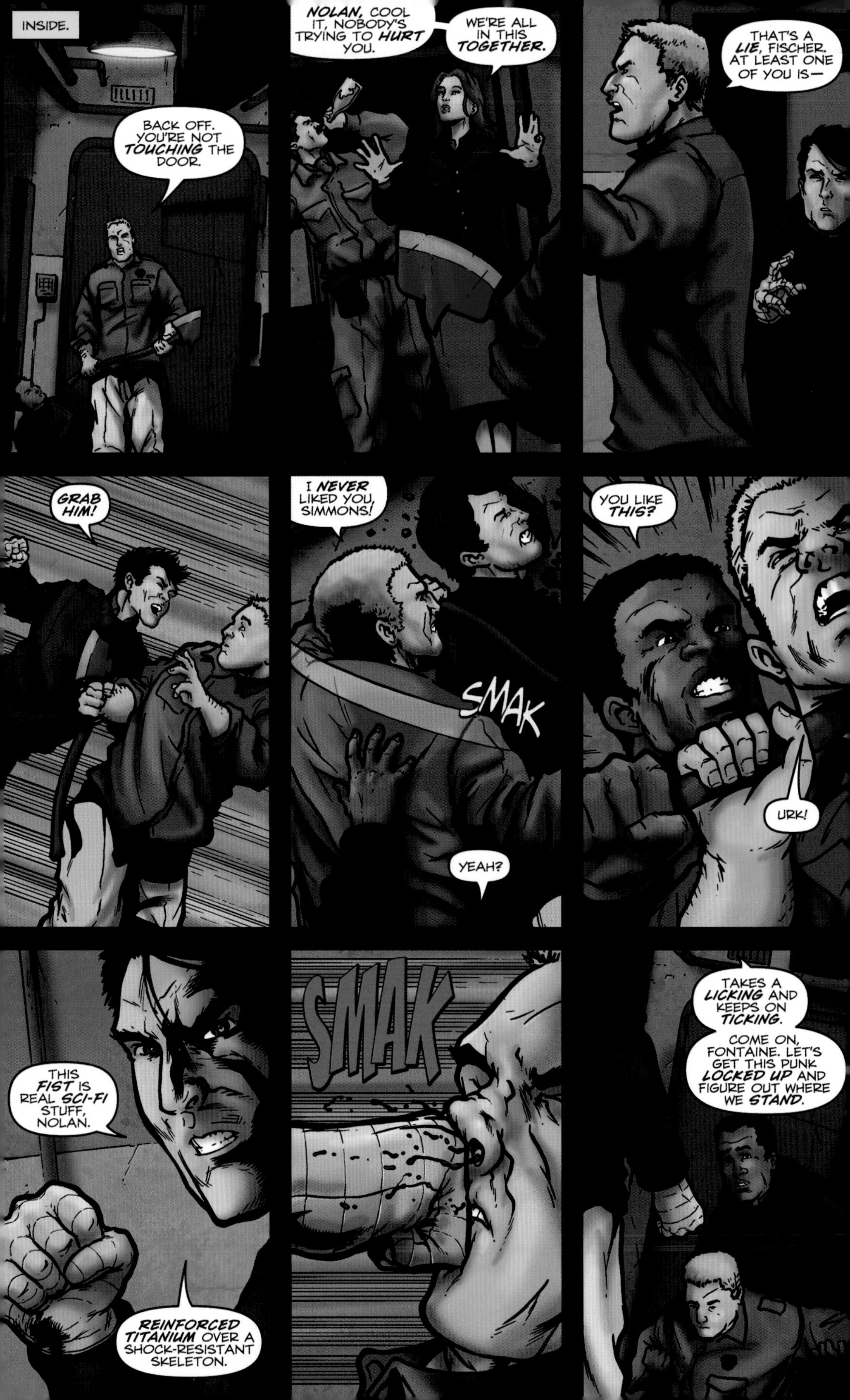
INSIDE.
BACK OFF. YOU'RE NOT TOUCHING THE DOOR.
NOLAN, COOL IT, NOBODY'S TRYING TO HURT YOU.
WE'RE ALL IN THIS TOGETHER.
THAT'S A LIE, FISCHER. AT LEAST ONE OF YOU IS—
GRAB HIM!
I NEVER LIKED YOU, SIMMONS!
SMAK
YEAH?
YOU LIKE THIS?
URK!
THIS FIST IS REAL SCI-FI STUFF, NOLAN.
REINFORCED TITANIUM OVER A SHOCK-RESISTANT SKELETON.
SMAK
TAKES A LICKING AND KEEPS ON TICKING.
COME ON, FONTAINE. LET'S GET THIS PUNK LOCKED UP AND FIGURE OUT WHERE WE STAND.

YOU'LL SEE— ONE OF **US** IS ONE OF **THEM!**

YOU CAN'T TRUST **ANY** OF US!

RELAX, **NOLAN**... THAT'S A BULLETPROOF POLYMER WINDOW. **STRONGER** THAN MY FIST.

MISS FISCHER, YOU HOLD ON TO THIS KEY.

NOLAN GOT TO THE **RADIO**— LOOKS LIKE **ROCKY MARCIANO** WENT A COUPLE ROUNDS WITH IT.

FINE. LET'S GET TO **WORK** ON THE DOOR.

DON'T BE AN ASS, **SIMMONS!**

THE LOCKDOWN WAS **SPECIFICALLY** SET UP FOR CIRCUMSTANCES LIKE—

LOOK, **KID.** JUST **SHUT UP** AND WAIT FOR YOUR **COURT MARSHAL.**

YOU LOOK, OLD MAN!

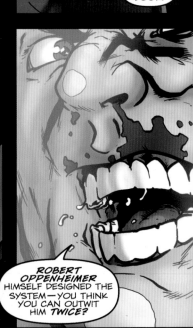

ROBERT OPPENHEIMER HIMSELF DESIGNED THE SYSTEM— YOU THINK YOU CAN OUTWIT HIM **TWICE?**

"OLD MAN" IS MY **GRANDFATHER'S** NAME, AND **OPPENHEIMER** WAS A **COMMIE.** WE'LL GET **OUT** OF THIS—

DANCO— WHAT DO YOU KNOW ABOUT **FURNACES?**

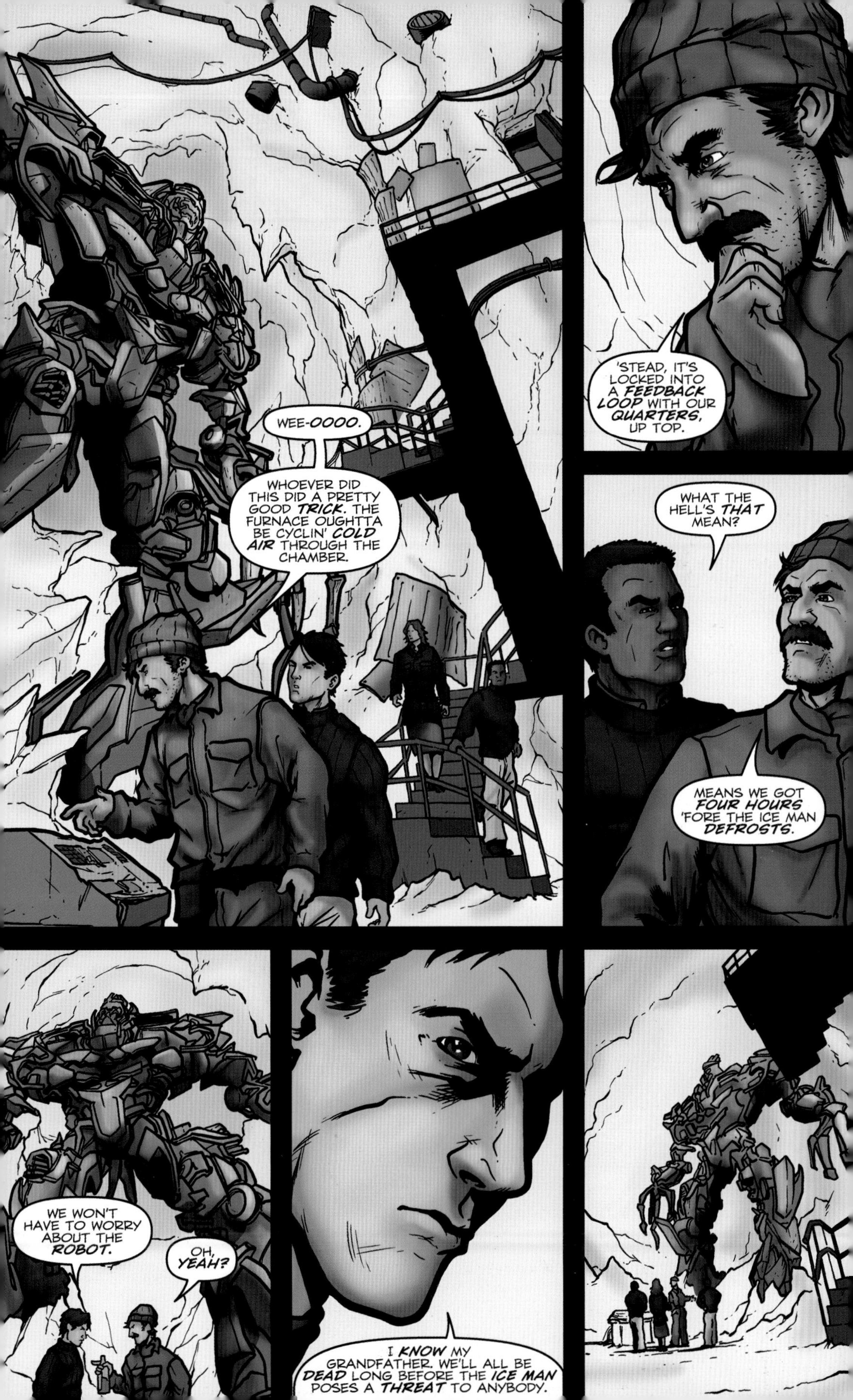
WEE-OOOO.
WHOEVER DID THIS DID A PRETTY GOOD TRICK. THE FURNACE OUGHTTA BE CYCLIN' COLD AIR THROUGH THE CHAMBER.
'STEAD, IT'S LOCKED INTO A FEEDBACK LOOP WITH OUR QUARTERS, UP TOP.
WHAT THE HELL'S THAT MEAN?
MEANS WE GOT FOUR HOURS 'FORE THE ICE MAN DEFROSTS.
WE WON'T HAVE TO WORRY ABOUT THE ROBOT.
OH, YEAH?
I KNOW MY GRANDFATHER. WE'LL ALL BE DEAD LONG BEFORE THE ICE MAN POSES A THREAT TO ANYBODY.

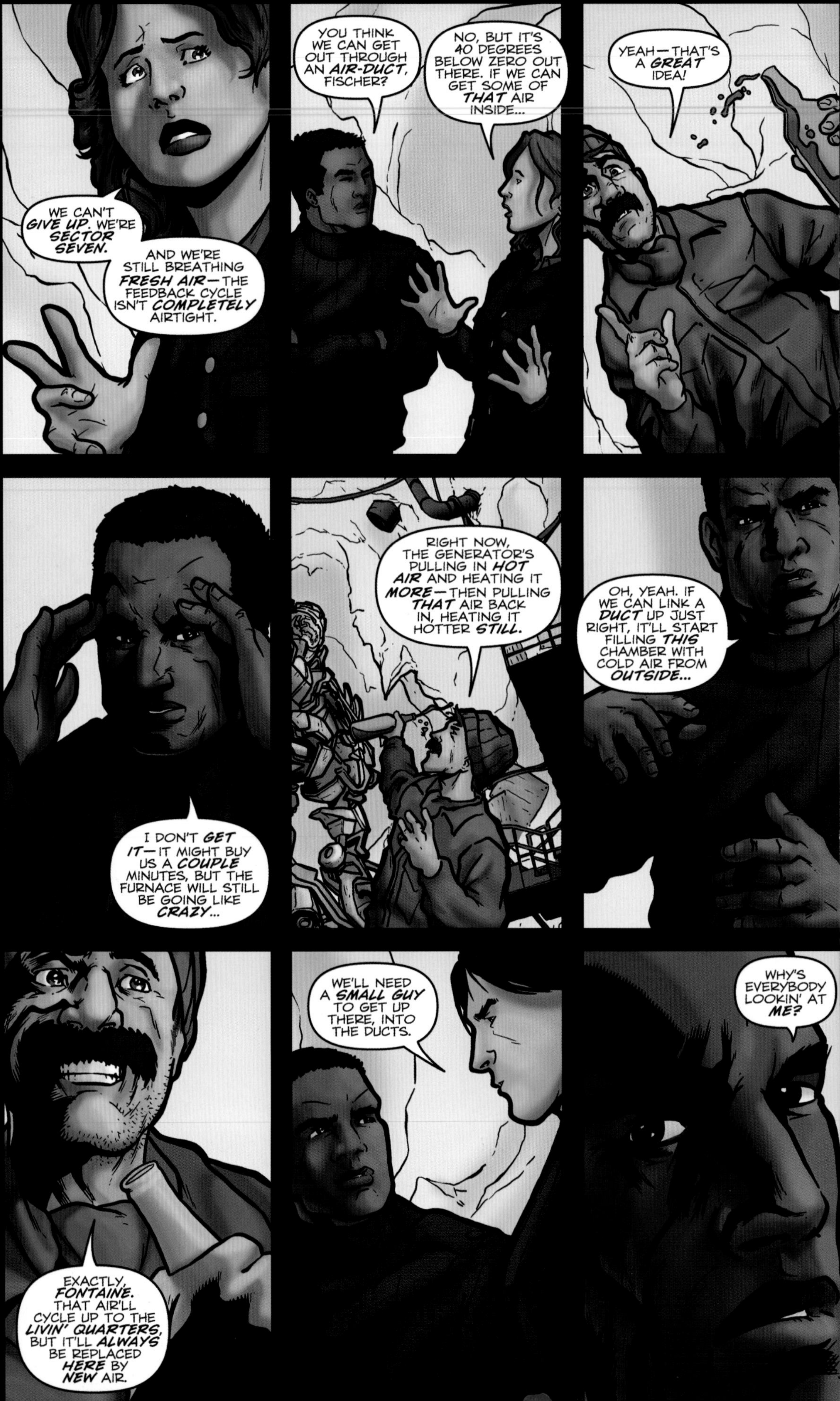
WE CAN'T GIVE UP. WE'RE SECTOR SEVEN.
AND WE'RE STILL BREATHING FRESH AIR—THE FEEDBACK CYCLE ISN'T COMPLETELY AIRTIGHT.
YOU THINK WE CAN GET OUT THROUGH AN AIR-DUCT, FISCHER?
NO, BUT IT'S 40 DEGREES BELOW ZERO OUT THERE. IF WE CAN GET SOME OF THAT AIR INSIDE...
YEAH—THAT'S A GREAT IDEA!
I DON'T GET IT—IT MIGHT BUY US A COUPLE MINUTES, BUT THE FURNACE WILL STILL BE GOING LIKE CRAZY...
RIGHT NOW, THE GENERATOR'S PULLING IN HOT AIR AND HEATING IT MORE—THEN PULLING THAT AIR BACK IN, HEATING IT HOTTER STILL.
OH, YEAH. IF WE CAN LINK A DUCT UP JUST RIGHT, IT'LL START FILLING THIS CHAMBER WITH COLD AIR FROM OUTSIDE...
EXACTLY, FONTAINE. THAT AIR'LL CYCLE UP TO THE LIVIN' QUARTERS, BUT IT'LL ALWAYS BE REPLACED HERE BY NEW AIR.
WE'LL NEED A SMALL GUY TO GET UP THERE, INTO THE DUCTS.
WHY'S EVERYBODY LOOKIN' AT ME?

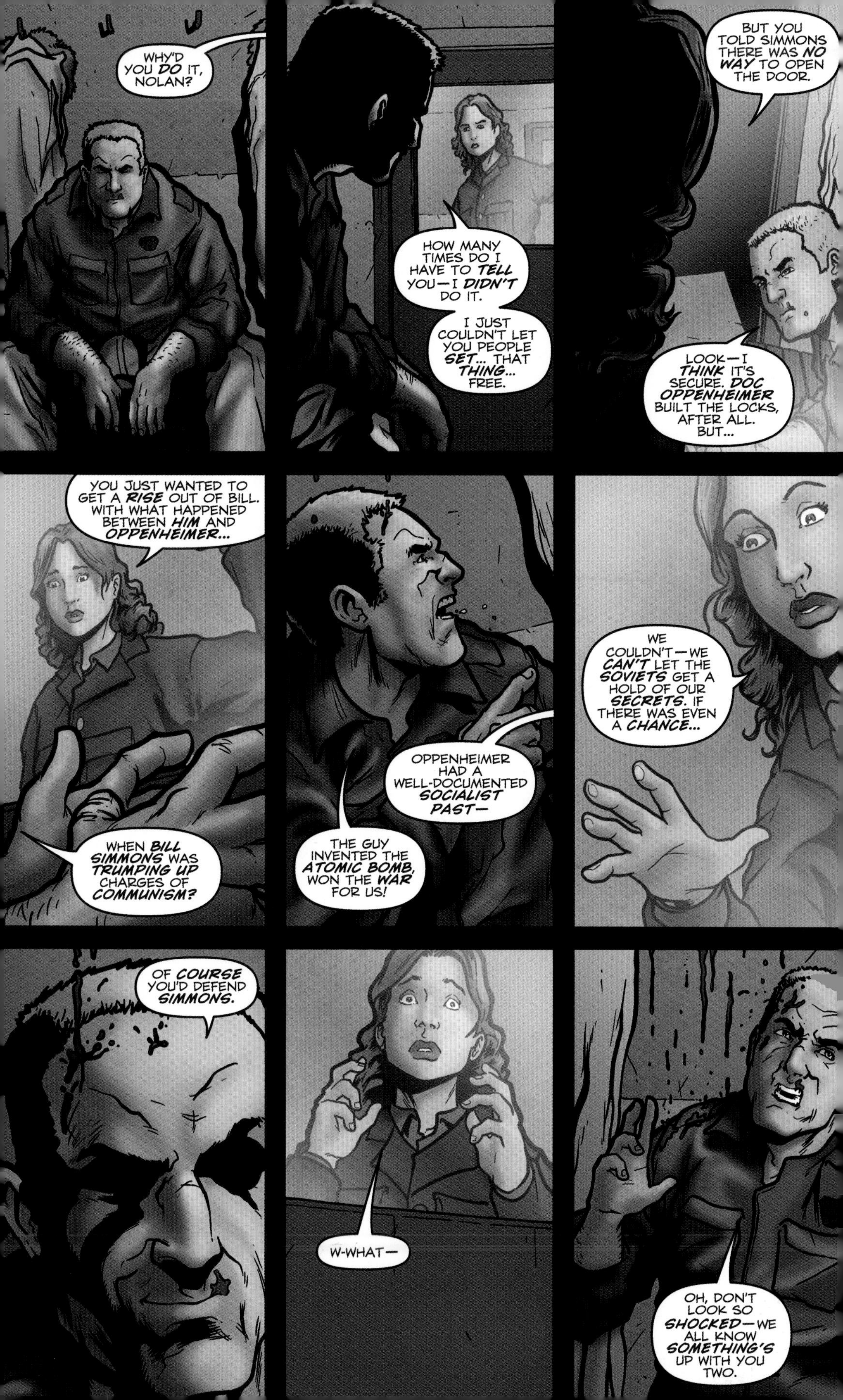
WHY'D YOU DO IT, NOLAN?
HOW MANY TIMES DO I HAVE TO TELL YOU—I DIDN'T DO IT.
I JUST COULDN'T LET YOU PEOPLE SET... THAT THING... FREE.
BUT YOU TOLD SIMMONS THERE WAS NO WAY TO OPEN THE DOOR.
LOOK—I THINK IT'S SECURE. DOC OPPENHEIMER BUILT THE LOCKS, AFTER ALL. BUT...
YOU JUST WANTED TO GET A RISE OUT OF BILL. WITH WHAT HAPPENED BETWEEN HIM AND OPPENHEIMER...
WHEN BILL SIMMONS WAS TRUMPING UP CHARGES OF COMMUNISM?
OPPENHEIMER HAD A WELL-DOCUMENTED SOCIALIST PAST—
THE GUY INVENTED THE ATOMIC BOMB, WON THE WAR FOR US!
WE COULDN'T—WE CAN'T LET THE SOVIETS GET A HOLD OF OUR SECRETS. IF THERE WAS EVEN A CHANCE...
OF COURSE YOU'D DEFEND SIMMONS.
W-WHAT—
OH, DON'T LOOK SO SHOCKED—WE ALL KNOW SOMETHING'S UP WITH YOU TWO.

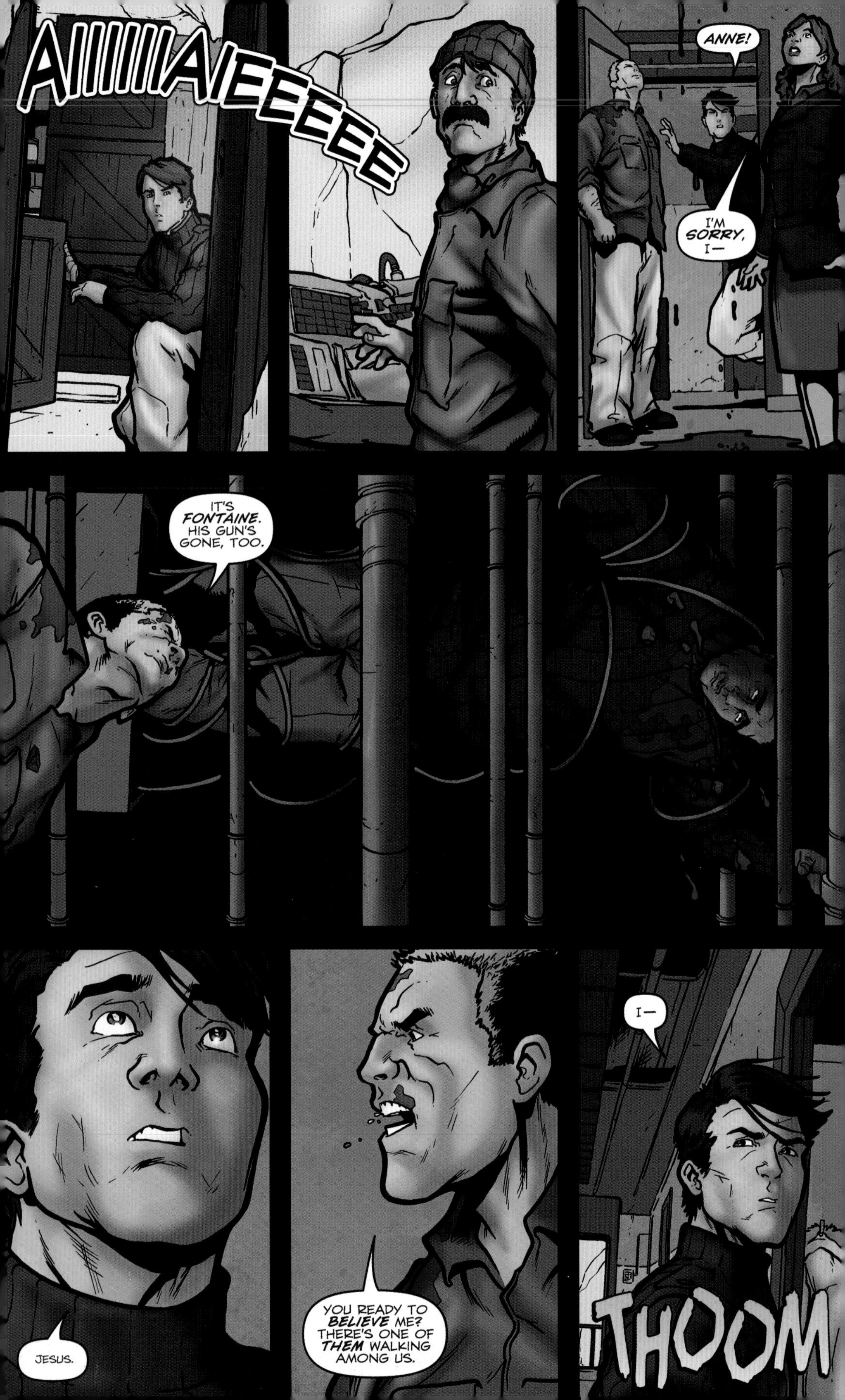
AIIIIIIAIEEEEEE
ANNE!
I'M SORRY, I—
IT'S FONTAINE. HIS GUN'S GONE, TOO.
JESUS.
YOU READY TO BELIEVE ME? THERE'S ONE OF THEM WALKING AMONG US.
I—
THOOM

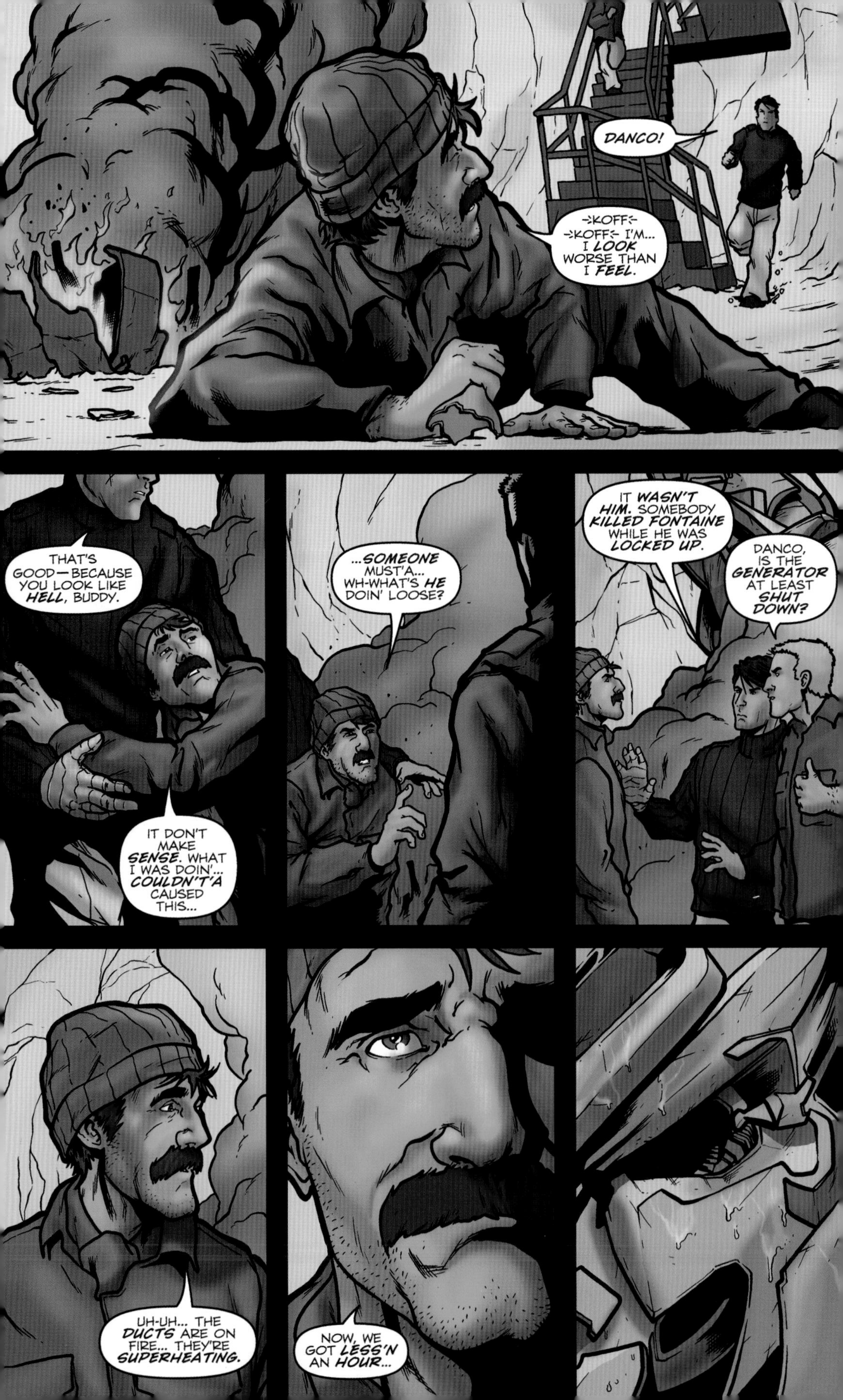
DANCO!
-KOFF- -KOFF- I'M... I LOOK WORSE THAN I FEEL.
THAT'S GOOD—BECAUSE YOU LOOK LIKE HELL, BUDDY.
IT DON'T MAKE SENSE. WHAT I WAS DOIN'... COULDN'T'A CAUSED THIS...
...SOMEONE MUST'A... WH-WHAT'S HE DOIN' LOOSE?
IT WASN'T HIM. SOMEBODY KILLED FONTAINE WHILE HE WAS LOCKED UP.
DANCO, IS THE GENERATOR AT LEAST SHUT DOWN?
UH-UH... THE DUCTS ARE ON FIRE... THEY'RE SUPERHEATING.
NOW, WE GOT LESS'N AN HOUR...

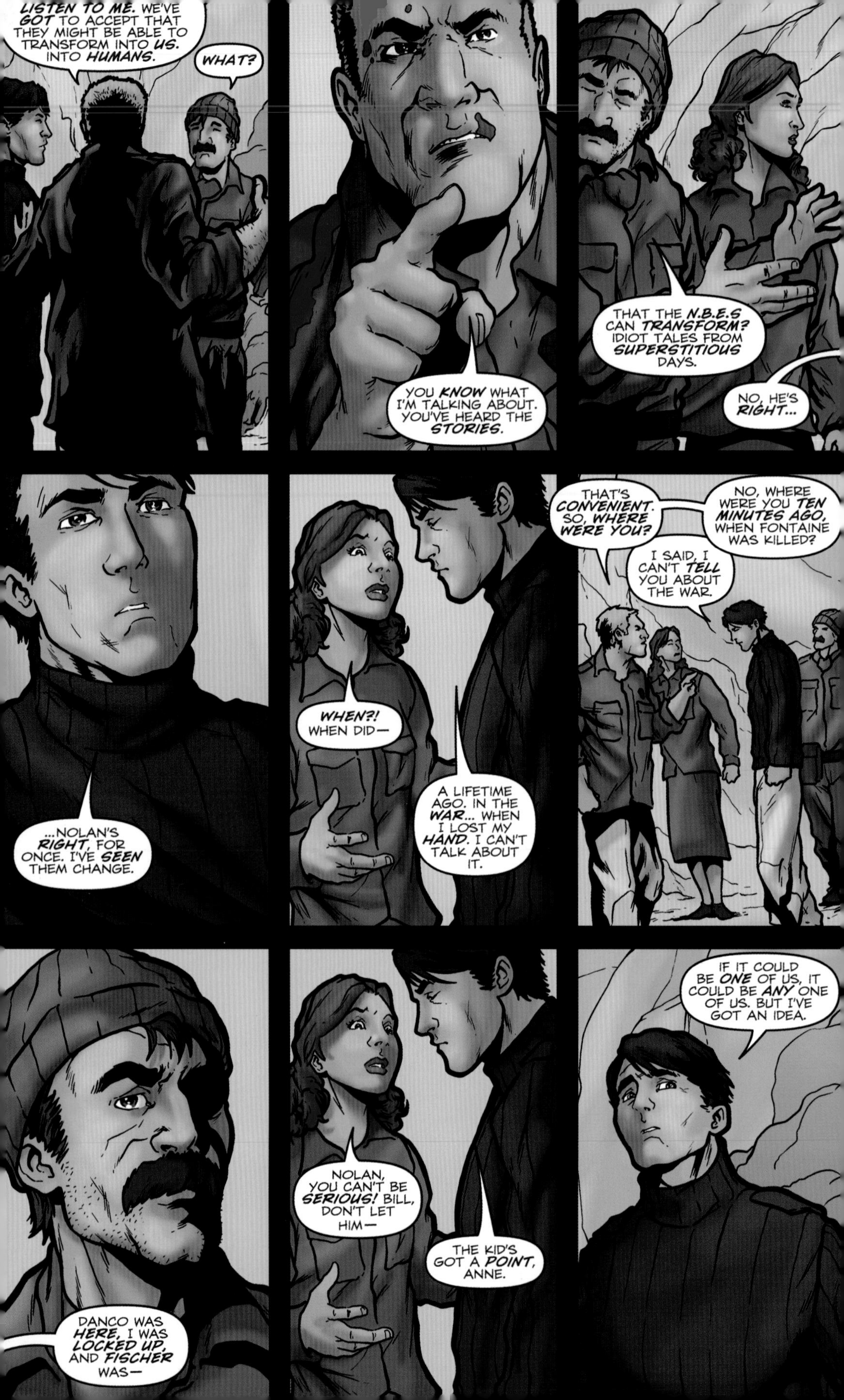
LISTEN TO ME. WE'VE GOT TO ACCEPT THAT THEY MIGHT BE ABLE TO TRANSFORM INTO US. INTO HUMANS.
WHAT?
YOU KNOW WHAT I'M TALKING ABOUT. YOU'VE HEARD THE STORIES.
THAT THE N.B.E.S CAN TRANSFORM? IDIOT TALES FROM SUPERSTITIOUS DAYS.
NO, HE'S RIGHT...
...NOLAN'S RIGHT, FOR ONCE. I'VE SEEN THEM CHANGE.
WHEN?! WHEN DID—
A LIFETIME AGO. IN THE WAR... WHEN I LOST MY HAND. I CAN'T TALK ABOUT IT.
THAT'S CONVENIENT. SO, WHERE WERE YOU?
I SAID, I CAN'T TELL YOU ABOUT THE WAR.
NO, WHERE WERE YOU TEN MINUTES AGO, WHEN FONTAINE WAS KILLED?
DANCO WAS HERE, I WAS LOCKED UP, AND FISCHER WAS—
NOLAN, YOU CAN'T BE SERIOUS! BILL, DON'T LET HIM—
THE KID'S GOT A POINT, ANNE.
IF IT COULD BE ONE OF US, IT COULD BE ANY ONE OF US. BUT I'VE GOT AN IDEA.

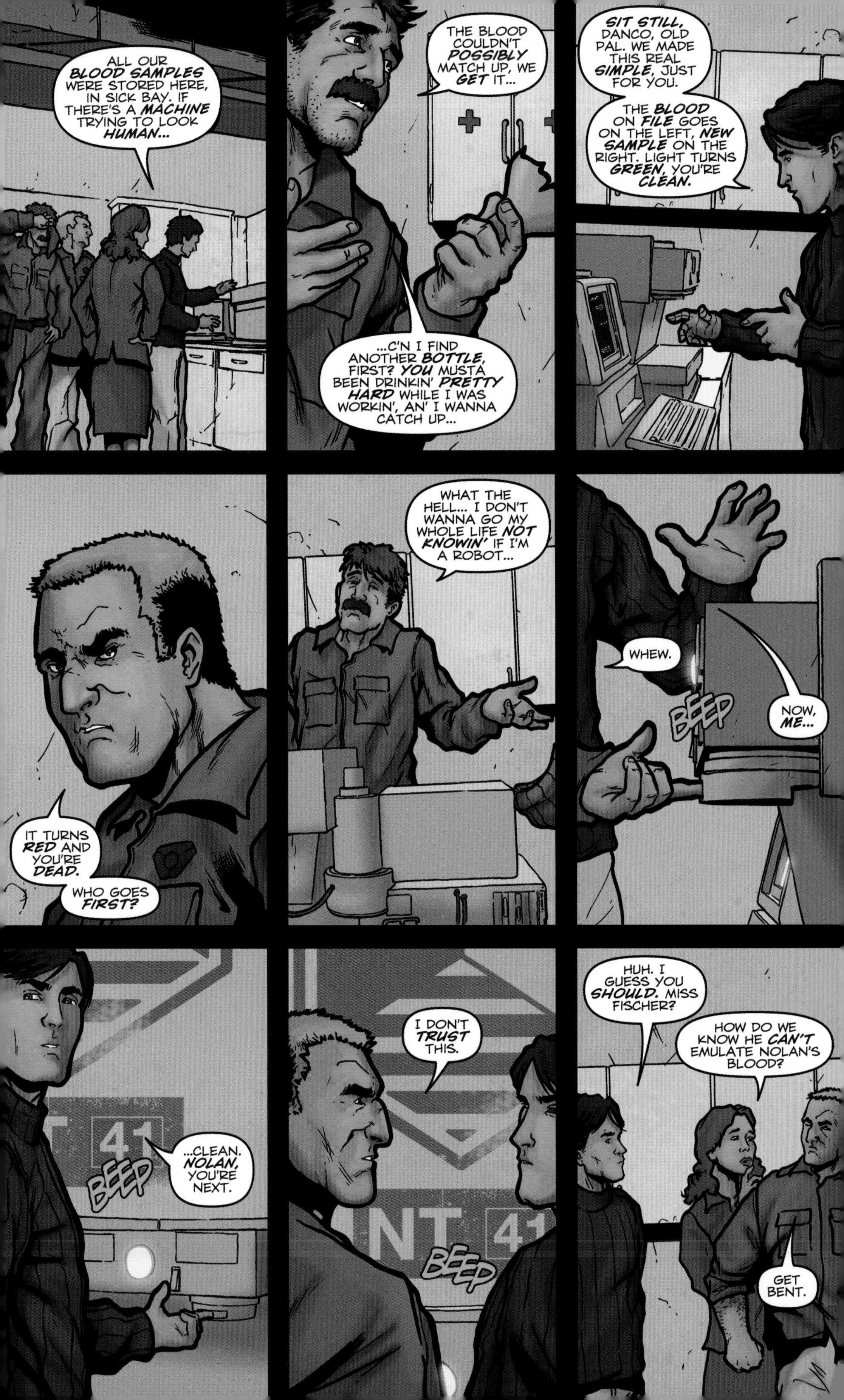
ALL OUR BLOOD SAMPLES WERE STORED HERE, IN SICK BAY. IF THERE'S A MACHINE TRYING TO LOOK HUMAN...
THE BLOOD COULDN'T POSSIBLY MATCH UP, WE GET IT...
...C'N I FIND ANOTHER BOTTLE, FIRST? YOU MUSTA BEEN DRINKIN' PRETTY HARD WHILE I WAS WORKIN', AN' I WANNA CATCH UP...
SIT STILL, DANCO, OLD PAL. WE MADE THIS REAL SIMPLE, JUST FOR YOU.
THE BLOOD ON FILE GOES ON THE LEFT, NEW SAMPLE ON THE RIGHT. LIGHT TURNS GREEN, YOU'RE CLEAN.
IT TURNS RED AND YOU'RE DEAD.
WHO GOES FIRST?
WHAT THE HELL... I DON'T WANNA GO MY WHOLE LIFE NOT KNOWIN' IF I'M A ROBOT...
WHEW.
BEEP
NOW, ME...
41
BEEP
...CLEAN. NOLAN, YOU'RE NEXT.
I DON'T TRUST THIS.
NT 41
BEEP
HUH. I GUESS YOU SHOULD. MISS FISCHER?
HOW DO WE KNOW HE CAN'T EMULATE NOLAN'S BLOOD?
GET BENT.

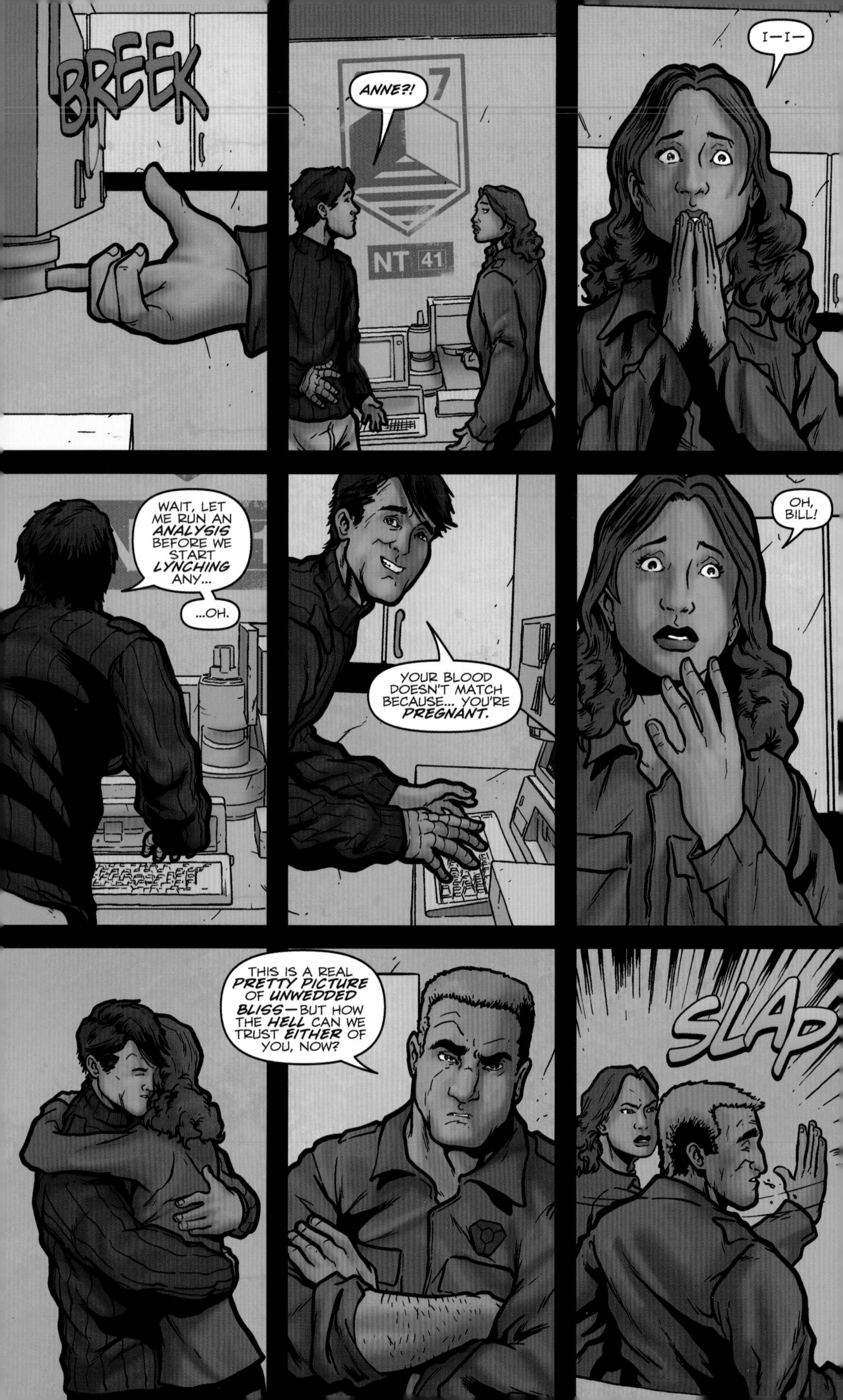
BREEK
ANNE?!
NT 41
I—I—
WAIT, LET ME RUN AN ANALYSIS BEFORE WE START LYNCHING ANY...
...OH.
YOUR BLOOD DOESN'T MATCH BECAUSE... YOU'RE PREGNANT.
OH, BILL!
THIS IS A REAL PRETTY PICTURE OF UNWEDDED BLISS—BUT HOW THE HELL CAN WE TRUST EITHER OF YOU, NOW?
SLAP

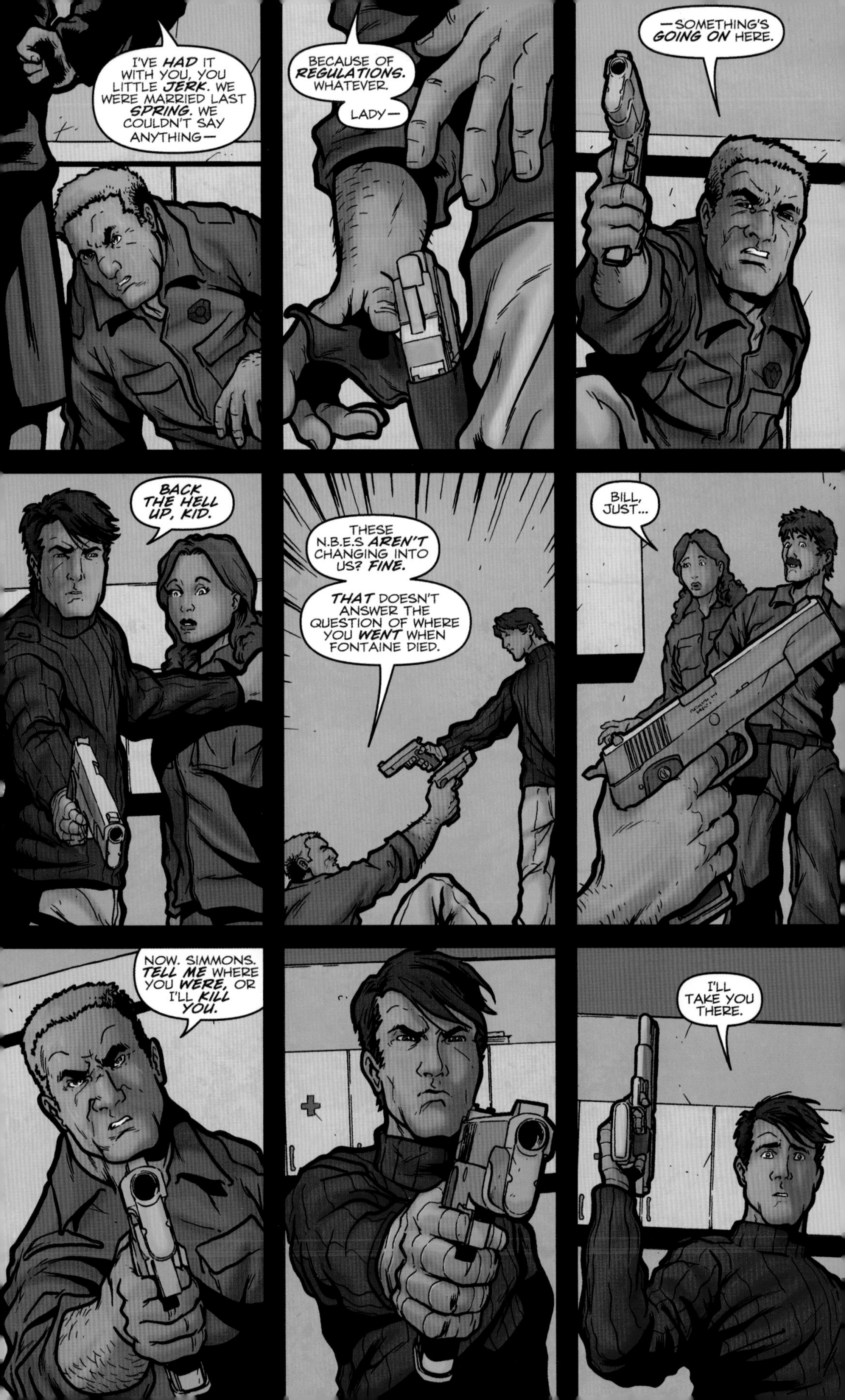
I'VE HAD IT WITH YOU, YOU LITTLE JERK. WE WERE MARRIED LAST SPRING. WE COULDN'T SAY ANYTHING—
BECAUSE OF REGULATIONS. WHATEVER.
LADY—
—SOMETHING'S GOING ON HERE.
BACK THE HELL UP, KID.
THESE N.B.E.S AREN'T CHANGING INTO US? FINE.
THAT DOESN'T ANSWER THE QUESTION OF WHERE YOU WENT WHEN FONTAINE DIED.
BILL, JUST...
NOW. SIMMONS. TELL ME WHERE YOU WERE, OR I'LL KILL YOU.
I'LL TAKE YOU THERE.

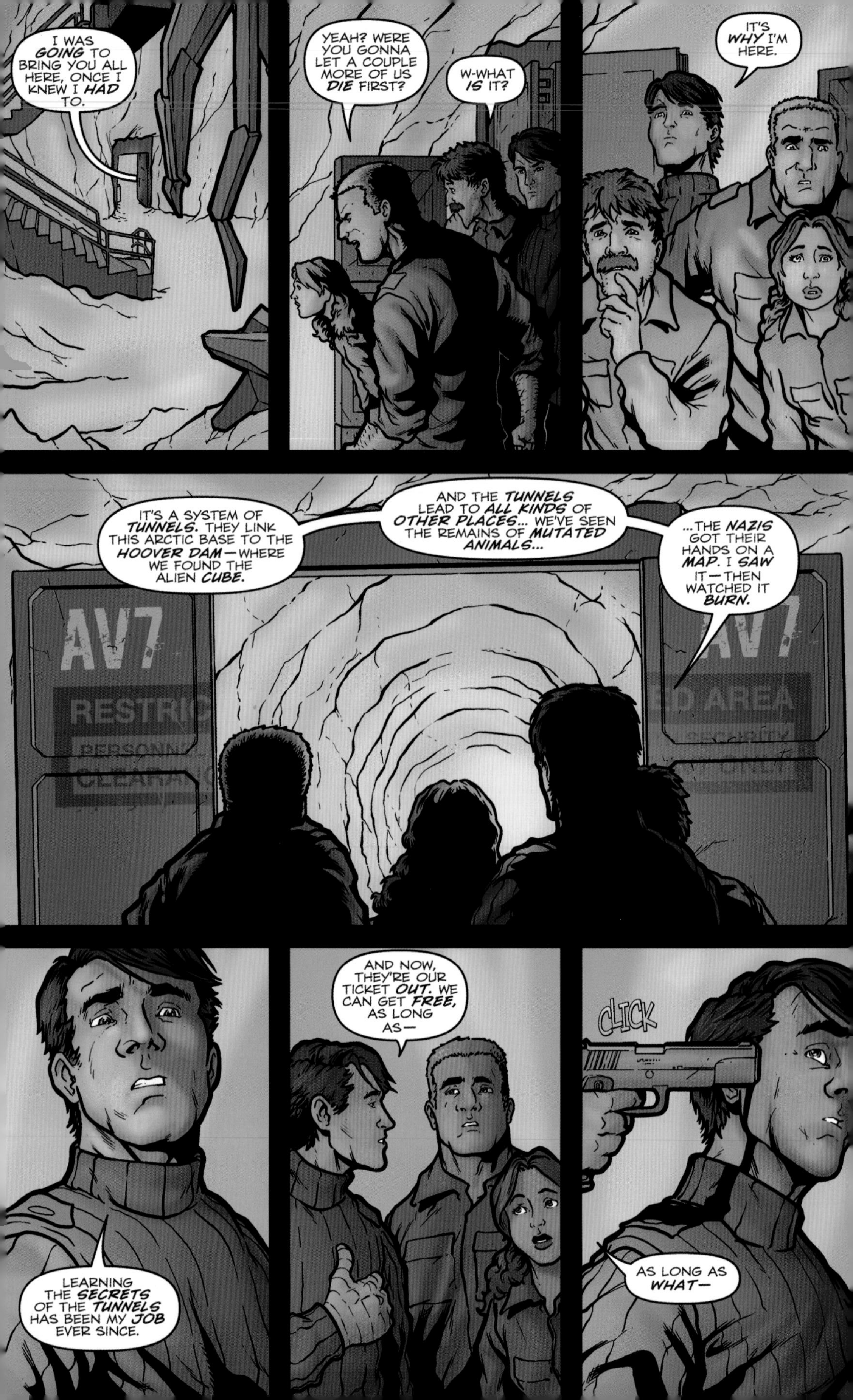
I WAS GOING TO BRING YOU ALL HERE, ONCE I KNEW I HAD TO.
YEAH? WERE YOU GONNA LET A COUPLE MORE OF US DIE FIRST?
W-WHAT IS IT?
IT'S WHY I'M HERE.
IT'S A SYSTEM OF TUNNELS. THEY LINK THIS ARCTIC BASE TO THE HOOVER DAM—WHERE WE FOUND THE ALIEN CUBE.
AND THE TUNNELS LEAD TO ALL KINDS OF OTHER PLACES... WE'VE SEEN THE REMAINS OF MUTATED ANIMALS...
...THE NAZIS GOT THEIR HANDS ON A MAP. I SAW IT—THEN WATCHED IT BURN.
AV7
AV7
LEARNING THE SECRETS OF THE TUNNELS HAS BEEN MY JOB EVER SINCE.
AND NOW, THEY'RE OUR TICKET OUT. WE CAN GET FREE, AS LONG AS—
CLICK
AS LONG AS WHAT—

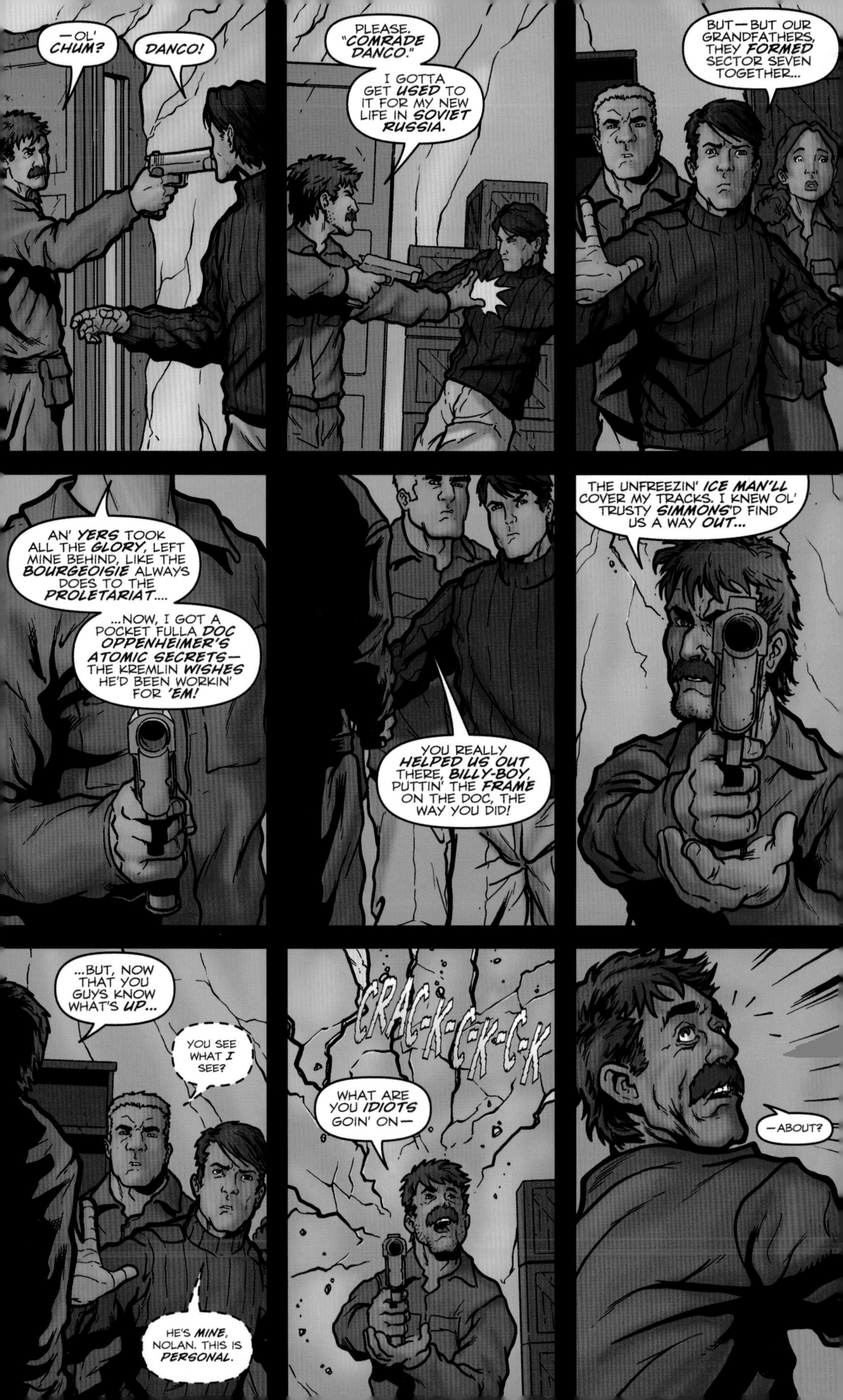
—OL' CHUM?
DANCO!
PLEASE. "COMRADE DANCO."
I GOTTA GET USED TO IT FOR MY NEW LIFE IN SOVIET RUSSIA.
BUT—BUT OUR GRANDFATHERS, THEY FORMED SECTOR SEVEN TOGETHER...
AN' YERS TOOK ALL THE GLORY, LEFT MINE BEHIND, LIKE THE BOURGEOISIE ALWAYS DOES TO THE PROLETARIAT....
...NOW, I GOT A POCKET FULLA DOC OPPENHEIMER'S ATOMIC SECRETS—THE KREMLIN WISHES HE'D BEEN WORKIN' FOR 'EM!
YOU REALLY HELPED US OUT THERE, BILLY-BOY, PUTTIN' THE FRAME ON THE DOC, THE WAY YOU DID!
THE UNFREEZIN' ICE MAN'LL COVER MY TRACKS. I KNEW OL' TRUSTY SIMMONS'D FIND US A WAY OUT...
...BUT, NOW THAT YOU GUYS KNOW WHAT'S UP...
YOU SEE WHAT I SEE?
HE'S MINE, NOLAN. THIS IS PERSONAL.
CRAC-K-C-K-C-K
WHAT ARE YOU IDIOTS GOIN' ON—
—ABOUT?

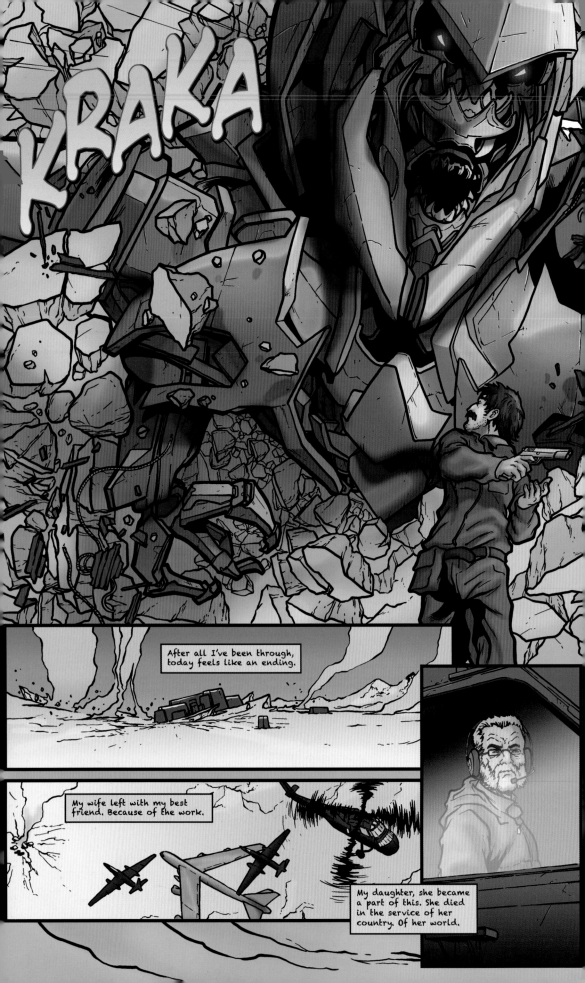

KRAKA

After all I've been through, today feels like an ending.

My wife left with my best friend. Because of the work.

My daughter, she became a part of this. She died in the service of her country. Of her world.

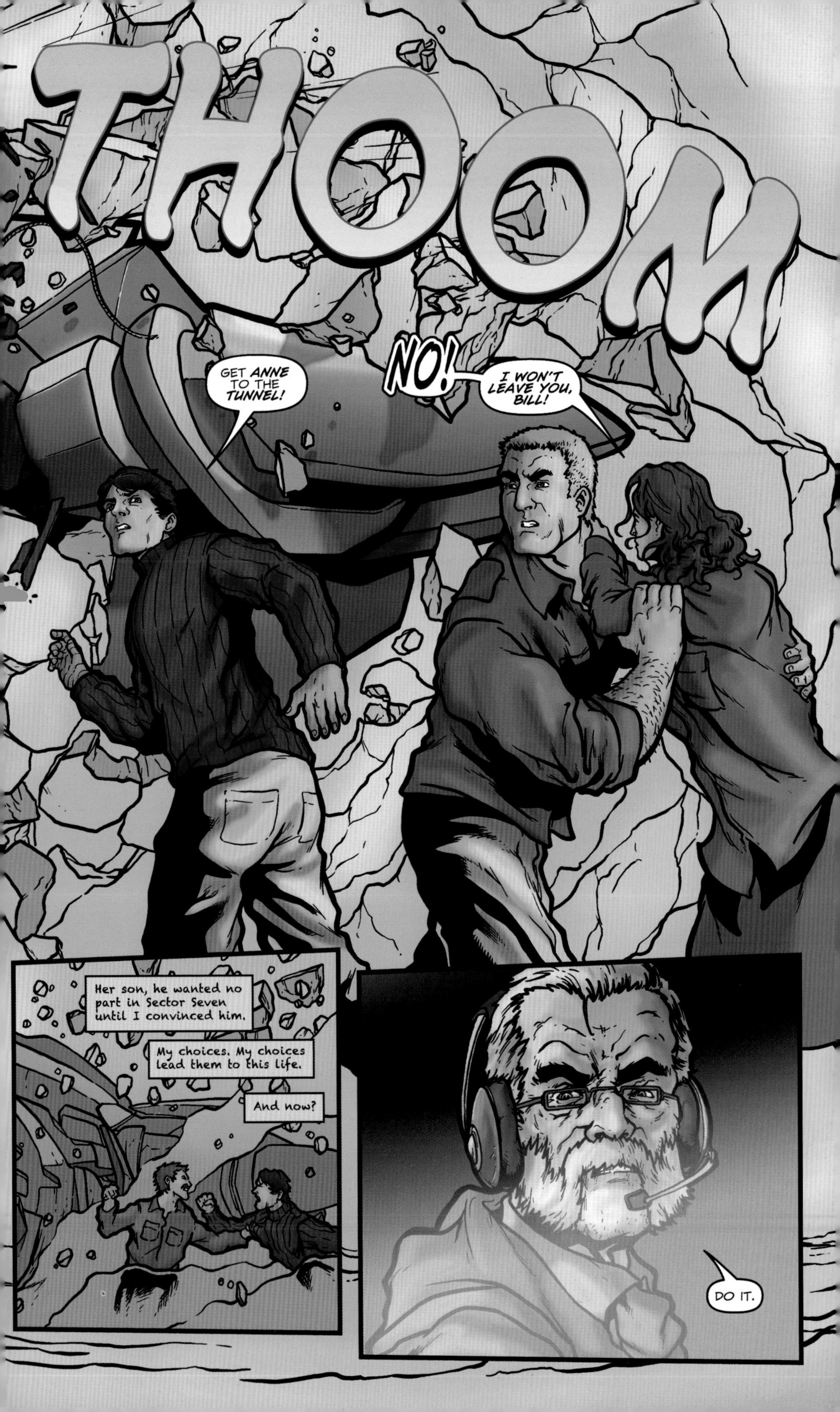
THOOM
GET ANNE TO THE TUNNEL!
NO!
I WON'T LEAVE YOU, BILL!
Her son, he wanted no part in Sector Seven until I convinced him.
My choices. My choices lead them to this life.
And now?
DO IT.

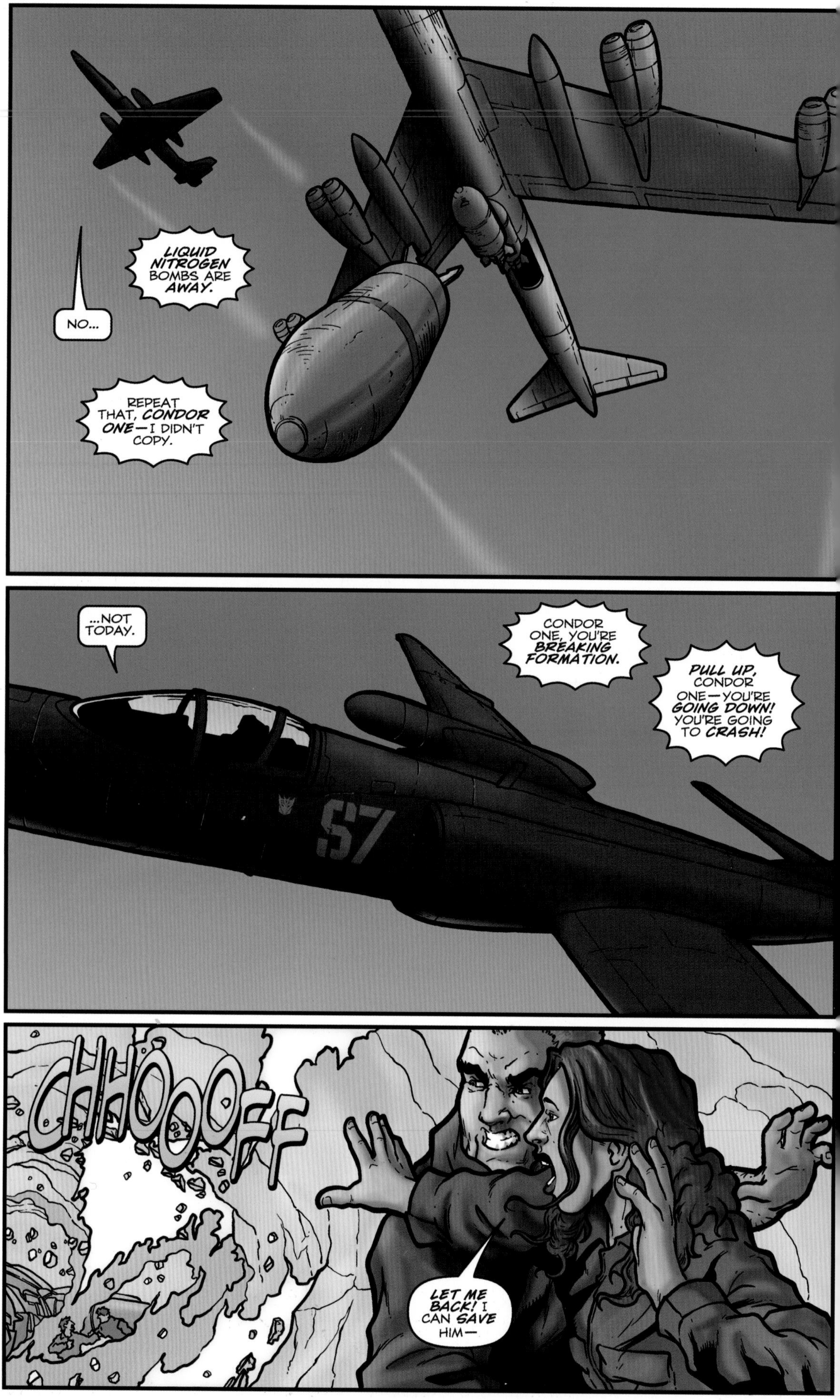
LIQUID NITROGEN BOMBS ARE AWAY.
NO...
REPEAT THAT, CONDOR ONE—I DIDN'T COPY.
...NOT TODAY.
CONDOR ONE, YOU'RE BREAKING FORMATION.
PULL UP, CONDOR ONE—YOU'RE GOING DOWN! YOU'RE GOING TO CRASH!
S7
CHHOOOFF
LET ME BACK! I CAN SAVE HIM—

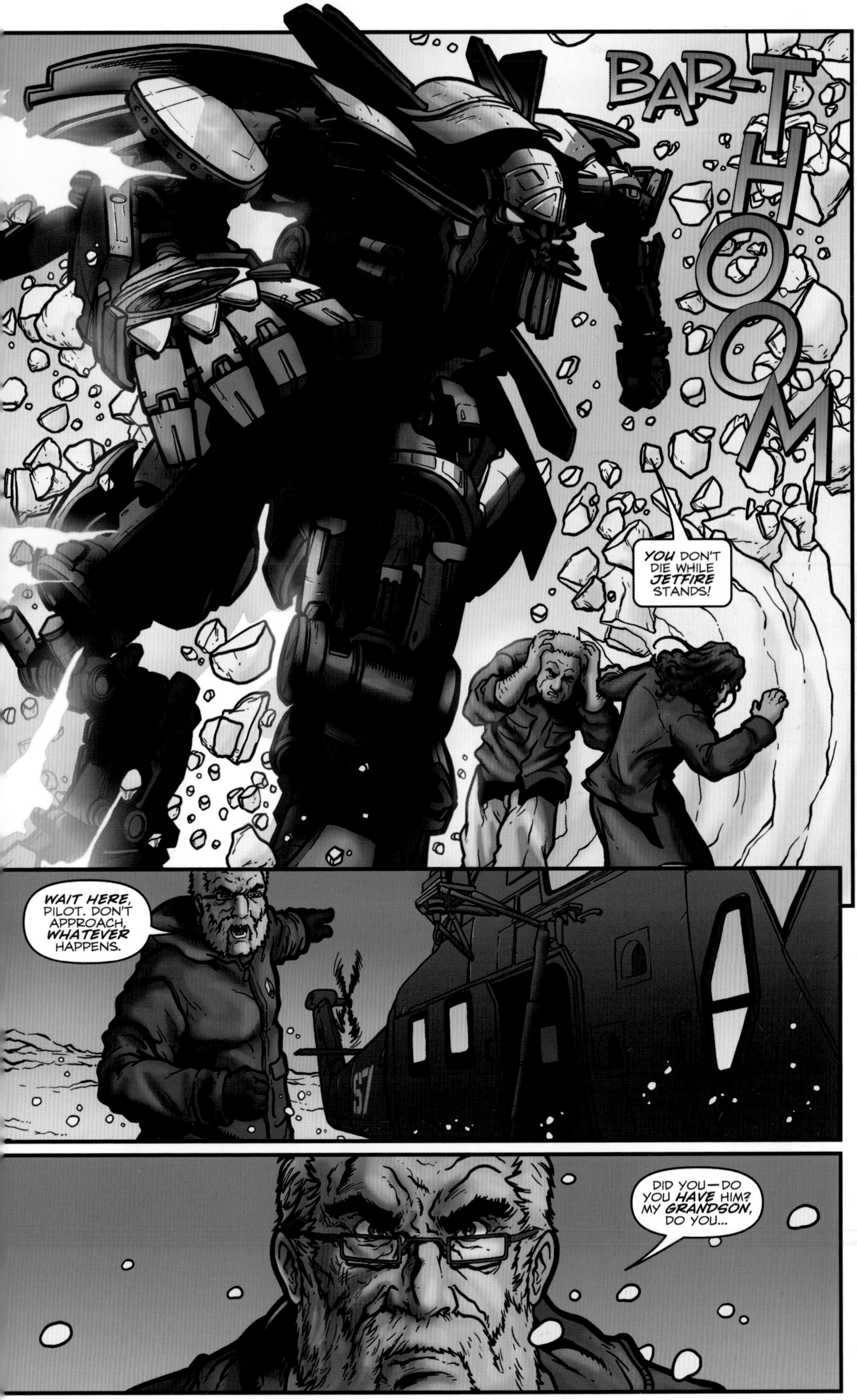

BAR-THOOM
YOU DON'T DIE WHILE JETFIRE STANDS!
WAIT HERE, PILOT. DON'T APPROACH, WHATEVER HAPPENS.
DID YOU—DO YOU HAVE HIM? MY GRANDSON, DO YOU...

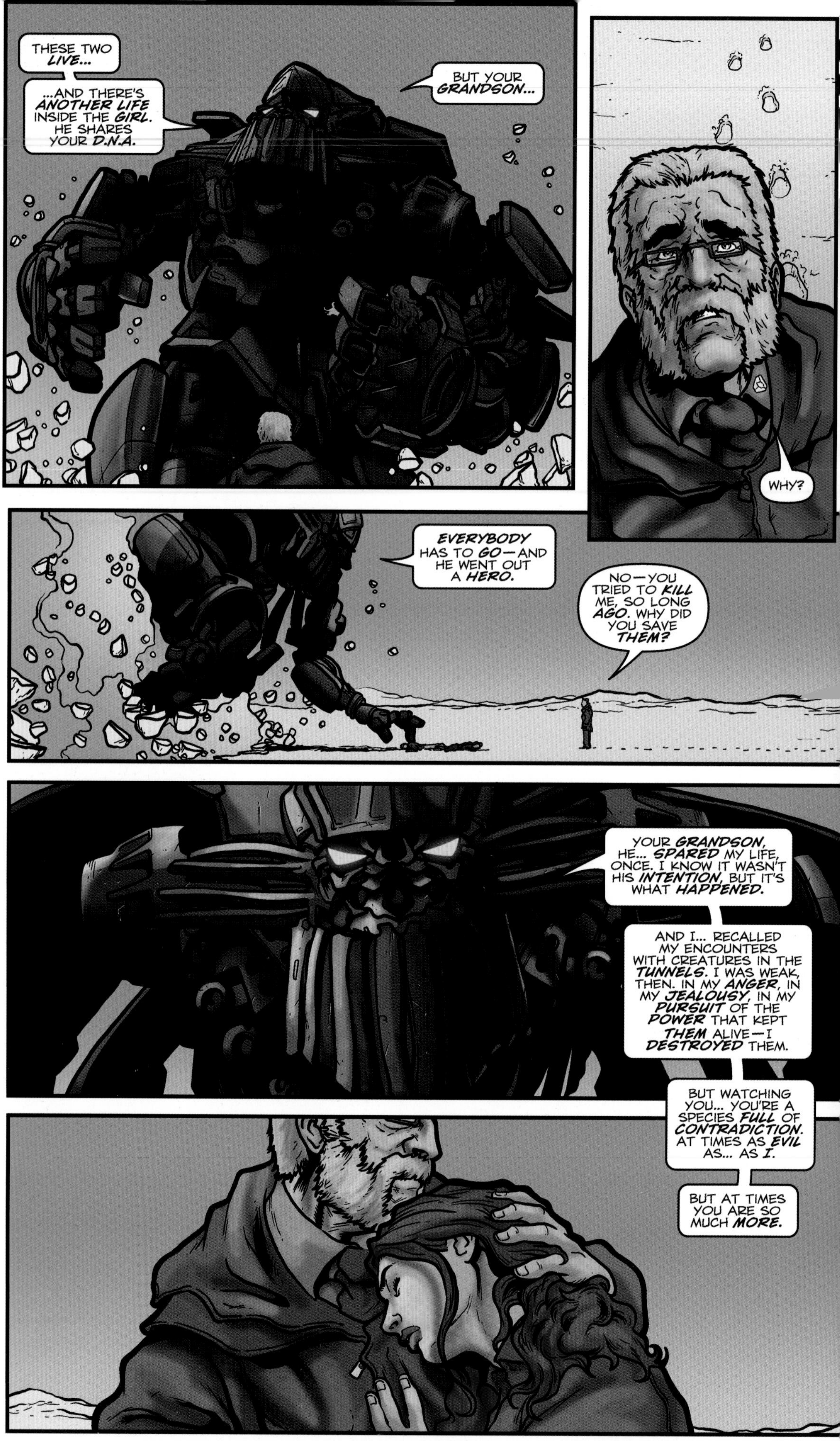

THESE TWO LIVE...
...AND THERE'S ANOTHER LIFE INSIDE THE GIRL. HE SHARES YOUR D.N.A.
BUT YOUR GRANDSON...
WHY?
EVERYBODY HAS TO GO—AND HE WENT OUT A HERO.
NO—YOU TRIED TO KILL ME, SO LONG AGO. WHY DID YOU SAVE THEM?
YOUR GRANDSON, HE... SPARED MY LIFE, ONCE. I KNOW IT WASN'T HIS INTENTION, BUT IT'S WHAT HAPPENED.
AND I... RECALLED MY ENCOUNTERS WITH CREATURES IN THE TUNNELS. I WAS WEAK, THEN. IN MY ANGER, IN MY JEALOUSY, IN MY PURSUIT OF THE POWER THAT KEPT THEM ALIVE—I DESTROYED THEM.
BUT WATCHING YOU... YOU'RE A SPECIES FULL OF CONTRADICTION. AT TIMES AS EVIL AS... AS I.
BUT AT TIMES YOU ARE SO MUCH MORE.

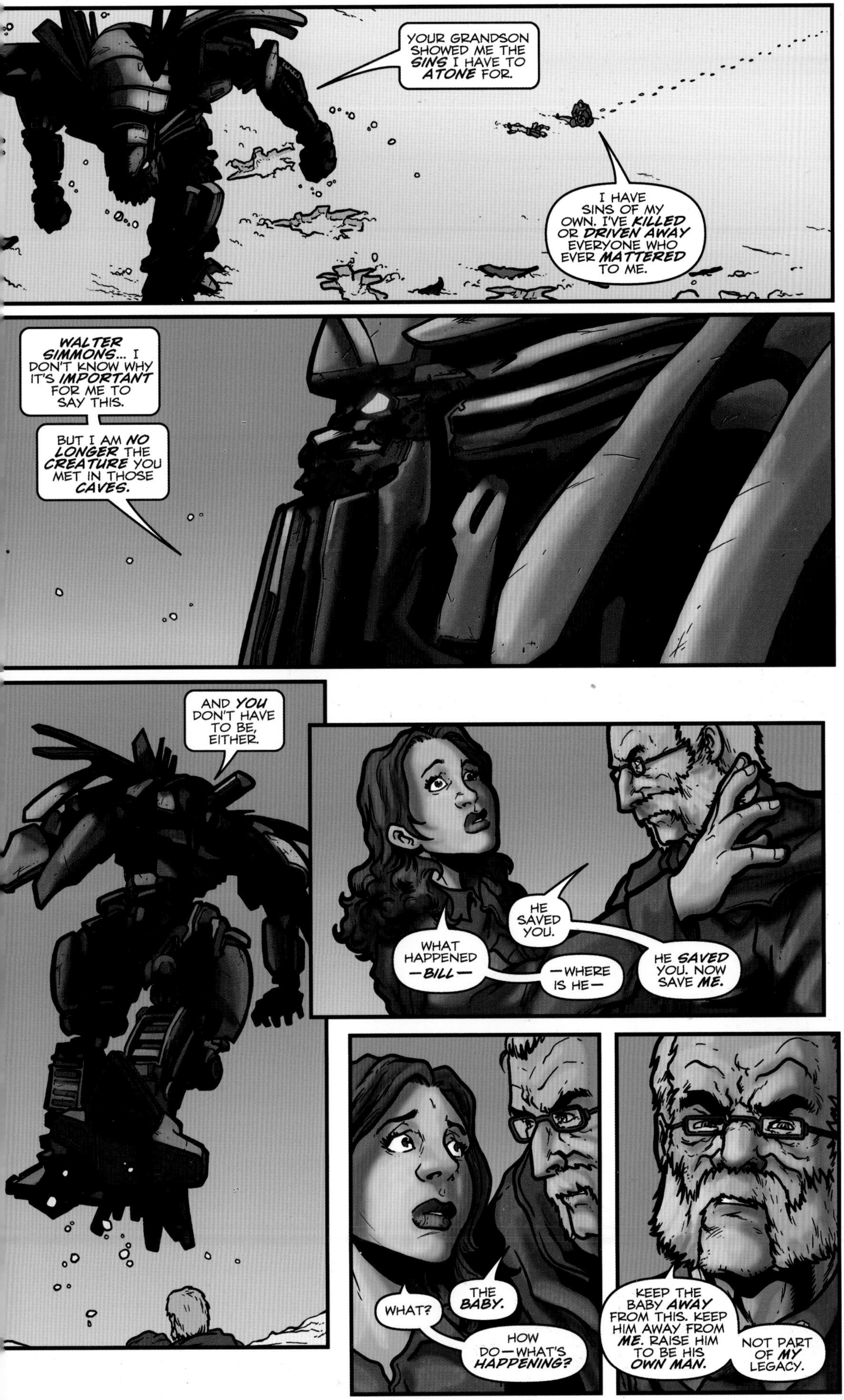

YOUR GRANDSON SHOWED ME THE SINS I HAVE TO ATONE FOR.
I HAVE SINS OF MY OWN. I'VE KILLED OR DRIVEN AWAY EVERYONE WHO EVER MATTERED TO ME.
WALTER SIMMONS... I DON'T KNOW WHY IT'S IMPORTANT FOR ME TO SAY THIS.
BUT I AM NO LONGER THE CREATURE YOU MET IN THOSE CAVES.
AND YOU DON'T HAVE TO BE, EITHER.
WHAT HAPPENED —BILL—
HE SAVED YOU.
—WHERE IS HE—
HE SAVED YOU. NOW SAVE ME.
THE BABY.
WHAT?
HOW DO—WHAT'S HAPPENING?
KEEP THE BABY AWAY FROM THIS. KEEP HIM AWAY FROM ME. RAISE HIM TO BE HIS OWN MAN.
NOT PART OF MY LEGACY.

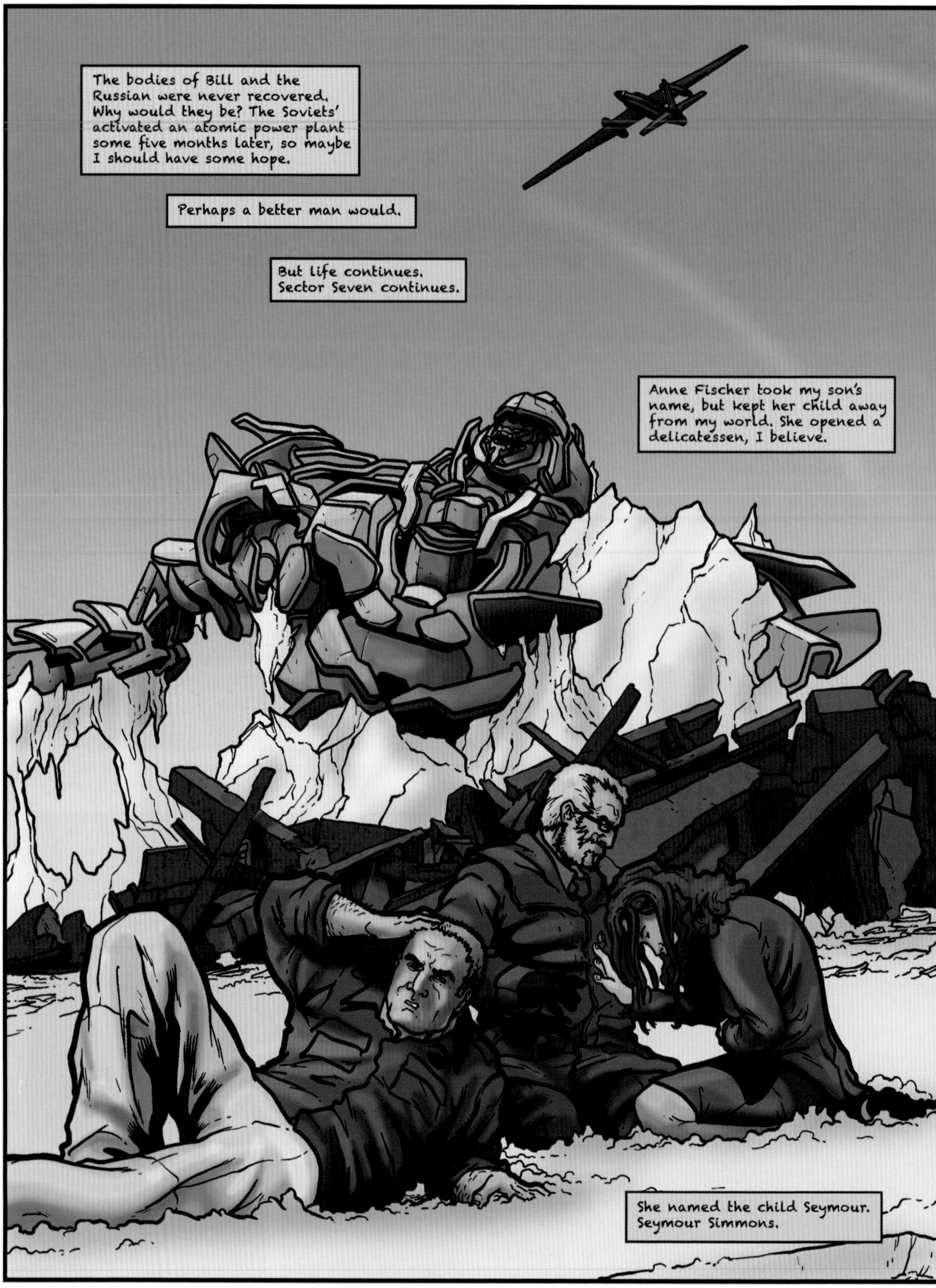

The bodies of Bill and the Russian were never recovered. Why would they be? The Soviets' activated an atomic power plant some five months later, so maybe I should have some hope.
Perhaps a better man would.
But life continues. Sector Seven continues.
Anne Fischer took my son's name, but kept her child away from my world. She opened a delicatessen, I believe.
She named the child Seymour. Seymour Simmons.

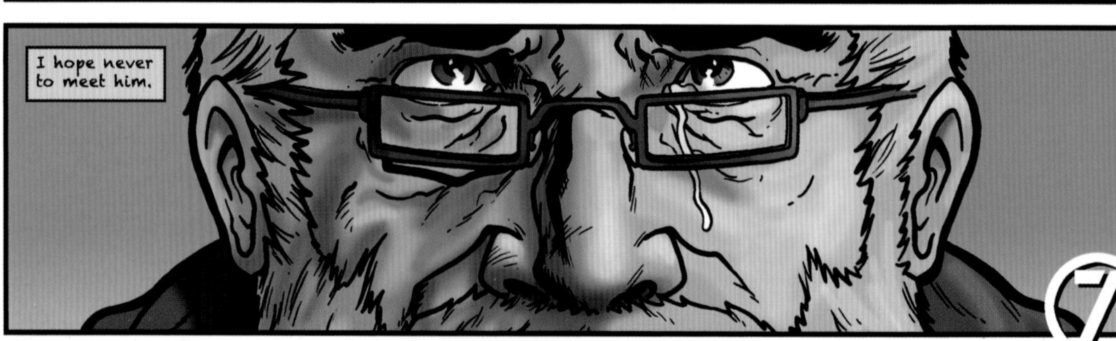

I hope never to meet him.

PROPERTY OF
U.S. GOVERMENT
ARCHIVES
4NS2BD7
TRS
AV7 GS548

SECTOR
AV7 7 TRS
TRANSFORMERS

ART GALLERY

CLASSIFIED
X3T2V3
DOCUMENTS
E7

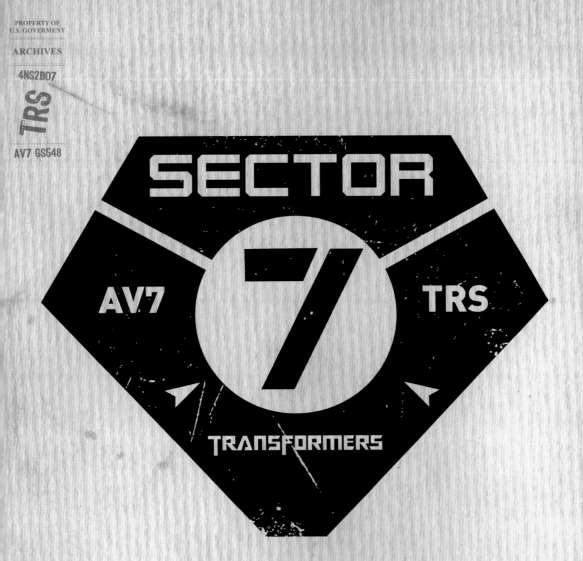

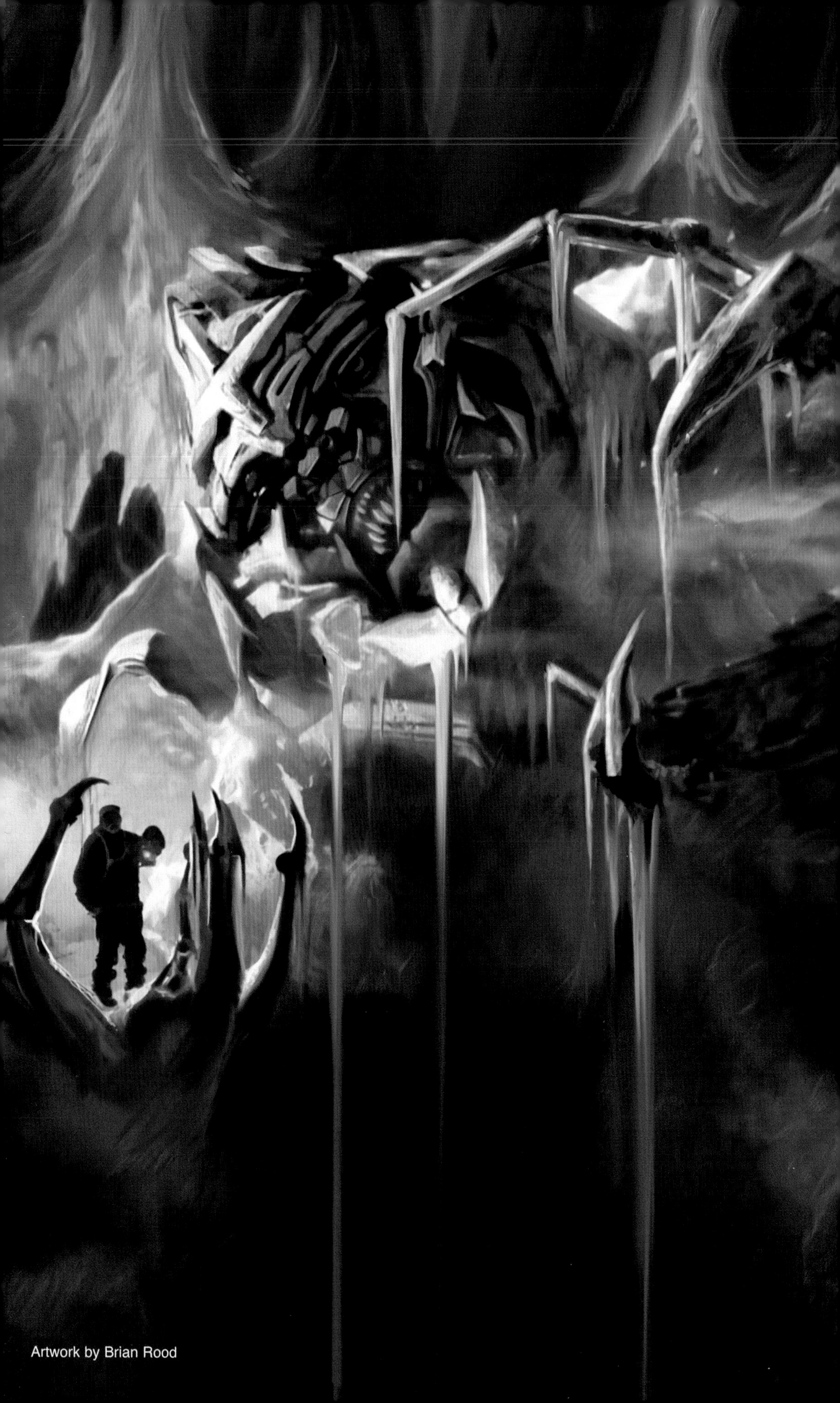

Artwork by Brian Rood

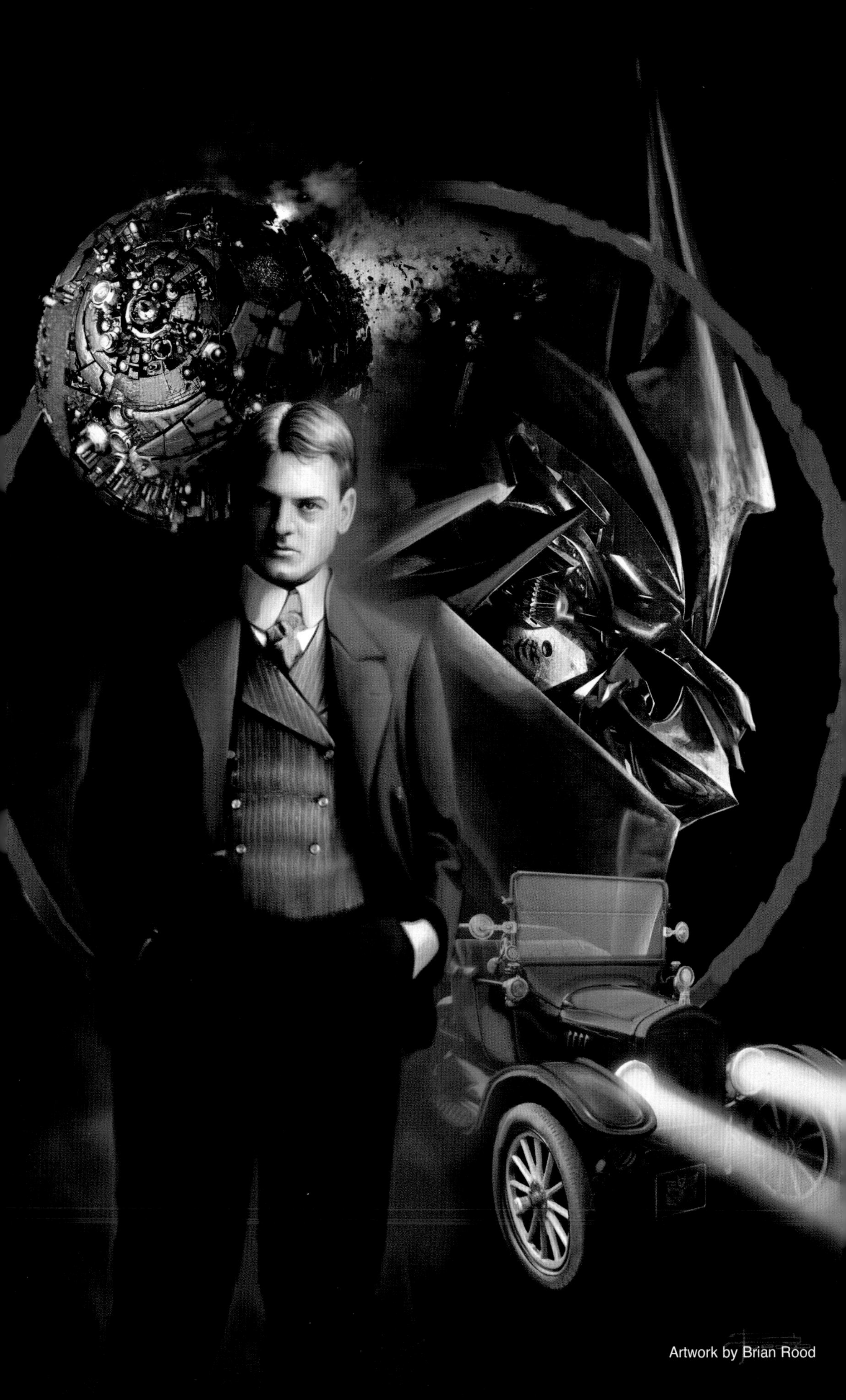

Artwork by Brian Rood

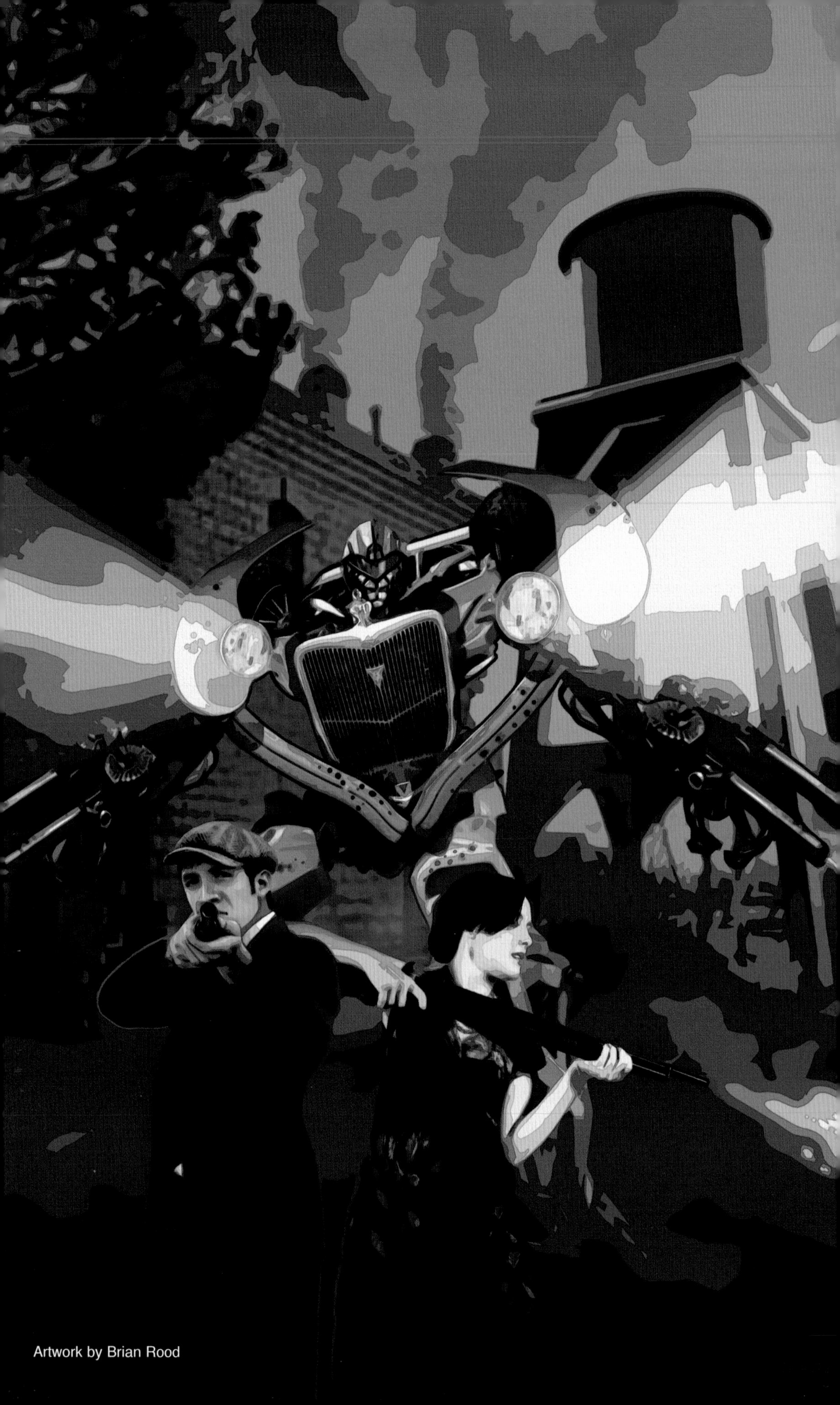
Artwork by Brian Rood

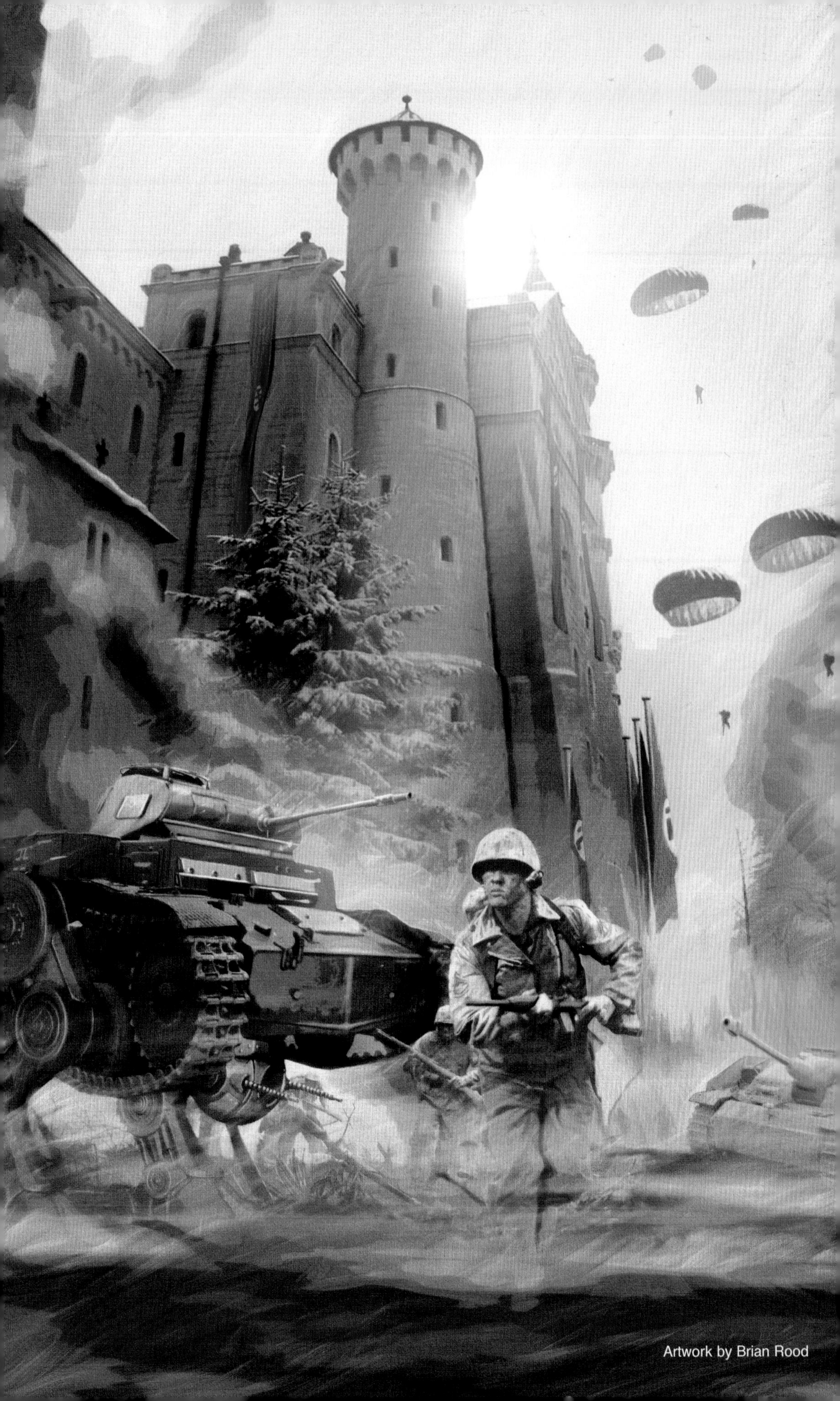

Artwork by Brian Rood

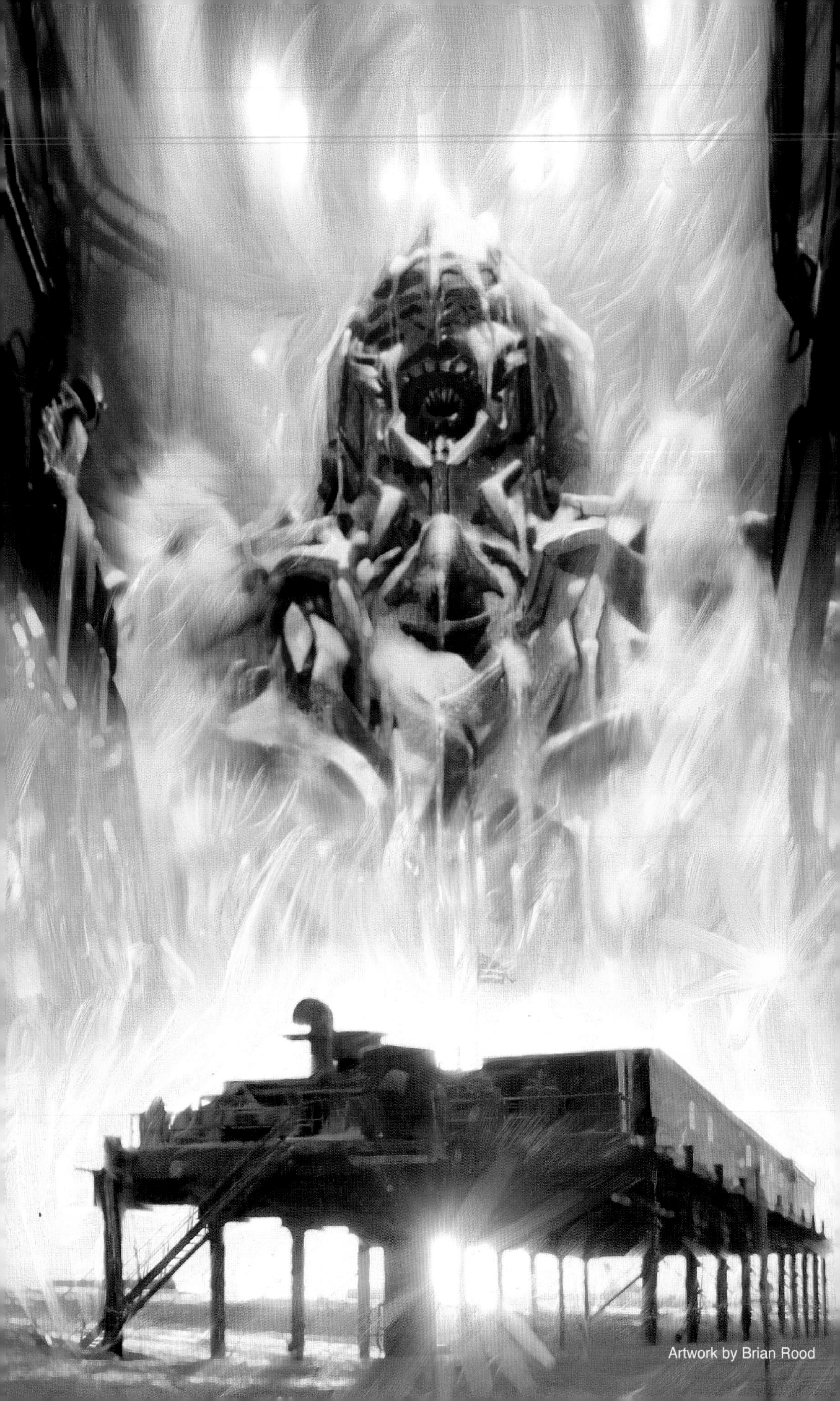

Artwork by Brian Rood

Ralph Bond, Captain

Lepus Viperidae Decipis

...Westf...
...ian Brews...
...erson Whittin...
...Wilson Clairn...
...ar Jennings Cro...
Vance Milhaus Laws...

Subject of the Welfare
ll presently be advise
Secure Hospital of Bo
itwicky was brought u
curred whilst Capt. Wi
Strength of Cold of
n in a Cavern made of
itude of Lights of th
anity that has overco

nset of Insanity incl
e a Giant Living in t
reatment of the Insan
a "cure" for Capt.
of Modern Medico-Psyc
ng Procedures:

r, in
ll rest

Benjamin Vane

Artwork by Joe Suitor

Dr. Benjamin Vane, M.D.

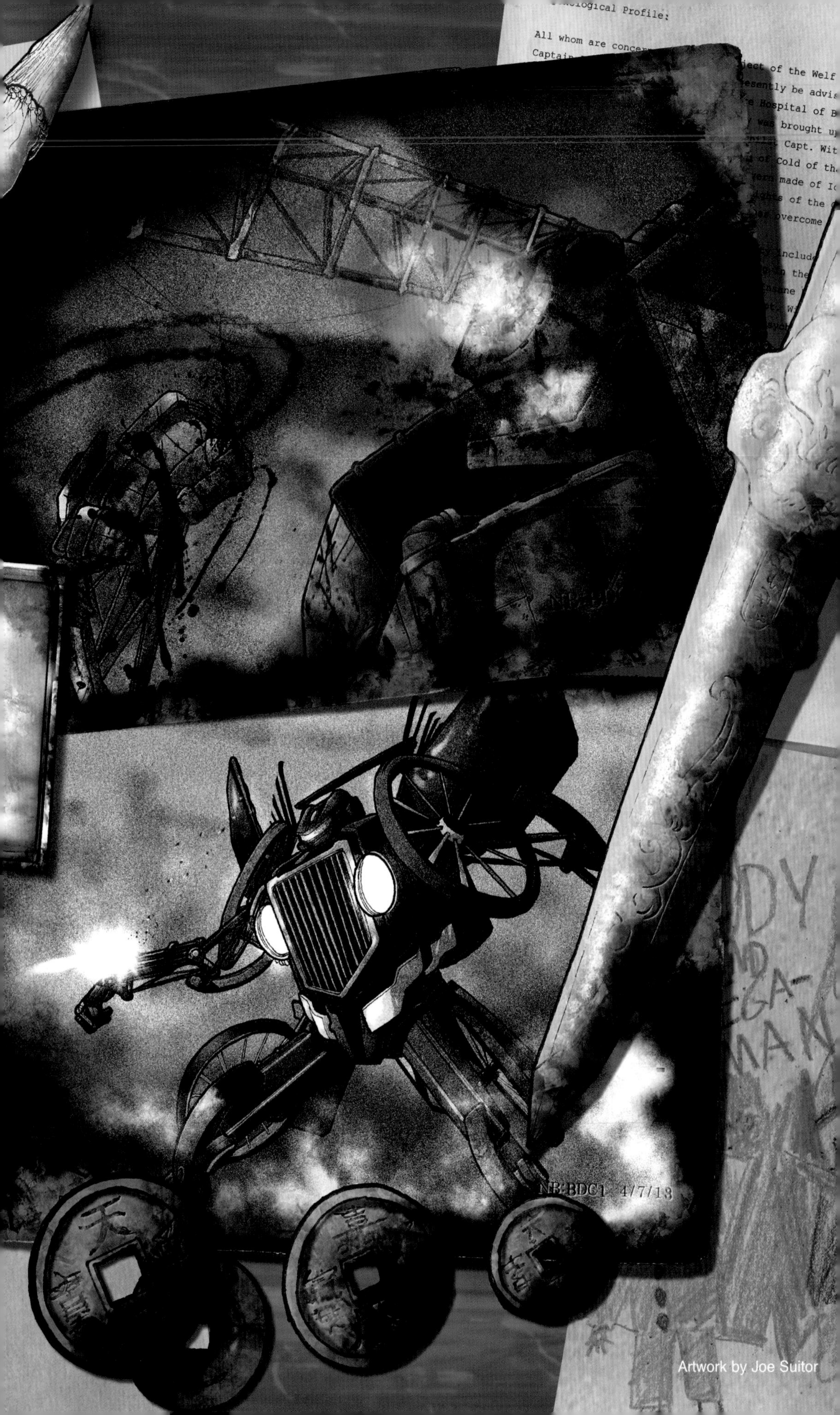
ological Profile:
All whom are conce
ject of the Welf
Hospital of B
was brought u
Capt. Wit
of Cold of th
made of I
of the
overcome
NB:BDC1 4/7/18
Artwork by Joe Suitor

...'ve read the story of Jesse James
...f how he lived and died.
...f you're still in need;
...something to read.

...e Are Slain By Police And Fe...

Mystery Creature S...
Near Barber Falls

...andits And Car Are Riddled With Bullets

Highway Ambush Ends Criminal Career

The War on Crime

...w and Bonnie Parker were kille...
...fficers of an unknown fede...

...d Is Sudden

...ork Beacon
...arrow, notorious...
...r, and his trigg...
...onnie Parker, we...
...ter with T...

57-013

to act like citiz...

BP

...d "bad man," who was accused
...lve murders, and his companion rushed
...into a carefully-laid death trap. Before they
...d use any of the weapons in the small ar...
...rangers and oth...

...down together
...them side b...

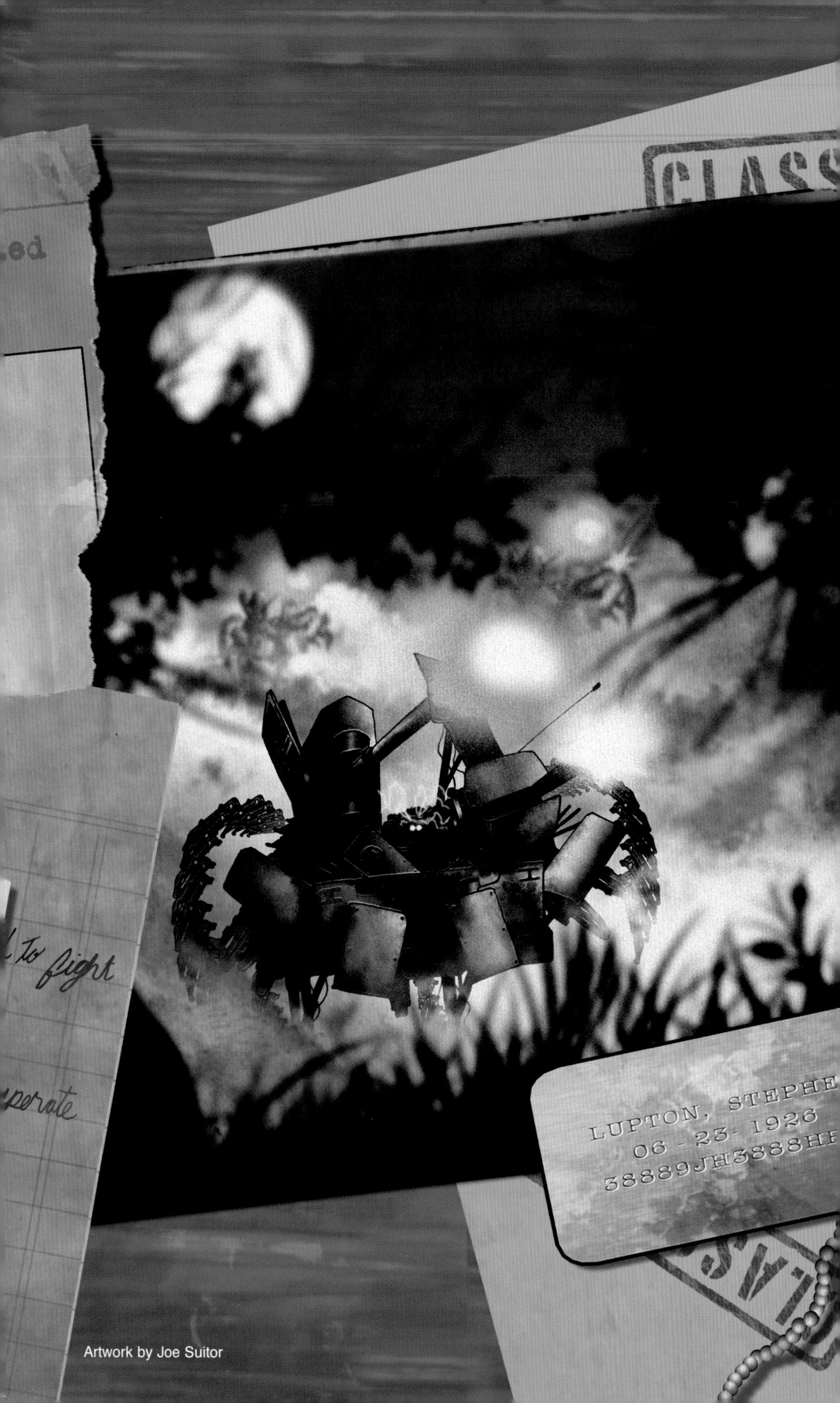
ed
CLASS
l to fight
sperate
LUPTON, STEPHE
06 - 23 - 1926
38889JH3888HF
Artwork by Joe Suitor

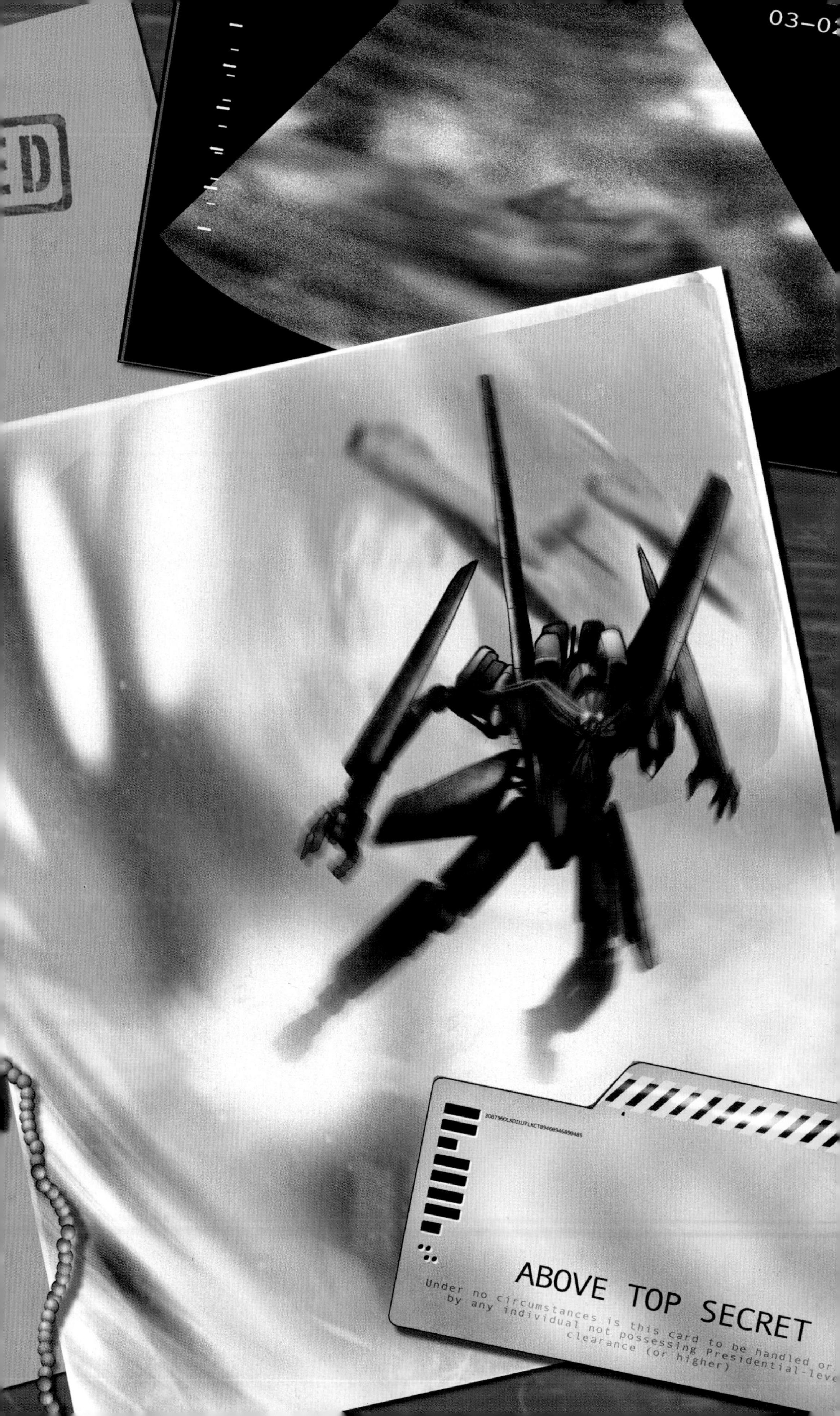
03–0
ED
ABOVE TOP SECRET
Under no circumstances is this card to be handled or
by any individual not possessing Presidential-leve
clearance (or higher)

PROPERTY OF
U.S. GOVERMENT

ARCHIVES

4NS2BD7

TRS

AV7 GS548

SECTOR

AV7

7

TRS

TRANSFORMERS

FIELD NOTES

CLASSIFIED

X3T2V3

DOCUMENTS

E7

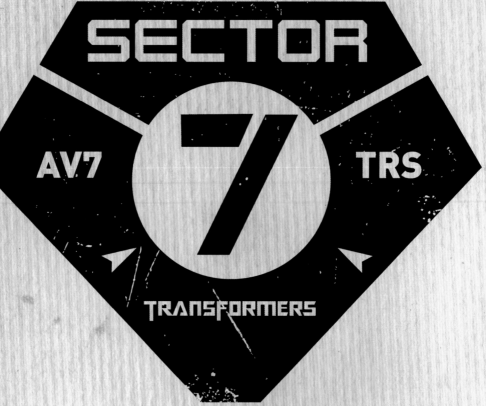

CHAPTER ONE

i. I'm John Barber, the writer of this tale. Hope you njoyed it, because artist Joe Suitor and I have four ore coming your way! Editor Andy Schmidt asked me o sort through the mix of Transformers mythology and ctual historical happenings that we've got going on ere, none of which is integral to actually enjoying the omic (I hope!)—but here goes:

ages 3-6: We'd met Walter Simmons and Theodore Vells in the first *Transformers: Movie Prequel* comic, but ow we learn their names. The *Prequel* established that ese guys were adventurers, and their collection of ophies indicated that their forte was the strange and nusual. Later in the *Prequel* we learn that the great-randfather of the *Transformer* films' Agent Seymour immons was one of the people who had captured an .B.E., so it's a short jump to figure out that he's one of ese guys.

t this time, America was just transforming (no pun tended) into the industrial juggernaut it would be in the 0th century, but the disparity between urban, East oast America and the west was stronger than probably ny time before or since. I thought we could emonstrate that incongruity by having a cowboy joining p with these Jules Verne/H.G. Wells gentlemen cientist-adventurers, so meet Agent North.

ages 7-9: This scene is an extension of a scene in the *requel* comic. Danco first appeared as a member of Vitwicky's crew in the *Prequel*, and a guy working with immons' group a few pages later looked enough like im that I figured they were the same fellow.

age 10: Now we meet our group of seven for the first me, having only seen them as a photograph in the *ansformers* movie. They're meant to encompass isparate bits of the era. We've got Bowen, who's asically then-contemporary writer Oscar Wilde as an xplosives expert; Grant, a rugged hero in the mold of . Rider Haggard's fictional colonialist Allan uatermain; and Arden, who's a throw-back to the pre-ndustrial Revolution master/apprentice era which was uickly vanishing. Joe came up with a look for each of ese guys, and we promptly cover them up with parkas. orry, Joe.

ages 11-13: The list we see—the ship's manifest—is a tle easter-egg for really hardcore fans. The only place efore this comic) where there's a list of the original roup of seven was a promotional website for the first ransformers movie, but that website doesn't exactly ke place in continuity. The site "reveals" that the ansformers are all real, and the toy line and movies re attempts by Sector 7 to confuse people by making it ok like the Transformers are fictional characters. Taken s part of the comic-book reality, this triggers a ecursive effect that causes my head to explode. But at's where the list of names comes from; and it turns ut they're aliases.

ages 14-15: In 1823, the United States issued the lonroe Doctrine, which basically declared that the U.S. ould not stand for any European nation to have olonies in North or South America. An exemption was

made for the Spanish colony of Cuba. However, within Cuba, there was a U.S.-supported desire for independence—which was finally granted on January 1, 1898, after negotiations between the U.S. and Spain.

A few days later, tensions mounted between Cubans and Spanish soldiers in the capital city of Havana. Rioting broke out, due in no small part to Spanish anger at the efforts of American newspaper magnates William Randolph Hearst and Joseph Pulitzer, who had been fanning the flames of U.S. mistrust of Spain in an effort to sell newspapers. This would come to be called "Yellow Journalism"; the term originated because both the Hearst and Pulitzer newspapers published versions of the comic strip *The Yellow Kid,* which is another story entirely, but, see—it all comes back to comics.

President McKinley sent in the *U.S.S. Maine* to protect American assets in Cuba, and on February 15, an explosion caused the *Maine* to sink, killing 266 of its crew. The American newspapers loudly proclaimed that a Spanish mine had sunk the ship, a theory confirmed by initial military reports. Thus, the U.S. declared war on Spain. In subsequent years, studies would suggest that the sinking of the *Maine* was more likely due to ammunition being accidentally set off—though there's really no way to be sure. Well, now *we* know for sure—Jetfire carelessly sunk the *Maine* and started the Spanish-American War. Sorted.

Pages 16-17: Bowen is reading the direct antecedent for all alien invasion stories, *The War of the Worlds* by H.G. Wells, whose style of gentleman-adventurers helped provide the inspiration for Simmons and Wells (as well as Wells' name). The novel was serialized in 1897 and released as a book in 1898, of which Bowen must have a snagged a copy pretty early, because it's only February.

Pages 18-20: In the comic book *Transformers: Revenge of the Fallen: Tales of the Fallen*, we see that, having arrived on Earth 19,000 years ago, Jetfire wanders the Earth and a caption tells us "time becomes meaningless" before he spots an SR-71 Blackbird spyplane and transforms into that, which is where we find him in the *Revenge of the Fallen* movie. This *Sector 7* series takes place in that (massive) time gap. And since he's been on Earth since well before there was an Optimus Prime or a Megatron, he certainly has no idea who Megatron is. The symbol of the Fallen that Jetfire wears was (much) later adopted by Megatron for his Decepticon army (see the *Transformers: Revenge of the Fallen: Defiance* comic).

Pages 21-26: With North dead, so ends the first and last adventure of the original seven. See you here next time when we learn just who is "Irreplaceable"!

John Barber
August, 2010

Hi—writer John Barber here again, with some historical and continuity-based notes on this story! Hope you liked it!

Pages 27-29: We're in Nevada here, not far from where the Hoover Dam will someday be built. It's not a big deal, but artist Joe Suitor and I talked this bit out: that's a little high-tech super-science electrical generator outside the house in panel one, providing electrical power to Clara and Margaret Wells. Not exactly regular tech for the era (electricity was, I mean the portability) but these aren't regular folk.

Page 30-31: Here we introduce real life people Herbert and Lou Hoover, the future President and First Lady of the United States. We meet them in Tianjin, China, during the Boxer Rebellion—an uprising against colonial power and Christian missionaries in China (hence the line about being a Christian). The "Boxers" were a group called the "Society of Righteous and Harmonious Fists"—the martial arts they practiced led to westerners calling them by their pugilistic nickname. The uprising lasted from 1898 to 1901.

Tianjin was (along with Beijing) one of the main hot points of the Boxer Rebellion, and the Hoovers were indeed trapped there. They were, in fact, funneling information on Boxer troop movement to American forces, which they're depicted as doing here. Now, Lou probably didn't walk around packing pistols, but she was a geologist and metallurgist, and Herbert was—at this point—an expert in mining who was a reasonably well-known professional lecturer. In the context of this comic, I'm of course suggesting that their adventures were a lot more fantastical than the real life ones, but there's actually some basis in reality!

Pages 32-35: In the first *Transformers* movie, it's mentioned that the AllSpark was found and recognized as alien in 1913, but in the *Transformers: Movie Prequel* comic, it's clearly located in 1902. Here we learn the truth: it was located in 1902 but excavated in 1913, when it was pretty undeniably proven to not be from Earth.

So, um, why aren't they underwater here? They're in the Colorado River basin! In real life, the Colorado River was rerouted around the area that the Boulder Dam—later renamed Hoover Dam—was being built. Construction began in 1931. Also in real life, Boulder Dam is actually renamed Hoover Dam in honor of Herbert Hoover, who helped get the Dam built—first as Secretary of Commerce, then as U.S. President.

In the Transformers timeline, it seems like 30 years is a long time to wait between locating the AllSpark and getting it out of the water. But here we learn that, upon finding the AllSpark, the Seven bring in Herbert Hoover, an expert in soil and mining and that sort of thing, to secretly reroute the Colorado River. He accomplishes this in about a decade, completing it a little while before we open this comic.

Incidentally: At this stage, our group of heroes isn't officially called "Sector 7" yet, though the number seven appears with astonishing regularity in their lives, including the designation of the location they plan to move the AllSpark to. As of 1913, the group-that-will-someday-become-Sector-7 is always composed of seven members. Three of them (Herbert Hoover, Lou Hoover, and Roy Thompson) joined between last issue and this, replacing North (who died last issue) and Arden (the metallurgist that Lou Hoover explicitly replaced) as well as at least one other member. With Simmons and Wells still there, the identities of the remaining two—who are in the Arctic Alpha Base, where Megatron is—are open to question.

Page 34: Just to note, here and for the future: the bureaucrats in Washington only grant official N.B.E. status to Transformers they have material evidence of (e.g. an actual body or a solid, clear, unimpeachable recording plus physical evidence, like they got of Bumblebee in the *Prequel* comic—reports, eyewitnesses, and blurry recordings like Starscream and company destroying the Beagle probe on Mars don't cut it). So that's why, even as we learn that Sector 7 has encountered Transformers between the discovery of Megatron and the capture of Bumblebee, Bumblebee is N.B.E.-2.

Pages 36-41: Jetfire plummeted to his apparent death last issue, but you knew he'd be back, right? Evidently, these tunnels extend through the Earth all the way up to the Arctic.

Pages 42-44: The AllSpark has the power to bring to life mechanical devices that touch it—and here's where humanity learns that.

Pages 45-48: The Colorado River floods again, and after this issue, Herbert Hoover goes on to have a political career, in which his chief goal is to ensure the area around the AllSpark is rebuilt with a more permanent housing for the AllSpark… and that's the secret origin of the Hoover Dam. No wonder they named it after him!

And, uh-oh, looks like one of the AllSpark spawns got away. We'd all better meet back here next month and see what happens…

CHAPTER THREE

Writer John Barber here, welcoming the fantastic artist Chee to this issue! And a sad note—as this issue was in production, film director Arthur Penn, who directed the 1967 film *Bonnie and Clyde,* passed away. While this comic doesn't have much in common with that film (beyond sharing a couple characters), Penn's movie certainly helped keep the legend of Bonnie and Clyde alive and was an inspiration to both of us. With respect and admiration, Chee and I asked to dedicate this issue to his memory. Now on to the notes…

Page 49: We open on a bank robbery, being perpetrated by the famous real-life outlaws Clyde Barrow (25 years old) and Bonnie Parker (23). At this point, their run of robberies and murders had been going on for about a year and a half, and the duo were already famous. In an era of gangsters as celebrities, these two were rock-star bank robbers—hence Clyde's dialog to the bank patrons. Driving the car here is W.D. Jones, who had joined with Bonnie and Clyde around Christmas, 1932. At the time of this story, he's actually only 17 years old.

Pages 50-52: This particular robbery isn't based in reality (as the appearance of the Transformer may have tipped you off) but Sowers, Texas, was the site of a November 1933 shoot-out involving Bonnie and Clyde. But in real life—or at least given the facts that Sector 7 was allowed to be public—W.D. was not captured here, at this time. The Transformer is the lost AllSpark-spawn we met last issue, and has presumably been wandering around for the last 20 years or so. It also seems to have developed a more apparent (if rudimentary) intelligence than some of the other machines we've seen transformed by contact with the AllSpark.

Pages 53-55: We met Roy Thompson last issue, then the newest recruit in Walter Simmons' and Theodore Wells' organization. Now, we learn that group has officially become "Sector 7" and Thompson is a veteran officer. Margo Simmons, the daughter of Walter Simmons, is also a familiar face: we met her when she was a child last issue. In the intervening years, she's been married and had a child… but clearly something happened to her husband, causing her to revert to her maiden name. Death? Divorce? Perhaps a future story will tell, but her father has tried to get her a job—not easy in the Great Depression—and placed her on what he assumes will be a safe, simple mission investigating reports that will prove to be nothing.

Pages 56-57: Bonnie Parker was well known for writing poetry, much of it about her bank-robbing escapades.

This one—"The Trail's End," later known as "The Story of Bonnie and Clyde"—is probably the most famous, and was published in newspapers two weeks after Bonnie's death.

Pages 58-64: Clyde led a breakout at Eastham Jail on January 16, 1934, largely in retaliation for (as he saw things) the murder of his brother by Texas lawmen. Moreover, Clyde himself had been incarcerated in Eastham years earlier, and in fact had committed his first homicide while he was a prisoner. A prison guard was killed in the escape (one of nine lawmen killed by the Barrow Gang, all told) and this was the final straw for lawmen—they wouldn't let Bonnie and Clyde survive for long, after that… Reality alleges that no robots (or W.D. Jones, for that matter) were involved. And, while the Texas Rangers were not lying in wait for Clyde, the lead ranger here is based on former Ranger Frank Hamer, who was brought in to chase the criminals—and in fact was part of the posse responsible for killing the duo.

Pages 65-70: The death of Bonnie and Clyde has long been controversial. On May 23, 1934, on a Louisiana road, Bonnie and Clyde were shot to death in their car by a posse of lawmen. Whether they were given a chance to surrender has been the source of controversy. Now (as I've said before) we know the truth. Following their deaths, dozens of so-called "Bonnie and Clyde Death Cars" appeared as roadside attractions across the United States. Many of them still exist. But are any of them the real one?

That's it for now—see you next time as artist Lou Kang brings us into the heart of Nazi Germany in World War II.

John

PROPERTY OF U.S. GOVERMENT

ARCHIVES

CHAPTER FOUR

4NS2BD7

Hi again! Writer John Barber here, welcoming my great friend Lou Kang, who handled the art chores on this issue! Historically speaking, there's less going on here than in the last couple issues. World War II was an actual war… but beyond that, we took a few liberties…

AV7 GS548

Page 71: That's Margo Simmons, from issues 2 and 3, and young Bill Simmons in the photo. And that's Roy Thompson there, too, who it seems stuck around with Margo… But it doesn't sound like she got the happy ending we might have hoped for. Walter Simmons is still alive and kicking and dragging his family into his obsession, though.

Page 72-73: Hoover Dam was completed in the mid-1930s. As we saw in issue 2, it was built to house the AllSpark, but the plan has always been to move the Mega-Man (a.k.a. Megatron) in. So why isn't he here? In fact, back in the first *Transformers* film, you might recall Tom Banachek (of Sector 7 Advanced Research Division) telling Sam Witwicky and Mikaela Banes that Megatron was moved to Hoover Dam in 1934 (which was actually before the Dam was completed, for whatever that's worth).

Well, in the Alan Dean Foster novel (based on a story by David Cian) *Transformers: Ghosts of Yesterday,* Megatron is being moved to the Hoover Dam in 1969. Why the erroneous dating by Banachek, then? Well, he had no motivation to actually tell Sam or Mikaela the truth—plus he didn't exactly have a lot of time to go into details—so he just, well… *didn't* tell the truth. He's Sector 7, after all—that's probably second nature.

The reality of moving Megatron presented a series of logistical problems; we saw the original dam destroyed in issue 2, and the final dam wasn't completed until the middle of the Great Depression—at which point getting the Mega-Man from the North Pole to America may not have been top priority. Once WWII broke out, priorities again shifted. The biggest thing, though, was getting the coolant system to work. This was a system that simply couldn't be allowed to fail, and it was replacing a natural cooling system that seemingly *wouldn't* fail. See next issue for the final motivation that gave the push to get Megs moved by 1969.

One more thing on this spread: in previous issues, and in the first film, "N.B.E." has referred to "Non-Biological Extraterrestrial." In some of the comics—and in this scene—though, it's been phrased as "Non-Biological Entity." Here Simmons is using "Entity" deliberately. He strongly suspects the Nazis have captured the same Transformer he encountered in 1898 and in 1913, but even with the photo as evidence (on the wall behind the soldiers) he's not *sure* it's the same creature, or even of the same alien race. He is sure it's an "entity" of some kind—a pretty safe bet. This phrasing caught on over the years, so it's not totally incorrect in the present day to use the terms somewhat interchangeably.

Page 74: "Fulton Recovery" is real: surface-to-air recovery system ("STARS"). A balloon carries a line up to be intercepted by an aircraft, dragging the agent afte it. Robert Edison Fulton, Jr. developed it for the CIA in the early '50s; Sector 7 was using it in 1944.The group is flying in a modified Douglass C-47 Skytrain. The guns they're carrying are mostly the military version o the Thompson submachine gun, with Garcia carrying Browning .30 caliber light machine gun.

Page 76: Lou tells me the tanks are based on an amalgam of German Panzer tanks with a bunch of other American and British design elements thrown in t make the tanks clearly modified, but not straying too fa from the era. I think they turned out great!

Incidentally, this is the first time (that we've seen in the Transformers movie universe, anyway) that humans have ever used a tactical energy weapon in combat. In real life, in our own time, laser weapons are gigantic—weighing in the range of three to six tons, and are just at the cusp of not being too unwieldy to be effective. In fact, the first successful tests (that we know of) have al occurred in the last three or four years, so having these kinds of weapons in 1944 would potentially give the Nazis an advantage…

Page 78-83: …but a well-placed shot can still bring them down. As unstoppable as the TF-tech would be tc a WWII soldier, this crude, first-generation version of human-Cybertronian amalgamated tech isn't *quite* as invincible.

Page 84: Neuschwanstein Castle is a real place and was, coincidentally, made into a cake on the TV show *Ace of Cakes* the same week I wrote this scene.

Page 88: Were the pilots volunteering soldiers or conscripts? Either way, it's pretty horrifying, and I can see why Bill Simmons didn't try to find out more. Meanwhile, the maps on the walls chart the underground tunnels that have been playing a role in this comic since issue 1… what can they mean?

Page 91: The inset scene playing back in Jetfire's memory is from *Transformers: Revenge of the Fallen: Tales of the Fallen* issue 3. Some of Jetfire's morality—the stuff that got him in trouble in the first place—is beginning to reassert itself.

Page 92: In real life, Neuschwanstein Castle wasn't destroyed by a giant robot. Or if it was, Sector 7 kept it on the down low and rebuilt it. Anyway, as in issues 1 and 2: there's just a swath of destruction—and no material evidence proving Jetfire's existence (the photo on pages 2-3 isn't enough for Sector 7). He hasn't got—and won't get—an N.B.E. number.

CLASSIFIED X3T2V3

One last thing: that's a Lockheed P-38 Lightning that Jetfire transforms into, the kind of plane my own grandfather, Roy Evans, flew in World War II.

DOCUMENTS

CHAPTER FIVE

...thanks to the fantastic Jon Davis-Hunt for drawing every one of those one million panels so well! One last time, here are some (inessential) notes on the story for historical and continuity context…

Pages 93-94: In the first *Transformers Movie Prequel*, we saw some glimpses that Sector 7 had built a base in the Arctic, but this is the first time we see it in this series. Those are Lockheed U-2 spyplanes in the air above the Arctic base. "Officially" they didn't make their first flight until 1955, and didn't enter service until a couple years after that, but as is often the case, Sector 7 had the technology earlier than was generally reported. Likewise, the customized Sikorsky S-58 helicopter that Old Man Simmons arrives in would first fly (officially) the following month, and would come to be used by the Army, Navy, and Marines by the end of the decade.

Pages 95-96: And here's (most of) our cast. Fontaine is a new character. Bill Simmons you (hopefully) remember from last issue; as we learn later, he's made good on his vow to follow up on the tunnel system he saw laid out in the Nazi stronghold a decade ago. Anne Fischer will turn up again, in *Transformers: Revenge of the Fallen*, somewhat older. Nolan—who's definitely not as crazy as he seems here—next shows up in the Alan Dean Foster novel (based on a story by David Cian) *Transformers: Ghosts of Yesterday,* where he's part of the crew that finally moves Megatron to Hoover Dam, in 1969. And Danco is another new character, but his grandfather appeared in *Sector 7 #1* (as well as in the *Transformers Movie Prequel*) as one of the founding members of what would eventually be called Sector 7.

Bill Simmons lost his right hand last issue, and here we learn he's got a top-of-the-line Sector 7 mechanical right hand. The line about his hand being "shock resistant" is a reference to a contemporary Timex watch ad featuring baseball player Micky Mantle. "Takes a licking and keeps on ticking" was the Timex slogan for many years, and boxer Rocky Marciano—mentioned by Danco—also appeared in a Timex ad around this time.

Pages 97-98: As stated in last issue's notes, Megatron is still frozen solid in the Arctic. The disaster presented in this issue results in two things: the damage sustained delays the transfer again; but it simultaneously seals the deal that Megatron can't stay in the Arctic. Knowing that the Arctic cool takes care of Megatron wasn't an incentive to move him, but now Sector 7 can see it's not entirely safe up north. *Ghosts of Yesterday* demonstrates, again, how unsafe it is.

Page 99: In the Transformers movie universe, J. Robert Oppenheimer was first mentioned as being affiliated with Sector 7 in the *Transformers Movie Prequel,* and his name has come up a few times during the course of this series; "Doc Oppenheimer" was instrumental in creating many of Sector 7's high tech devices.

In real life, Oppenheimer was instrumental in the Manhattan Project, which created the first atomic bombs during World War II. After the war, Oppenheimer lobbied for international arms control, including the development of an international authority to control fissionable material. But, after some initial doubts, he worked on the fusion-based hydrogen bomb—the most powerful explosive weapon mankind has ever developed.

The Cold War was a time of massive paranoia about the spread of Soviet-style Communism. Oppenheimer had been under observation by the FBI since the early 1940s for alleged Communist sympathies. The first actual accusations came in 1950, and were discredited. Nevertheless, this seemed to fuel the FBI's fire, and Oppenheimer's security clearance was suspended on December 21, 1953.

That's where he is in this story, and it's clear that Bill Simmons was instrumental in stripping Oppenheimer of that clearance. Hearings would begin in April of 1954, and Oppenheimer would come to be seen as a security risk. His clearance would not be reinstated, and he would spend the rest of his life lecturing and writing on science. He died in 1967 of throat cancer, likely due to his chain-smoking.

Page 100-101: Danco killed Fontaine and slipped him into the roof of Nolan's "cell" between pages 6 and 7, before Fischer arrived. Then Danco went back to the furnace, which he set to a higher temperature before blowing up the controls. "I look worse than I feel," he says. How would he know how he looks? Because he's lying and he staged the whole thing.

Page 102: It seems that nobody's seen a Transformer in the field for a while. There was a time—issues 1 and 2—when every active member of what would be Sector 7 had seen those guys in action.

Pages 103-105: This whole issue took inspiration from *John Carpenter's The Thing,* this scene especially so. Thank you, John Carpenter. And that's little Seymour Simmons in Anne Fischer's tummy.

Pages 106-107: If you want to be really pedantic, Reginald Danco and Walter Simmons didn't form Sector 7 together; the group they formed became Sector 7 later. However, Danco is being literal when he says that the Kremlin wishes Oppenheimer had been working for them. Despite his public disgrace, it's become clear (in the years since the fall of the Soviet Union) that Oppenheimer was not working for the Soviets, though that they had attempted to recruit him on multiple occasions. Bill Simmons, an honorable guy, realizes (correctly) that he's done a very dishonorable thing.

Pages 108-110: Jetfire was hiding out as a U-2. The U-2 would later be largely replaced by the Lockheed SR-71 Blackbird, which is Jetfire's alternate mode in *Revenge of the Fallen*.

Pages 111-114: The Soviet nuclear power plant in Obninsk went on-line on June 27, 1954. It was actually the first nuclear power plant anywhere on Earth, but from the context of the issue we might infer that Sector 7 was already operating some. And Mrs. Simmons—née Miss Fischer—doesn't succeed in keeping little Seymour away from Sector 7, of course, as seen in both Transformers films.

But did Seymour ever meet Walter? Did Bill survive? Those are all stories for another time, and that's where I hope to see you all again. Thanks for joining us on this adventure!

John Barber
November, 2010

PROPERTY OF
U.S. GOVERMENT

ARCHIVES

4NS2BD7

TRS

AV7 GS548

SECTOR

AV7

7

TRS

TRANSFORMERS

IDW™

www.IDWPUBLISHING.COM

CLASSIFIED

X3T2V3

DOCUMENTS

E7

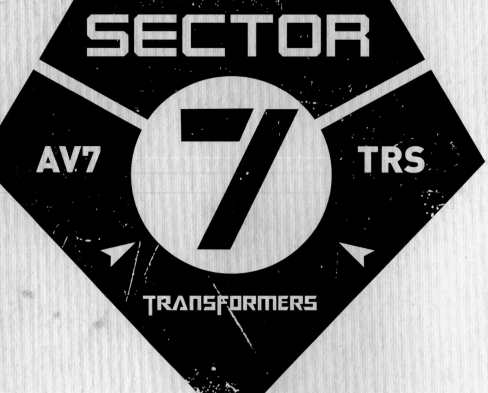

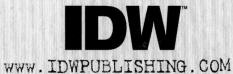